Women and Capital Punishment
in America, 1840–1899

ALSO BY KERRY SEGRAVE
AND FROM MCFARLAND

Actors Organize: A History of Union Formation Efforts in America, 1880–1919 (2008)

Women Swindlers in America, 1860–1920 (2007)

Ticket Scalping: An American History, 1850–2005 (2007)

America on Foot: Walking and Pedestrianism in the 20th Century (2006)

Drive-in Theaters: A History from Their Inception in 1933 (2006 [1992])

Suntanning in 20th Century America (2005)

Endorsements in Advertising: A Social History (2005)

Women and Smoking in America, 1880 to 1950 (2005)

Foreign Films in America: A History (2004)

Lie Detectors: A Social History (2004)

Product Placement in Hollywood Films: A History (2004)

Piracy in the Motion Picture Industry (2003)

Jukeboxes: An American Social History (2002)

Vending Machines: An American Social History (2002)

Age Discrimination by Employers (2001)

Shoplifting: A Social History (2001)

Movies at Home: How Hollywood Came to Television (1999)

American Television Abroad: Hollywood's Attempt to Dominate World Television (1998)

Tipping: An American Social History of Gratuities (1998)

American Films Abroad: Hollywood's Domination of the World's Movie Screens from the 1890s to the Present (1997)

Baldness: A Social History (1996)

Policewomen: A History (1995)

Payola in the Music Industry: A History, 1880–1991 (1994)

The Sexual Harassment of Women in the Workplace, 1600 to 1993 (1994)

Women Serial and Mass Murderers: A Worldwide Reference, 1580 through 1990 (1992)

BY KERRY SEGRAVE AND LINDA MARTIN
AND FROM MCFARLAND

The Continental Actress: European Film Stars of the Postwar Era; Biographies, Criticism, Filmographies, Bibliographies (1990)

The Post-Feminist Hollywood Actress: Biographies and Filmographies of Stars Born After 1939 (1990)

Women and Capital Punishment in America, 1840–1899

Death Sentences and Executions in the United States and Canada

KERRY SEGRAVE

McFarland & Company, Inc., Publishers
Jefferson, North Carolina, and London

LIBRARY OF CONGRESS CATALOGUING-IN-PUBLICATION DATA

Segrave, Kerry, 1944–
　　Women and capital punishment in America, 1840–1899 :
death sentences and executions in the United States and
Canada / Kerry Segrave.
　　　　p.　　cm.
　　Includes bibliographical references and index.

　　ISBN 978-0-7864-3823-5
　　softcover : 50# alkaline paper ∞

　　1. Capital punishment — United States — History — 19th century.
2. Capital punishment — Canada — History — 19th century.
3. Women death row inmates — United States — History — 19th
century.　　4. Women death row inmates — Canada — History —
19th century.　　I. Title.
HV8699.U5S36　　2008
364.66082'0973 — dc22　　　　　　　　　　　　　　　2008005200

British Library cataloguing data are available

©2008 Kerry Segrave. All rights reserved

*No part of this book may be reproduced or transmitted in any form
or by any means, electronic or mechanical, including photocopying
or recording, or by any information storage and retrieval system,
without permission in writing from the publisher.*

Cover photograph ©2007 Shutterstock

Manufactured in the United States of America

*McFarland & Company, Inc., Publishers
　Box 611, Jefferson, North Carolina 28640
　　www.mcfarlandpub.com*

Contents

Preface 1

1. Women and Capital Punishment 3

2. 1840s and 1850s

Elizabeth Van Valkenburgh	17	Mary Twigg	33
Mary Runkle	18	Mary Hartung	34
Ann Hoag	20	Ann Bilansky	43
Elizabeth Harker	23	Executions of Women	
Henrietta Robinson	25	in the 1840s and 1850s	47
Charlotte Jones	31		

3. 1860s

Martha Grinder	49	Hester Vaughn	74
Mary Surratt	56	Harriet Grier (Crittenden)	75
Bridget Durgan	62	Executions of Women	
Lucy Parnell	69	in the 1860s	76
Sarah Victor	70		

4. 1870s

Mary Wallis	79	Phoebe Campbell	85
Laura Fair	80	Susan Eberhart	88

Table of Contents

Libby Garrabrant	89	Jennie Smith	99
Elizabeth Workman	93	Kate Sothern	105
Lodecea Fredenburg	94	Executions of Women	
Anna Hollenschied	95	in the 1870s	109
Johanna Turbin	98		

5. 1880s

Margaret Meierhofer	111	Matilda Jones	140
Lucinda Fowlkes	113	Sarah Jane Robinson	141
Catherine Miller	115	Sadie Hayes	143
Mary Booth	115	Mary Garrett	144
Matilda Carter	117	Axey Cherry	145
Ella Moore	117	Chiara Cignarale	146
Lucinda Teasdale	118	Sarah Jane Whiteling	151
Emeline Meaker	118	Milly Poteat	153
Barbara Miller	121	Pauline McCoy	154
Margaret Harris	123	Executions of Women	
Angenette Haight	125	in the 1880s	154
Roxalana Druse	128		

6. 1890s

Elizabeth Potts	157	Maggie Tiller	176
Emily Boon	161	Elizabeth Nobles	177
Margaret Lashley	161	Mary Snodgrass	179
Amanda Umble	161	Martha Place	179
Anna Tribble	161	Cordelia Poirier	185
Milbry Brown	162	Emily Hilda Blake	186
Caroline Shipp	163	Executions of Women	
Lizzie Halliday	163	in the 1890s	186
Maria Barberi (Barbella)	169		

Chapter Notes 189
Bibliography 199
Index 209

Preface

Compared to men, women commit murder much less frequently, making up perhaps 10 percent of the total across time in the United States. It was rarer still for a woman to be executed for the crime of murder, with women making up no more than two to three percent of those executed in the United States across several centuries. And it was even more unusual for a white woman to be executed. For the period covered by this book slightly over 70 percent of the women executed were black.

This book profiles women executed in the United States during the period 1840 to 1899 and also profiles women sentenced to death in that period but who escaped the gallows. Usually their sentences were commuted to life imprisonment but a few won new trials and were acquitted. Only judicial executions are covered, not lynchings. An unclear number of women were lynched in America during the period covered and those were also disproportionately black women. Also profiled are all the women executed in Canada from its formation as a nation in 1867 through 1899.

Women were less likely to be executed than men because of the idea that women were "special" people, more moral, less violent, and so on. As well, it was just not considered manly to execute women. Because of the characteristics and traits ascribed to women, there was a debate throughout this entire period on the general question as to whether or not females should be executed. Editorial comment in the first 30 years covered by this book was generally opposed to the idea; in the last 30 years it was more obviously in favor of their execution, cloaked under the rhetoric of equality under the law but, perhaps, a backlash against a rising feminism taking hold in America. Public opinion seemed to move more and more behind the idea that women should not be executed and that put many state governors on the spot as they considered whether or not to commute a woman's death sentence. State legislators, on several occasions, got involved with various attempts to pass laws that would have banned the capital punishment of women, or of a specific woman. Although there was a small segment of American society that opposed capital punishment completely, the vast majority of the American people, in all walks of life, supported the death penalty, at least when it was imposed on men.

The book is divided into chapters by decades rather than, say, an alphabetical listing or a listing by type of crime, as the chronological approach makes it easier to see the changes that took place in the positions of newspaper editors and other opinion makers toward the execution of females. It was an opinion that seemed to move in an opposite direction to that of the general public. As well, the influence of the woman's movement of the time is easier to see from a chronological listing. At the end of each chapter is a more or less complete listing of all women executed in the United States during each period. From that one can see, for example, the overrepresentation of black women, especially in the first three decades.

The women mentioned in this book came from all parts of America and ranged in age from teenagers to senior citizens. Their status ranged from the lowest possible — slave — to a high-living mistress of a prominent judge. Some truly were fiends and monsters while others were the victims of outrageous injustices. One thing they had in common was that every one of them was sentenced to death by the American legal system.

1

Women and Capital Punishment

Women have always comprised a very small proportion of the total legal executions in the United States. According to one estimate approximately 567 women have been executed here over the period 1632 to 2005, about 2.8 percent of the roughly 20,000 executions carried out in that time. Of the 7,837 executions that took place from 1900 to 1999, women accounted for just 0.5 percent of the total. It was rarer still to execute a white woman. For the period covered by this book, 1840 to 1899, a total of 100 women were executed. Totals by decade were as follows, respectively: 18, 28, 25, 5, 13, 11. Thus, the execution of women declined from 71 in the first 30 years covered by this book down to 29 for the remaining 30 years. And that was due to the disappearance of slavery. Characteristics were reported for 97 of the 100 condemned women and broke down as follows: 50 black slaves, 20 free blacks, three Hispanics, 24 whites. Breakdown by decade was as follows: 1840s (12 black slaves, two free blacks, four whites); 1850s (24 black slaves, one Hispanic, three whites); 1860s (14 black slaves, three free blacks, two Hispanics, five whites, one unknown); 1870s (two blacks, two whites, one unknown); 1880s (eight blacks, five whites); 1890s (five blacks, five whites, one unknown). During the period covered by this book, lynching was a regular part of the American scene, and an additional number of women lost their lives to lynch mobs. According to one estimate, of the more than 3,000 people lynched in the United States between 1882 and 1902, about 60 were women, of which 20 were white.[1]

During 1891 some 6,000 murders were committed in the country, which led to 123 legal executions, the greatest number of executions in 10 years. No women were put to death legally that year. For the same year the number of lynchings totaled 189 men and six women; of those, 129 were blacks. Over time, very roughly, women have been responsible for 10 percent of all murders, perhaps a bit less. However, the number put to death legally has never been near that proportion. That is, there has always been a much greater reluctance to execute a woman than to execute a man, and that disinclination has been evident in lynching to about the same extent as it has manifested itself in judicial executions.[2]

It was only from the mid–1800s onward that the question of whether or not women should be executed, if convicted of a capital crime, became a major issue and one that stretched nationwide. Newspapers and periodicals became much more pervasive and widely available, and were relatively affordable. An increasingly literate population turned to them more and more. As well, improvements in telecommunications meant that through, for example, the press wire services, news was available across the nation, and published in newspapers within a day or two, and even less later, of its occurrence. This timeliness allowed the topical discussion of, and comment on, such things as capital murder cases. Still, there was little editorial comment on the execution of women in the 1840s, 1850s, and 1860s, with much more attention devoted to the issue in the last 30 years of the century, as the above-cited factors took on increasing importance. During the 1840s through the 1860s what little comment was made was mostly against the execution of women. During the 1844 trial in New York of Polly Bodine for the murder of two people (she was ultimately acquitted), the *Brooklyn Eagle* editorialized, "To hang a man is bad enough, but to hang a woman in this day of light and knowledge, is awful."[3]

A decade later the same newspaper commented on a pair of recent death sentences. In one case it noted the *Albany* (New York) *Transcript* was anxious to have the law "vindicated" in the case of the murderess Henrietta Robinson of Troy, New York, by having the death sentence carried out. The editor first chastised the Albany paper and then mentioned the second case. "The *Transcript* ought to be ashamed of such sentiments. To hang a woman would be a disgrace to any civilized community," he fumed. "An unfortunate woman named [Ann] Hoag was recently hanged at Poughkeepsie for murder, and we never wish to see the State disgraced by a repetition of such barbarity. It is ... [unworthy of] intelligent Christians."[4]

With respect to the Robinson death sentence an editor on the *New York Times* stated that even if the evidence against her was of overwhelming guilt "we should deem the execution of a woman, in the present state of the public mind, as certain to do far more harm than good. It is easy to make an argument to show that it ought not to be so, but the fact remains that the great mass of the community do not regard the hanging of a woman with the same feelings which would be excited by the hanging of a man." Even when her crime was as great as a man's and as clearly proved, even when she was just as vicious in character and in life, and even when logic dictated the same kind and degree of punishment for her and for him, it did not matter. Because, he argued, "the public sense is, and will be, shocked at it, nevertheless. It will forever seem an ignoble and a cowardly thing for the State, through its armed officers and with all the military parade of an execution, to seize upon a woman and hang her by the neck until she be dead. It seems useless and therefore inhuman — for certainly the State has bolts and bars enough to keep a woman from committing more murders. Her weakness is her defense." Additionally, he worried about the possible effect the execution of a woman would have on the general status of capital punishment. "In the case of a woman, and especially of one upon whom so much of public attention and curiosity has been expended as upon Mrs. Robinson, we have no doubt whatever that her execution would inspire the public mind with horror and disgust" the editor reasoned. "It would do more, in our judgment, than anything else to stimulate hostility to capital punishment in any case; yet much as many may desire its abolition, we presume no one would desire to have it hastened by such a cause. We trust that the sentence will be commuted."[5]

A year later, in 1856, the *Brooklyn Eagle* declared, when a motion in favor of abolishing capital punishment was lost in the U.K. House of Commons, "The execution of women has more opponents, however, and is undoubtedly a barbarous practice unworthy of the age." In the House of Lords a member of that body — Lord St. Leonards — asked if the government intended to introduce a bill for the abolition of capital punishment in the case of women, as "two most atrocious [female] criminals had had their sentences commuted." In reply, the government said no such bill would be introduced.[6]

One of the newspapers taking a harder line was the *Cleveland Plain Dealer* in 1858. In the wake of the execution of a woman in New York State and in response to the general query as to whether or not women should be hanged for murder, the publication editorialized, "We are as much admired of true women as any one but we think that exempting them from capital punishment, when guilty of murder, merely because they are women, is carrying politeness towards them altogether too far."[7]

When New York State Governor Edwin D. Morgan declined to commute the death sentence of Mary Hartung, he said of the issue generally, "It is urged upon me that, even though she is guilty, public opinion demands that her punishment should be commuted to imprisonment for life; and that if this is not done, no woman will ever again be convicted of murder in this state. Even if this were true, I should see in it no reason for my interference. It is not a matter to be decided by public feeling, by the impulses of those who have not had time or inclination to scan the evidence carefully, and many of whom are influenced by an objection to capital punishment in general, or by a horror of hanging a woman, or both." Morgan added, "Moreover, though there is undoubtedly a great repugnance in the public mind to the infliction of capital punishment upon a woman, I do not think that it is so general as is assumed, or that it interferes essentially with the course of public justice."[8]

A reprint of an article that appeared first in the *Liverpool Mercury* mentioned the possibility that William Ewart would introduce a motion into the U.K. House of Commons for the abolition of the capital punishment of females. Ewart's reasons for wanting such a measure applied equally to the U.S.A. and detailed much of the reasoning as to why women were "special," at least in regard to the death penalty. Reason number one was "the peculiarly disgusting and revolting nature of the cold-blooded strangulation of females in a Christian age and country." Second on his list was the extra time and difficulties always encountered both as to the verdict and execution when a woman faced a capital charge. That is, it was harder to seat a jury since more potential members of the panel opposed the death penalty for women than were against the death penalty for men. Also, there was a belief that a woman facing a potential capital punishment would be less likely to be convicted on the same evidence as would be a man — a more stringent degree of proof was needed. The third reason listed by Ewart was "the peculiar liability of women to influence of sudden, unexpected or previously latent, violent, insanity arising from puerperal cause or other sexual and physiological conditions." The fourth reason was the complications that arose if a woman convicted of a capital crime was found to be pregnant after sentence was passed and before the slated execution date. Obviously, the execution was postponed until after the birth, but Ewart fretted that the execution was rarely ever rescheduled and thus, somehow, justice was perverted. His fifth reason was the possibility a woman who was pregnant would be hanged without anyone knowing of her condition and thus an innocent life would be lost. Ewart, though, admitted such a situation was extremely unlikely. His sixth and last reason was "the peculiar insanity of females to temptation and crime through their circumstances of weakness and of frequently compelled submission to the violence of male ruffians." An example he gave for his last reason (and one of egregious injustice) was the case of Elizabeth Benyon, condemned to death in 1863 at Liverpool. Aged just 17, she had murdered her child of one year by drowning it in a canal. "Her own father had compelled her to horrible and unnatural immorality and had afterwards turned her and her child into the streets." Ewart's reasons caused the editor of the *Mercury* to conclude, "The illustrations of the peculiar and unavoidable evils connected with the capital punishment of females are in themselves sufficient to justify the prompt abolition of exhibitions so revolting as the judicial strangulation of women."[9]

Editorial comment on the issue turned against the idea that women should not be hanged, from about 1870 through the 1890s, even though public opinion likely moved more strongly behind the idea. Some newspapers became harsh and strident against any exemption to the death penalty for women, either in general or in individual cases. Most likely reason for the shift was the rise of feminism, which took on a greater visibility and importance from the end of the 1860s onward. Two national women's organizations for suffrage were established in 1869. And the case of Hester Vaughn's death sentence was perhaps the first in America to garner strong opposition from feminist groups and to present feminist arguments for commutation. Her case was not unlike that of Benyon in that Vaughn was also the victim of outrageous injustice. While getting the vote was the prime factor for the rise of feminism, the women lobbied for reforms in many other areas. Newspaper editors had been willing to advocate no hanging of women because they were "special," but that perhaps held only so long as they remained docile, knew their place, and kept to it. Once those special people got too demanding, though, it was a different story.

Early in May 1871 the Union Woman Suffrage Association passed a resolution that the sentencing of women to death was wrong because the right to a jury of peers was not observed since the jury was all male. Therefore, said the resolution, the execution of women was "murder." Declaring he had no wish to disparage the work done by the Association, an editor on the *New York Times* went ahead and did exactly that. He admonished the group to put its demands in "a logical form." As an example he observed that an association of "roughs" might get together and pass a resolution that the trial of "a rowdy by a jury of honest men is unconstitutional" and such a move would make about as much sense as what the women were arguing. "It is extremely bad logic to assume that the execution of a woman, convicted by a jury of men must be 'deliberate murder,'" he concluded. "But if the women's rights advocates will insist upon it, they must be prepared for unpleasant analogies by way of demonstrating its absurdity." The argument cited above would be used by feminists from 1870 through the end of the period covered by this book. It was always treated with disdain and contempt by men.[10]

In 1872 the *Brooklyn Eagle* expressed the opinion there was a growing disinclination to hang people. "The disinclination to hanging is especially strong in regard to women. It must be a very positive public opinion that can send a woman to the gallows," declared the editor. "And it must be admitted that the argument against the execution of the most awful sentence against the more delicate sex has very great weight with very many people." He wanted to see more honesty and felt if society really was against the capital punishment of women then a statutory exemption should be made in their behalf because "the other policy, which in terms establishes sexual equality on the scaffold but in effect destroys it, brings justice and law into contempt. The result is that nobody now expects a woman to be punished for an extreme crime." He worried that the opposition to the hanging of a female with a conviction involving it was "substantially unattainable."[11]

An editorial in that same year in the *New York Standard* also felt that to obtain a conviction of a woman for murder in the first degree was "impossible," citing as an example the case of Laura Fair and a couple of others. Declaring that public opinion apparently failed to find women and men equal before the criminal law in capital cases, the editor said that those rare cases in the previous few years in which females had been convicted usually ended in a commutation to a term of imprisonment or an outright pardon after a short time in prison. "We do not now, as a rule, hang women," he concluded. He, too, thought it would be more consistent if governments were to conform by statute to that fact and expressly enact a law limiting the penalty for a woman convicted of a capital crime to imprisonment for life, "with the reasonable hope of pardon by the next governor." Any such change in the law, he reasoned, would be a great relief to juries that would not have to labor under the stress of imposing a capital sentence on a woman. "For the benefit of juries, will not some of our reformers propose this change? It should not much effect the accused, but would so relieve jurors."[12]

With regard to the Anna Hollenschied case, an 1875 editorial in the *St. Louis Globe Democrat* remarked that one of the saddest duties imposed on society was the imposition of the death penalty, "and all the horror of this stern duty is intensified when the punishment is wrought upon a woman. But, unless we are prepared to say that women shall have impunity to murder, there is no other alternative than to mete out regardless of sex the penalty for that crime in which all distinctions of sex are swallowed up. Between the murderess and the murderer we can make no distinctions; that is demanded alike by the abstract claims of justice, and by the interests of society." At the time arguments favoring Hollenschied reasoned that married women were subjugated under the law to their husbands. However, it was an argument the editor attacked. Whenever a woman was found guilty of a capital crime, he declared, an appeal for a commutation was almost always made, but not due to evidence or facts, "not because manhood's natural instinct revolts at the hanging of a woman, but because — so runs the appeal — the legal subjection of a wife to her husband renders her incapable of incurring such a responsibility." As far as he was concerned, such an argument was less a protest against the execution than against the legal relations between man and wife, and less an appeal from a just sentence than an argument to show that all sentences against married women were unjust. So anyone advancing such an argument "takes refuge behind the theory that woman's subjection — woman's pupilage — has reduced her to the state of an irresponsible being; of one to whom murder is merely a technicality of the law."[13]

The Honorable Charles P. Johnson delivered a lecture in St. Louis under the auspices of the Bank Clerks' Association on the subject of "Character in Murder." After starting with some general observations such as, "Your Englishman makes the most determined burglar; your Frenchman the most expert pickpocket," he went on to discuss the differences between men and women with respect to the crime of murder. "Woman makes an able accessory before the fact, but a poor principal in the first degree. Her instincts revolt against immediate contact with the act. But as the projector, the agitator and the deviser of combinations to obtain criminal results she stands unrivaled," Johnson explained. "She plays with the fiercest passions of man with utter recklessness. She arouses the form, she nerves the arm, she directs the will, but she does not strike the blow. She leaves that to her executioner. Woman is the intriguer in murder, and with intrigue cruelty is a corollary."[14]

Upon the execution in the U.K. of convicted murderess Mary Webster in July 1879, the *Hartford Courant* observed, "The right of the sex to be treated like men was vindicated in London on Tuesday by the hanging of a woman for murder. Such an ending is against public sentiment here, although it seems to us female murderers are more common now than formerly."[15]

Early in 1880 U.S. President Rutherford Hayes remarked that an erroneous public impression existed as to his position on capital punishment. Not only was he not opposed to capital punishment, he explained, he was a staunch advocate of it. When he was governor of Ohio he had said that no woman should be hanged during his tenure in that office and he thought the erroneous impression stemmed from that pronouncement. With respect to any convicted murderess in the District of Columbia when he was in the White House, Hayes emphasized "that no merely sentimental considerations should have any weight but that any mitigations or commutations of sentence would be due to reasons which properly should weigh."[16]

At the start of 1881 the editor of the *Indianapolis Journal* discussed the case of Mrs. Brown and Mr. Wade, both convicted of the murder of the woman's husband. Wade was then under a sentence of death for the crime, while his paramour Mrs. Brown had been sentenced to life in the Indiana Reformatory. Since the pair had planned and carried out the murder together, the editor argued "There is, therefore, no room for sympathy on the ground of her possible innocence.... Neither is she entitled to any sympathy on account of her sex. Justice makes no distinction between the sexes in defining the quality or punishment of crime." He was annoyed by what he saw as discriminatory sentences for the same crime, adding, "It is true the popular mind does revolt somewhat from the idea of hanging a woman, but this sentiment grows out of a confusion of ideas in regard to the administration of justice, and a real, though perhaps unavowed opposition to capital punishment." As long as capital punishment existed on the statute books he believed it should be imposed on the sexes with an equal hand. "There is something revolting in the idea of hanging a woman, but there is also something revolting in the idea of a woman committing a murder. Murder itself is revolting."[17]

Weighing in on the subject early in 1887 was Henry Ward Beecher, who wondered in print if women should be hanged. His answer to his question was, "Why not? There are many as well fitted for it as men. I do not see any reason why they should be denied the rights of the gallows!" Actually, his article was very much in favor of equal rights for women in all spheres of activity. Beecher concluded, "As long as men are to be hanged, let no one deprive a woman of the privileges of the gallows on the same edifying conditions.... But is it best to hang men? I do not think it is."[18]

When a bill to abolish capital punishment for women failed to become law in New York State in 1887 an editor with the *New York Times* declared, "Happily, murder in the form and manner that can be clearly proved is rarely committed by women, but when it is it loses none of its atrocity, and it is hard to give a reason why the prescribed penalty should not be insisted upon." However, he did argue the "weaker sex" had certain advantages on their side in such cases, sentiment being one. Also, it had to be a pretty clear case in which there were few extenuating circumstances that would result in the conviction of a woman for murder in the first degree and for the imposition of the death penalty.[19]

In the wake of the execution of Roxalana Druse at Herkimer on February 28, 1887, the *New York Times* editorialized, "There is no doubt a far stronger feeling of repulsion — not so much, perhaps, against the infliction of capital punishment as against our method of inflicting it — in the case of a woman than of a man. It is very possible that executions of women would have been more frequent if the idea of choking a woman to death were less horrible or if some less brutal mode of giving effect to the law were provided, even as an alternative."[20]

Later in 1887 the *Brooklyn Eagle* delivered one of its many editorials in favor of executing women. It commented on the Druse execution, then three months old, and the more recent case of Chiara Cignarale. The editor felt the conviction of the latter "is an additional proof that juries are overcoming that 'sickly sentimentalism' which for so many years has given point to the sneer that no woman could be convicted of a capital crime in the State of New York. There is no chivalry in espousing the cause of a deliberate murderess. Cold blooded assassination effectually obliterates the respect which every properly constituted man feels for members of the opposite sex." Continuing on, he added, "If it is to be conceded that the majority of men shrink from the thought of hanging a woman with a repugnance which they do not feel in the case of a man, it must also be admitted, in view of the case of Mrs. Druse and Mrs. Cignarale, that the disposition to permit that repugnance to override the law and defeat the ends of justice is rapidly yielding to a more rational view of the duties of jurymen."[21]

Also prodded to take editorial action by the Cignarale case was the *Hartford Courant*, but from a different position. "It does not seem as if a woman was made to be hung. It shocks all our ideas of the sex, all our notions of tenderness and protection.... We are shocked extremely when a woman commits a murder, it seems more horrible than the same crime in a man. We do not think of her as a woman at all, but as a fiend in woman's form." And, he explained, "This comes from a noble survival in us of our original idea about women — that they are so much above us generally in delicacy, and purity, and goodness. And then their physical weakness pleads for them." He allowed that one could reason if a man was subject to capital punishment, then so should a woman in similar circumstances, "but we cannot feel so. Wicked and abandoned as she is, she is still a woman, and the spectacle of her dangling on the gallows is revolting, and is somehow repugnant to our civilization."[22]

Adding to the debate in 1887 was an editorial from the *New York World* that declared, "The hanging of a woman is revolting. Likewise the hanging of a man.... Neither the law of God nor the moral law takes cognizance of sex. The consequences of infraction are unpitying." Thus, argued the editor, it was not possible for the courts or for the governor to create a sex distinction for capital punishment.[23]

After Mrs. Potts and her husband were hanged in 1889, the *Carson (Nevada) Tribune* editorialized, "In capital cases the mere fact of sex alone should not blunt the sword of justice. When a woman dyes her hands in human blood deliberately it removes her from the immunities of her sex, and the good of womanhood at large is best subserved by her punishment the same as though she were a man."[24]

1. Women and Capital Punishment

Speaking of the execution of an unnamed woman in the U.K. in 1896, the *Brooklyn Eagle* fumed, "There are sentimentalists who will argue that because she was a woman, she should have been spared the final and supreme disgrace of the gallows and her punishment commuted to imprisonment for life. The only argument for such a conclusion is found in mere sentiment, and it is mawkish sentiment at the best." The editorial added, "If a woman forgets the gracious distinctions of her sex and the humanity which is her chiefest ornament, and willfully imbues her hands in the life blood of a fellow creature, then she has forfeited all claims to distinction from any other criminal, and should receive no more consideration than as accorded to any other murderer." In conclusion he thundered, "There is neither humanity nor justice in the doctrine that because a criminal is a woman she should be treated more leniently in the matter of punishment than a man guilty of the same offense."[25]

Later in 1896 the same newspaper delivered another editorial on the subject. "The *Eagle* believes in capital punishment for women as well as for men when capital crimes have been done," the editorial explained. "Women have been hanged in this state. Of course few of them have met such a death because few women are guilty of murder. But the fact that they have been convicted of murder in the first degree and have paid the legal penalty for their crime is proof of the possibility of executing the law upon women."[26]

A year and a half later the *Brooklyn Eagle* discussed the case of Elizabeth Nobles, a white woman on death row in Georgia, and the black man she had hired to commit the murder, also on death row. At that point the case had dragged on for over two years, "but public sentiment is so decidedly against the death sentence [for Nobles only] that for once the delays of the law have received public countenance." Speculating on the final outcome of the case, the editor thought Nobles would "undoubtedly" escape the gallows but "a poor, ignorant wretch of a negro whom she hired to help her in the murder will be hanged. The exemption of women from hanging does not imply any tenderness on the part of the community toward violators of the law. It is rather a token of respect for the sex that furnishes so few of the criminal and vicious." Both Nobles and the black man had their death sentences commuted to life imprisonment.[27]

Another to comment on the Nobles case was the *Montezuma Journal* from Cortez, Colorado. It said that the petitions that had been circulated to save Nobles were "all based on the theory that no court of that state should condemn a woman to hang.... There is a deeply rooted sentiment in that state against the hanging of women, especially those of the white race." Reportedly, only two women had been legally executed in Georgia; Polly Baker was hanged in Wilkes County for poisoning a rival, around 1800; and Susan Eberhart, hanged in 1872. Regarding the execution of the latter, the paper said, "Public sentiment was so strong against the hanging of a woman that Governor Smith lost all political influence when he permitted Miss Eberhardt to ascend the scaffold. His career ended with the fall of the drop."[28]

Later in 1898 the *Washington Post* delivered an editorial on Martha Place, then under a death sentence, declaring that all that could be urged by petitioners for clemency was the sex of the convict. "While cold reason condemns the granting of clemency on that ground, the sentiment of the American people is intensely hostile to the execution of a woman for any cause. This feeling has rendered it extremely difficult to convict a woman of a capital crime. Evidence that would convict a man often acquits a woman." He argued that if there were no way of avoiding the putting to death of female murderers, the death penalty laws would all be repealed. The editor said he could frame no logical argument for executive clemency in the Place case but also did not believe she would be put to death because "Sentiment will again prevail over logic." Place was executed.[29]

In March 1899, the *Washington Post* stated it was a well-known fact that it was difficult to inflict the death penalty on a woman, but in other countries there was much less reluctance on the part of juries, judges and executives to convict, sentence, and execute a woman guilty of murder. No examples or details were given. "And it may be added that the degree in which that reluctance obtains in different nations comes very near being a fair gauge of their respective advancement in civilization." Declaring itself not to be an advocate of abolition of the death penalty, the *Post* concluded, "Whether logical or otherwise — and we are inclined to think it the latter — the sentiment against putting women to death is strong and steadily growing stronger. And it cannot be denied that this is an indication of a tendency the reverse of decadent. Argue as one may against the absurdity of sex discrimination in crime, we still feel that the manliest of men are those who would be most reluctant to send a woman to death or to take part in her execution."[30]

1. Women and Capital Punishment

As 1899 came to a close the U.K. publication *The Spectator* discussed the topic, calling it "monstrously unreasonable" to retain the death penalty for one sex and not the other, since "morally the woman who murders is often more guilty than the man. She is more trusted, her instrument — poison — is more treacherous, and she is almost invariably sober. She has, if anything, a keener conscience to overcome, and a natural impulse of pity for all physical suffering which she has to beat down before she can obtain the necessary callousness." Wondering why, then, female murderers were so often spared the gallows, compared to men, *The Spectator* concluded, "Simply because the execution of a woman is rather more painful to a sensitive society than the execution of a man. That is the real reason, and it is quite time that society recognizing it, should ask itself whether some at least of its modern philanthropy, its horror of giving pain, does not spring either from pure selfishness or from enfeebled nerves." Arguing that to make the law effective it had to, on occasion, inflict pain, and to do so on both sexes equally, the publication warned, "The argument that a woman should not be executed for murder because of her weakness is an argument against all punishment whatsoever."[31]

2

1840s and 1850s

Elizabeth Van Valkenburgh

Elizabeth Van Valkenburgh [perhaps Valkenburg] was executed in Johnston, New York, on February 24, 1846, for having murdered her husband by administering poison to him, probably in 1845. Reportedly, great efforts were made to have the governor commute her sentence but those efforts failed. Prior to the governor's stating he would not alter the sentence, Van Valkenburgh, 47, maintained her innocence. However, when all hope was gone she confessed the crime. On February 22, just two days before her execution, she made a full confession to the crime for which she was to die, "and acknowledged the justice of the sentence" in the presence of the district attorney, the sheriff, and Judge Watson. In that confession she denied having poisoned her first husband, whom it had been reported and rumored she had also murdered. Then, on the morning of February 23, she made an addition to her confession in which she admitted giving her first husband a dose of arsenic. It was a dose that did not kill him immediately but was ultimately the cause of his death.[1]

According to a reporter, "We are informed by those who witnessed the execution that the scene was awful. ... when brought from her cell, her face showed a most haggard appearance, and the visage of despair was depicted upon her countenance." After a prayer was offered by a clergyman, Van Valkenburgh spoke a few words to those present, warning that if any "drunkards or transgressors" were present they should take warning from her fate. "The drop was then let fall and as the rope straightened upon her neck and just as she was raised from her feet, she gave a shriek and passed from time to eternity. Thus ended the life of a lewd and wretched woman who had sent two husbands (perhaps unprepared) into another world."[2]

Mary Runkle

Late in August 1847, a man by the name of John Runkle, who lived on West Street in Troy, New York, was found dead in his house. His body was severely mangled and his wife Mary Runkle also bore marks of violence on her body. A coroner's inquest was held and in due course it rendered a verdict that Runkle's death was the result of a beating inflicted on him by Mary and by his 12-year-old daughter Elizabeth. Both were arrested. Those three people constituted the entire Runkle household and had lived in Troy for only a few months. Prior to that time they lived for several years in the community of Westmoreland. Originally, they hailed from Montgomery County, where they were, said a journalist, "respectably connected." Reportedly, while they were not intemperate, their character while they lived in Montgomery County was "an unenviable one." Reports connected them with the disappearance of a peddler. Two of their children had made suspicious remarks with respect to the peddler and soon afterwards they were both found drowned under such circumstances that the coroner's jury in that case declared the two children came to their deaths by the agency of person or persons unknown. During the latter part of their residence in Westmoreland they were engaged in much litigation. All three surviving family members were under recognizance to appear at the next recorder's court, on a charge of larceny in regard to allegedly stealing clothes from their neighbors.[3]

Runkle was described as a feeble man, having been in declining health for some time. His wife and daughter's account of his demise was that John was taken by a fit in the night; he got out of bed and fell down on the floor two or three times, thus sustaining the injuries that appeared on his person. As well, Mary claimed the marks on her body were sustained while she tried to assist her flailing and thrashing husband during his fits. In the morning of the day of John's death Elizabeth was sent to the neighbors for help. When they arrived they found Runkle laid out on the bed, dead and cold. There were traces of blood on the floor, which had been mopped up. When the house was searched a bundle was found concealed in the attic, containing shirts of the three, all soiled with blood. Accounts by the wife and daughter as to the change of clothing and the hiding of the soiled garments were conflicting and contradicted by the facts. The verdict of the coroner's jury was as follows: "That the said John Runkle came to his death in consequence of violence occasioned to him by Mary Runkle, in the presence of Elizabeth Runkle, and with the assistance of the said Elizabeth."[4]

At the time of her execution Mary was about 50 years old, having been born in Root, Montgomery County. She was married to her husband in her native town, claiming she became jealous of him about a year after the marriage. From that point forward a "continued series of difficulties has occurred between them," observed a news account. Mary acknowledged that she obtained goods by forgery about 10 years after her marriage and said that was her first crime. Some time later a peddler passed through the area where she lived, selling goods on a credit of four to five weeks. When he failed to return at the expected time to make his collections a search was launched. He was traced as far as the Runkle house but then no trace of him could be found. At school her children spoke about their new dresses, stating their mother had plenty of such cloth. Having repeated those remarks to the schoolteacher in their mother's presence, the two children were soon after found drowned in a tub that held only a few inches of water. While rumors swept the area that Runkle murdered all three, Mary always denied the allegations. Other crimes and charges were laid at her feet over the years, some of which she denied, some of which she admitted. One of the latter was the robbing of a church.[5]

On the day of her execution as estimated 1,000 people gathered in the streets of Whitesboro and around the courthouse although the execution was private, limited to the number required by law to be present. The gallows was erected in a room over the jailer's office and included a hole in the floor through which a rope with a noose was passed down to the victim seated in a chair in the jailer's office. Sometime before her execution she was said to have made a confession to the undersheriff and to a medical doctor. At a few minutes after noon on November 9, 1847, "she was taken into a room where some dozen people were present, and seated upon a chair, more dead than alive," said a journalist. "From a hole above her head came a cord, which was attached to a beam in a room above. She was hoisted out of existence, making no more resistance than would have been made by a sack of meal."[6]

As she was positioned for death, a reporter observed, "What a sight! A woman — a mother — a wife, charged with a number of murders, dressed in preparation for her execution, her arms bound down, seated under the instrument of death, silent and fixed, with but a few minutes of existence left. And not a motion visible.... The bell rang — the cord was cut — and she was launched into eternity. Not a word — not a motion but a little heaving of the breast.... Thus ended the earthly fate of Mary Runkle."[7]

Ann Hoag

Ann Hoag was born in the town of Milan, Dutchess County, New York, in the spring of 1821. She was deserted by her parents while still an infant and left a foundling in the public streets. Fortunately, the abandoned infant was taken into the family of Henry Taylor, a "wealthy gentleman" residing in the community of Red Hook in the same county and who adopted Ann into his family as his daughter. At the age of 12 she was sent to a boarding school for two or three years and received what was described as a "fair education." According to press reports, "She mingled among the friends and relatives of her adopted parents, and was respected and esteemed by all who knew her." When she neared her 18th birthday a resident of the same town by the name of Nelson Hoag became her suitor and after a brief courtship they were married. Nelson owned a small farm in the interior of Dutchess County where they reportedly lived happily together for several years. Subsequently they moved to the town of Dover where they lived in reduced financial circumstances due to "unfortunate speculations." Over time Ann became the mother of five children. It was reported that even in her days of adversity she conducted herself "with propriety, and proved herself a faithful and affectionate wife until about the beginning of the year 1851, when she contracted an unholy passion for a young man named William Sumners [perhaps Somers] whose paramour she subsequently became, and thus rapidly traveled the road of crime which has ended in an ignominious death." Engaging in highly exaggerated prose the reporter continued, "Led blindly by guilty passion, the ill-starred woman plunged into misery and degradation, renounced virtue, reputation, husband, and children, until at last she murdered her husband, with the deliberate purpose of removing all barriers to the complete abandonment of herself to crime." It was in June 1851 that she resolved to murder her husband and did so by mixing arsenic with his food. Nelson died on June 20, 1851. After killing her husband Ann ran off with Sumners but was quickly captured. She was tried and convicted in March 1852. Judge Barculo sentenced her to be executed on May 7, 1852.[8]

A reprieve was granted to Ann due to a circumstance unique to

2. 1840s and 1850s

women. Explained a reporter: "In an evil hour she fell a victim to the impulses of her animal nature. And now it is clear that she is pregnant for a period of some seven months by her paramour." When a judge imposed a capital punishment sentence he was obliged to set the date of execution at no less than four weeks and not more than eight weeks from the date of sentencing. But a provision of the statute directed the state governor to extend the time of execution in the case of females who were pregnant until after the birth of the child.[9]

On April 18 Ann gave birth to a female child in her cell at the county jail in Poughkeepsie. She was sentenced again to death, with the hanging to take place on July 30. In mid–July, New York State Governor Washington Hunt declined to commute Hoag's sentence.[10]

In a letter to Alonzo H. Morey, sheriff of Dutchess County, and the man in charge of the execution, Governor Hunt explained his reasoning. Since granting the pregnancy reprieve, he wrote, he had received from Dutchess County numerous communications urging the exercise of clemency in Hoag's behalf. He explained the pardoning power vested in him was not a personal prerogative to be exercised without reference to the provisions of law or the guilt of the offender. Hunt argued the granting of a pardon was legitimate only when the conviction was based on inadequate proofs, inconsistent with newly discovered facts, or when the crime was accompanied by mitigating circumstances that diminished the moral guilt of the offender. He found no such circumstances in the case of Ann Hoag, calling her clearly guilty and saying that no one disputed the justice of the verdict. "Her crime was of the deepest atrocity. Without even the poor plea of resentment, she destroyed a kind and confiding husband, by mingling poison with his daily sustenance," wrote Hunt. "She destroyed her lawful protector to gain a paramour, and obtain free scope for the indulgence of a guilty passion. Having conceived this diabolical purpose, she proceeded to execute it with a degree of perseverance rarely equaled."[11]

The governor continued, "It is a murder made doubly detestable by the super-added crimes of treachery and adultery. The deliberate assassination of the husband by the wife has been contemplated with peculiar horror, and punished by the highest penalties in all countries, and in every stage of human society.... Of the various forms of murder, that which is inflicted under the disguise of kindness, disarming suspicion by professions of fidelity, must be acknowledged the most odious and revolting." Hunt acknowledged that many citizens, "yielding to sentiments of benevolence and forgetful of the enormity of the crime," had persuaded themselves it was the duty of the governor to shield the condemned person from the extreme penalty of the law because she was a woman and a mother. He argued that if he were at liberty to follow his sympathies it would be next to impossible to resist such appeals because the execution of a woman was "repugnant to the generous impulse of the heart, but the criminal code makes no distinction between the sexes in the punishment of crime." Elaborating on the theme, Hunt declared, "The woman who has renounced the virtue which adorns the female character, and profaned the laws of God and man by the deliberate murder of her only legitimate protector, appears before us disrobed of all those normal graces which entitle her to plead the prerogatives of the gentler sex. She ceases to be a woman; her hands are stained with the blood of the innocent, she presents a melancholy spectacle of the guilt and degradation to which our common nature may descend when the nobler affections are extinguished by depraved and licentious passions." Thus, Hunt refused to commute the sentence.[12]

During the morning of July 30 the scaffold was erected in the vestibule of the courthouse, attached to the jail, on Main Street, Poughkeepsie, under the direction of Sheriff Morey. A sheriff's jury consisting of 24 residents was assembled and seated directly in front of the gallows — to serve as official witnesses. As well, Morey admitted about 80 more people as general spectators. The jail was guarded on the outside by the Poughkeepsie Guards while a dense crowd of people milled about the area hoping to gain admission to the spectacle. Ann Hoag was hanged from the same scaffold and at the same time as was Jonas Williams, a 27-year-old black man. The pair were complete strangers to each other and faced death for separate and unrelated crimes. Late in the evening of July 29 Ann was attacked with what was called a "fit of insanity" and remained in that state of mind until daylight, when she became calm and appeared more reconciled to her fate. The condemned pair were attired in dresses of white cambric and at 20 minutes to midnight on the 30th they were conducted side by side to the scaffold. "The female looked exceedingly pale, and her bright blue eyes beamed with an expression of sadness and despondency," said a journalist. "She was about 5 feet 7 inches in height, slender form, small features, with fair skin and auburn hair. Her appearance was that of a female not over 22 years of age, although she was, in fact, past 31 years." At 14 minutes to midnight Morey shook hands with each and expressed a hope God had forgiven their sins. Ann replied, "I feel that I am to be saved. God bless you, dear Sheriff, for your kindness towards me." Their arms were pinioned, the white caps were drawn over their heads, and at midnight both ropes were severed and the upward-jerk hanging left both bodies suspended about two feet above the scaffold floor. Hoag had been attached to a 173-pound weight; Williams to one of 218 pounds. (Throughout some of the period covered by this book the upward-jerk gallows was used, giving way in latter years to the trap-door gallows with which we are more familiar. Both looked alike with a scaffold constructed above the ground and a noose hanging down. In the upward-jerk gallows a series of weights was set in motion which pulled the victim up, say, seven feet, and then allowed a drop of, say, six feet, leaving the victim suspended above the floor of the scaffold. The upward jerk method was less likely to break the neck — and deliver a theoretical quick and painless death — than was the trap-door gallows. However, the latter also regularly failed to break the neck. When the neck was not broken by the noose, the victim, of course, then strangled to death, which could take up to 10 or 15 minutes and resulted in a horrifying spectacle of a writhing and twisting body, often for the full ten minutes or so.) Reportedly Hoag died comparatively easy and in a few seconds her body was motionless. Williams writhed and twisted in agony for upwards of five minutes. After being suspended for about 30 minutes both bodies were cut down, deposited in coffins, and immediately interred in the grounds belonging to the courthouse.[13]

In the week before her execution Hoag made a full confession that ran to 70 pages, in which she declared Sumners to have been her confederate in the murder — he was in jail awaiting trial as an accessory before the fact. Upon her death, observed a reporter, Ann left "six unfortunate orphans who are left to the cold charities of the world." Hoag left her confession with a Mr. Pitt of the *Poughkeepsie American* newspaper with instructions to publish her confession in pamphlet form with any proceeds to be for the benefit of those six orphans.[14]

Elizabeth Harker

Some time in 1852 the husband of Elizabeth Harker died under mysterious circumstances in or around Huntington, Pennsylvania. Although those circumstances gave rise to rumor and suspicion the man was buried without a post-mortem examination. As time passed those suspicions faded away. However, about a year later, Harker's sister, with whom Elizabeth then lived, was seized by a violent illness exhibiting all the symptoms of a poisoning victim. She recovered but soon afterwards she was taken with the same terrible symptoms and died in great agony. Still, no suspicion fell upon Harker immediately. Bit by bit, though, fueled in part by the woman's "unfeeling conduct," people began to suspect Elizabeth of being a murderer. That led to the sister's body being exhumed and the finding of enough arsenic in the remains to have killed three people. After that the body of Mr. Harker was exhumed. It, too, was found to contain arsenic. Elizabeth was arrested and tried in Huntington in 1853. After two hours of deliberation the jury returned a verdict of guilty of murder in the first degree. Harker was sentenced to death in the fall of that year.[15]

Commenting on that verdict a news account declared, "The circumstances of the murder make it one of the most shocking cruelty and monstrous depravity. The murderess is a widow, sixty-five years of age, and is strongly suspected of having murdered her husband a year ago. [She was tried only for the murder of her sister.] Her object in the commission of the crime, of which she is convicted, seems to have been that she might become the wife of the widowed man and take the place of her murdered sister in his bed and at his board."[16]

Another contemporary account declared the evidence of her guilt to have been "very plain" and "disclosed a fiendish transaction sufficient to make humanity shudder. It appears that the woman poisoned her own sister for the purpose of becoming her successor in the household!" The reporter said that public opinion was so much against her that probably no effort would be made to have her reprieved.[17]

Pennsylvania Governor Bigler did step in by simply not issuing the death warrant. Since that was a necessary step in the trail of paperwork to be done before Harker's execution could be carried out it amounted to an indefinite stall in the execution of the woman. Officially, though, there was no commutation of sentence, no reprieve, no pardon. Elizabeth remained under a sentence of death in the Huntington jail. Bigler withheld the death warrant, said a journalist, "in consideration of her sex and extreme age." Early in November 1855, Harker died of natural causes in that jail, causing one commentator to observe that since her conviction "she was allowed to drag out a life of remorse and wretchedness, until called by Providence to her final account."[18]

Another newsman declared, a fortnight after her death, "Two weeks ago a stern summons came, and Elizabeth Harker, silvered by the frost of age, and charged with guilt such as has rarely stained the frame of mortals, passed to that tribunal where judgment is at once infallible and eternal."[19]

Henrietta Robinson

So much media attention was devoted to the trial and background of Henrietta Robinson that she was given a nickname by the press, becoming known across America as "the Veiled Murderess"— for her penchant for wearing a veil almost constantly. It was at Troy, New York, during the last week of May 1854 that her trial commenced, with the prisoner indicted for the murder of Timothy Lannagan, a 37-year-old man with a wife and four children, by administering poison to him on May 25, 1853. Lannagan's 25-year-old sister, Catherine Lubee, died at the same time as her brother and in the same fashion. And while Robinson was believed to have killed her also, she was never tried for that crime. When she was placed on trial she was around 35 years old and described as possessing a pretty face, fine form, and a foreign air. On her first day in court she was described thusly: "She was closely veiled, and remained so during her stay in Court. She was richly dressed in black silk, a finely worked collar and undersleeves, wearing a white shirred bonnet, ornamented with artificial flowers (overhung with a heavy blue veil), white kid gloves, black silk long shawl lined with white satin. Her whole apparel was of that fashionable description adopted to exhibit her form to the best advantage."[20]

During his opening address the district attorney outlined the history of the crime. Prior to May 25, 1853, Robinson had lived for a year or more in a house in the north part of the city of Troy. On the opposite side of the street, directly across from Henrietta, lived Lannagan, who had taken up residence there with his family in October 1852. He lived in one part of the house and ran a small grocery store in the other part. Robinson became a frequenter of the grocery store — the pair had no previous acquaintance. About four months before the pair died, trouble occurred between Timothy and Henrietta. She attended a party at the former's house and during the evening got involved in some sort of dispute with one or more men, during the course of which she drew a pistol on them. That incident prompted Mr. and Mrs. Lannagan to eject her from their house. Two or three days later she called at the Lannagan house before Timothy was out of bed and verbally abused Mrs. Lannagan. Some time elapsed before she resumed buying her groceries there. On May 25, 1853, she entered the store, bought a few items and left. She returned an hour or so later but some of the men from the fight were there and Mrs. Lannagan asked her to leave. Returning to the store at about 1:00 P.M., Henrietta found Mr. and Mrs. Lannagan and Lubee having a meal. Henrietta invited herself to join them and insisted they must all have some beer, her treat. It was purchased from the Lannagan store. Robinson also insisted on having sugar for the beer. People were up and down and in and out passing between the living quarters and the store — serving customers and so on — and Robinson was left alone for short periods of time during which she added sugar to the tumblers of beer. Apparently she also added arsenic. Neither Henrietta nor Mrs. Lannagan drank any beer but the other two did. Soon the pair got sick and both died, at around 7:00 P.M. Just two weeks before the deaths Henrietta had purchased arsenic, a quantity of which was found at her house — concealed under a carpet — after May 25th.[21]

At the end of May the jury, after being out for three hours, delivered a verdict of guilty of murder in the first degree. According to a news account, "She received the verdict very boldly, and exclaimed — 'Shame on you, Judge; you are prejudiced against me!' She also charged the Jury with being bribed." As well, the prisoner's manner after the verdict was rendered was described as "strange, and her language incoherent."[22]

Much curiosity existed as to the background of Robinson. Nothing was known about her prior to her arrival in Troy about one year before the murders. One story in circulation at the time of her conviction was apparently spread by Henrietta herself. It held that some 20 years earlier she lived near Quebec City, Canada, was a pupil at the seminary there, that her maiden name was Wood, and that her family was one of wealth, good standing and respectability. While in Quebec City she was said to have moved in the best circles, as did her three sisters, who also attended the seminary at different times; and she subsequently married an army officer in Canada. After he died she married a surgeon in the army, from whom she later separated. However, a William F. Wood (from the only family living in Quebec City with that surname and general description) wrote a letter refuting her story, after traveling to the Troy jail to visually inspect the woman. Wood had four sisters, who had been pupils at a seminary and who all then resided in Great Britain. One of them had married an officer of the British Army in Canada and, after his death, married in Quebec a Dr. Macintosh of the Royal Artillery, with whom she was then living in Scotland.[23]

On June 19, 1855, Judge Harris sentenced Robinson to be executed by hanging on August 3, 1855, at Troy. At the conclusion of the sentencing, when Harris commended her soul to God's mercy, she told him he had better pray for his own soul, declaring she was the victim of a political conspiracy. She was about to say more but her counsel managed to shut her up. As she was led out of the courtroom Henrietta turned, pointed her finger at the judge and exclaimed, "Judge Harris, may the Judge of Judges be your judge."[24]

That Henrietta Robinson might be insane, as mad as the proverbial hatter, was beginning to take hold. A month after the death sentence was passed an editorial in the *New York Times* stated it was known that New York Governor Clark was in daily receipt of petitions, numerous and "respectably" signed, urging him to commute Henrietta's sentence. "We trust the Governor will find it consistent with his sense of duty, and of public expediency, to grant the request of these petitioners," said the editor. "The guilt of Mrs. Robinson ... is not entirely free from doubt, nor is it quite certain that she has not been, and is not now, partially insane. Commutations have frequently been granted in cases less embarrassed by considerations of this sort than hers." Regardless of the particulars the editor was against the execution of women, period. "But without any reference to these circumstances, we should deem the execution of a woman, in the present state of the public mind, as certain to do more harm than good." He argued that the "great mass" of people did not regard the hanging of a woman with the same feelings as the hanging of a man. That editor was not opposed to capital punishment, per se.[25]

Speculation about the background of the woman, then referred to in the press almost always as the "Veiled Murderess," continued to swirl in 1856. A former prison officer at Sing Sing Penitentiary (where Robinson was incarcerated), who had several conversations with the prisoner, wrote a letter to a Troy newspaper supposedly about her background. In this version of her past it was said she was not a member of the Wood family but was a native of England who knew something about the Wood family from an acquaintance of their family in England, which perhaps explained her partial but incomplete knowledge of the family. According to this account Henrietta had been convicted in the United Kingdom of infanticide and sentenced to transportation and banishment to Van Dieman's Land (Tasmania). Through the intercession of friends the sentence was commuted to banishment from the country. She left for the U.S.A. and on the boat trip over ingratiated herself with a well-to-do woman returning home to New York by tending to her during a sickness. In gratitude the wealthy woman gave Henrietta a job working for her but Robinson stayed only a few weeks before decamping for Boston, where she "got into bad company and pursued the life of a wanton." Troy's newspaper editor did not know what to make of the story, unable to decide whether or not to believe it. "At all events, this much we know — Mrs. Robinson is Mrs. Robinson, the 'veiled murderess' — and a poor, wretched, passion-spoiled, pitiable, crazy wreck of humanity she is," concluded the editor. "That she has once and somewhere moved in refined circles; that she has enjoyed early educational and social advantages; that she was, withal, a beautiful and accomplished woman, no one who has seen and conversed with her freely can for a moment doubt. But what a fall, and how low she has fallen. Let the veil be drawn over her and the degradation forever more."[26]

New York State's governor soon intervened and commuted her sentence to life in prison. As of the summer of 1858 she remained incarcerated in the female prison at Sing Sing. It had 100 cells in the women's section and 108 prisoners. All were housed singly in the cells except for two each in eight cells. One of the inmates was Henrietta and of her it was said, "She is treated as a partial lunatic, but the officers of the prison do not fully believe that she has lost her reason. Her last fancy is a belief in the science of witchcraft." She professed an ability to bewitch any person, when it pleased her to do so. Supposedly she was convinced she had the power to make her associates sick or well, as the mood took her. As to her effect a reporter commented, "A tall, commanding figure, a haggard face, with the devil's own eye for accessories, enables her very strongly to impress these vagaries upon the ignorant and superstitious who are her companions. I will venture to say that more than one half of these degraded beings are firm believers in her capacity to raise the devil." So troublesome had Robinson become to the staff and inmates, that Mrs. Doge, matron of the women's section, had been forced to isolate her and confine her to her cell for most of the time. For an hour or two each day, while the other inmates were engaged in the workshops, Henrietta was left at liberty in the prison yard. She spent all her time there looking for four-leaf clovers, ingredients for the imaginary cauldron in her cell over which she muttered incantations.[27]

A certain amount of press attention was devoted in 1860 to excerpts from the book, *Life in Sing Sing*, by Reverend Luckey, chaplain of that institution for the previous 10 years. Based on his many talks with her he gave what he believed to be a "fairly" truthful account of her background. Henrietta was born in Canada East in 1827 to a wealthy family with all the advantages and was given a good education. At 16 she was sent to a distant institution of learning where she remained for two years. While there she fell in love with a man her parents did not approve of. To end that association her parents removed her from school and brought her back home. About one year after her return home she was married, despite her protests to her parents and the intended groom that she loved another. Her new husband was a young lieutenant in the British Army then stationed in Canada and with whom she shortly started for England. Continued Luckey, "Soon after marriage she began to manifest bursts of passionate and undisciplined rage, which ultimately merged into periodic fits of insanity, to which she owes her present degradation." She stayed with her husband in Europe for some two years but her dislike for him turned into such disgust that she determined to leave him and her two children and return to her parents in Canada. Upon her arrival at home she received such a torrent of "reproaches and upbraidings that she left her father's house on the night of her arrival and threw herself, unprotected and almost without means on the world."[28]

Regarding her status when her parents turned her out, Luckey said, "At this time she was in full bloom of womanhood, with more than an average amount of beauty and female accomplishments, of medium height, good figure, black hair and fair complexion, of dignified carriage, and winning manners and address. It does not appear, however improper may have been her conduct up to this period, that she had yet fallen from virtue." Shortly after being evicted from home she was found living in Troy, New York, under the assumed name of Henrietta Robinson, "and under the (so called) protection of one whose name shall not sully these pages," wrote a disgusted Luckey. That meant, perhaps, she was living openly with a man. After a year or so of living in sin she reportedly made an effort to "break the vicious bonds that held her" and return to her husband in

England. Thus, she left Troy clandestinely and reached Boston but was overtaken by her protector who induced her to return to Troy with him. "Her fall seemed now to be complete, and her case hopeless to herself," explained Luckey. "During the next few years of her life, she seems to have set at defiance all outward forms of modesty and respectability, to have become addicted to the use of intoxicating liquors, and to have completely surrendered herself to the impulses of her disposition already verging towards madness." She imagined a conspiracy had formed against her and she took to carrying pistols to protect herself from imaginary assaults. And that brought her story up to the time of Lannagan's house party from which she was ejected after the fight. By that time her protector had disappeared from the scene, probably having abandoned her. So far in the grip of madness was Henrietta then, said Luckey, "that we find her absolutely wandering about the streets of Troy in her night clothes, associating with drunken rowdies, involving the aid of the police for imaginary assaults, and acting as only a maddened woman would."[29]

People were reportedly still lobbying for a pardon for the woman in 1870. In 1873 she was transferred from Sing Sing to the state insane asylum at Auburn. To that date even her defense lawyers did not know her parentage, background, or even her real name. All the stories that had circulated with respect to her background were likely just that — stories. No evidence existed they were true in whole or in part and Robinson may just have been spinning out lies to the gullible and to those who hoped to use the tales for profit.[30]

Interest in the woman decreased over time but never completely disappeared. As late as 1898 the old story that she was a member of the Quebec City Wood family made the rounds again. This time it was supposedly verified by a woman whose name had never been cited in the past.[31]

The first 18 years of Henrietta's life sentence were passed in Sing Sing. She was then moved to the Auburn State Prison for the Insane where she remained for 17 years. In 1890 or so she was moved to the Asylum for the Criminally Insane at Mattewan, New York, where the woman of mystery died on May 4, 1905, after some 52 years in prison. Her lawyer at the end, who visited her at regular intervals, remained baffled as to her background. Even who paid and had paid all her legal fees over half a century remained unknown. That final lawyer said only that his services had been paid for by "certain influential personages" whom he was not at liberty to name.

All that was known of Henrietta Robinson was that she played the organ at Sing Sing with the touch of a "master musician" and that she died as she had lived — in silence and in mystery.[32]

A few days before her death, at a reported age of 89, when it was evident death was imminent, physicians at the asylum tried to get her to reveal her identity. She refused, saying that she had kept the secret for over 50 years and that it might as well die with her. Henrietta Robinson refused to say anything further.[33]

Charlotte Jones

On May 1, 1857, a double murder described as "most atrocious" was committed some two miles from McKeesport, Pennsylvania, 20 miles above Pittsburgh, during which an old man named George Wilson and his sister Elizabeth McMasters "were ushered into the presence of their maker." A niece of Wilson by the name of Charlotte Jones, 35, was arrested along with two men named Henry Fife and Monroe Stewart. All three were charged with murder.[34]

A few days later Charlotte made an affidavit before the mayor, correcting her original statement that implicated her brother William Jones and a man named James Williams in the double killing. In the amended document Charlotte charged the crime to Fife (her common-law husband) and Stewart.[35]

Money was said to have motivated the crime, as Wilson had about $400 in cash at his house while Elizabeth, who lived in the same dwelling, had $600 in gold and silver contained in a wallet she had tied to a rafter in the ceiling. A month earlier Charlotte's brother William told her that her uncle George kept money in his home, perhaps $900 or $1,000. From that information came the idea to rob the house. From the confession of Charlotte Jones it was revealed that in response to a summons from Henry, away from home at the time, she met Fife at a bar near Wilson's home on the evening of April 30. Charlotte journeyed there from Monongahela and met him at around 9:15 P.M. in the bar. Stewart arrived at 10 P.M. Both men had been drinking and all three drank after they met. Stewart told her he wanted her to go to Wilson's in order to steal the money. When Charlotte said she did not want to go, Stewart drew a knife and threatened her, according to the confession of Jones. When they went to the Wilson residence and knocked at the door, Wilson opened the door believing Charlotte, his niece, was outside by herself. After he opened the door to his relative the two men rushed in, with Fife stabbing Wilson to death. Stewart then beat McMasters to death. All the while, Charlotte claimed, she was yelling for the men not to kill the elderly pair. When it was all over the men swore Charlotte to silence, threatening to kill her if she talked. Sometime after 1:00 A.M. on May 1 the three set off walking to McKeesport. They drank all the while, finally turning up at a public house in McKeesport for breakfast at 7:00 A.M. or so. When the three were arrested all had extensive bloodstains on their clothing, including stains on Charlotte's dress, cape, and bonnet.[36]

One who testified during the trial of the trio was Andrew Moon, who overheard a jailhouse cell conversation between Fife and Charlotte (who had turned state's evidence). Moon had been in a cell between the cells occupied by Fife and Charlotte. Said Fife to Jones, "By your talk you have fetched us all to the gallows; you thought to save yourself but you'll have to hang with us." When he asked her why she had told everything she replied that she had been frightened into it.[37]

On July 11, 1857, in Pittsburgh the jury in the trial returned a verdict of guilty of murder in the first degree against all three.[38]

Toward the end of 1857 Jones and Fife confessed that they and they alone were guilty of the double murder. Each exonerated Monroe Stewart from all participation in the crime and from all guilty knowledge of it, either antecedent or subsequent to its commission.[39]

Charlotte Jones and Henry Fife were hanged at 2 P.M. on February 12, 1858, in the jail yard of the prison in Pittsburgh. That execution was witnessed by about 30 people — the number required by law to be present — but a very large crowd had gathered on the outside of the yard. Reportedly, "both murderers delivered addresses, acknowledging the justice of their sentence" and the innocence of Stewart. They had once in the past tried to get married but the official had rejected their application on the ground that Henry was too young. At the time of the execution Stewart was slated to die in two weeks' time, but as a consequence of the dying confessions of Charlotte and Henry, he was pardoned by Pennsylvania Governor Packer.[40]

2. 1840s and 1850s

Mary Twigg

With October 22, 1858, having been appointed the date for the execution of Mrs. Mary Twigg (perhaps Twiggs) in Danville, Pennsylvania, the whole town was reported to have been "alive with excitement." At an early hour in the morning a large concourse of strangers flocked into the place from the surrounding county. Twigg was convicted of the murder of Mrs. Catharine Ann Clark by poisoning her with arsenic. The husband of Mrs. Clark, and Mary's paramour, was convicted of the same charge and was hanged on September 20, 1858. Mrs. Clark had been on a visit to Philadelphia but returned to her home in bad health. The poison was said to have been administered in her medicine. Mary acted as the ailing woman's nurse, and she and Mr. Clark were the only people who attended her during her illness. Both were convicted on the basis of what was called "the strongest circumstantial evidence." In its account the *Chicago Tribune* spoke of Mr. Twigg having been poisoned to death by the pair, along with Mrs. Clark, and the executions being for both murders. Other news accounts spoke only of one murder and death — Mrs. Clark. After the death sentence was passed every effort was said to have been made to obtain clemency for Twigg. Petitions were extensively circulated and signed, but Governor Packer refused to grant any clemency. Public opinion was reportedly divided in regard to the guilt of Twigg. Many thought her innocent but a seemingly equal number told an inquiring reporter they believed her to be guilty. Since her imprisonment, Twigg had made one or two unsuccessful attempts to escape.[41]

The condemned woman passed her last night comfortably, sleeping well with her two children in her arms in her cell. On the morning of the 22nd she bade farewell to her brother and to her children and was taken to the scaffold at 10:15 A.M., leaning on the arm of a clergyman. After a prayer was offered, Twigg spoke for six to eight minutes, protesting her innocence, placing her trust in a "just Judge." Declaring her readiness to die, she said her only regret was leaving behind her two orphan children. A reporter described the scene thusly: "She was much affected throughout. The solemnity of the scene was made more impressive by her groans and sobs. Even after the cap was drawn over her face she appealed to God in the most earnest manner, and she asserted her innocence. At ten o'clock and thirty minutes the drop fell, and after struggling for a few moments the woman hung lifeless."[42]

Another account declared, "Mrs. Twigg is apparently about 35 years of age, and is a little over five feet in height. She is a native of Ireland and she has a very fiendish expression of the countenance." The scaffold and the rope itself used to execute Twigg were the same ones that had been employed on Clark.[43]

Mary Hartung

When Emil Hartung died in April 1858 near Albany, New York, the household consisted of himself and wife Mary as owners of the property; three boarders, Mr. and Mrs. Streit and William Rhineman [various spellings included Reimann and Rheinman]; and a young German maid. During Emil's April sickness the maid saw her mistress take something from a jar that contained "phosphorous paste" for rats and "put it in everything — tea, coffee, and beer soup." Despite that the maid was said to have interpreted that as meaning only that Mary was a devoted wife trying to cure Emil of his drinking habit. But it wasn't working fast enough for Mary so she sent her maid to the druggist for prussic acid, but he refused to sell the servant any on the ground the substance was too dangerous. Then Mary told her maid to go back to the druggist and get arsenic. When the maid refused to do so, Mary went herself. At the store she told the druggist that she wanted the arsenic for Mr. Streit, who used it in his hobby of stuffing birds. She bought four ounces of the poison. Emil kept getting worse and died screaming in pain. Soon gossip spread, with one of the rumors being that Mary and William were intimate. Rhineman was starting to act as master of the house. When the story of the arsenic's having been used to stuff birds came to the attention of Streit he explained he had no such hobby and had never stuffed a bird in his life. People urged Mary to consent to the idea of an exhumation of Emil's body to clear up the speculation circulating through the community. She promised she would go to the police and do so but suddenly she and Rhineman disappeared. However, William soon returned to the city alone and was taken into custody. Unbeknownst to the authorities, Mary was then working as a domestic. When the pair split up on the run it was agreed she would write to him as "Ferdinand Shultz" — a real person who lived near them. One of her letters to her paramour was misdirected to the real Shultz, who was familiar enough with Hartung to recognize her signature of "Mary Theresa Koehler" as the fugitive's maiden name. He passed the letter on to the police. That letter said, in part, "I dream of you every night, dear William. I do not know whether you love me still, or whether you have forgotten me: my heart clings to yours: you don't know how I love you or else I should not have committed this misfortune."[44]

And so on the afternoon of July 13, 1858, Mary Hartung was arrested for the murder of Emil by Sheriff Brayton, abut three miles west of Fort Lee, New Jersey. Brayton got a clue from the letter that indicated Mary might be in the north part of New York City. She was not there but Brayton found a woman who told him that a female of that description had left New York for New Jersey some six weeks earlier after engaging herself in a family as a seamstress. Following up that clue, Brayton discovered the girl had gone to the Fort Lee area in New Jersey. He went there and discovered that Dr. Weatherby of the community had hired a new girl some six weeks earlier. When he called at his house, Mrs. Weatherby told Brayton she had just one female servant, whose name was Elizabeth Shultz. Elizabeth was called into the room, whereupon the sheriff recognized her as Mary Hartung. Confronted thusly she admitted to being Hartung and agreed to accompany Brayton back to New York State.[45]

Near the close of her trial in February 1859, Hartung made a statement that was read to the court and to the jury by her counsel. In it she declared she had been induced to buy the arsenic by her paramour for an innocent purpose, as he informed her, and that she had no suspicion that her husband's death had been caused by poison until some time after the fact. Apparently nobody believed that because on February 7, 1859, she was found guilty by the jury of murder in the first degree. A reporter described her, in the dock, as follows: "The prisoner is quite young and handsome, and her case has created the greatest sympathy." As far as an editor with the *New York Times* was concerned there was no doubt the husband died of arsenic poisoning and there was equally not the slightest doubt the poison was administered by the wife, or by Rhineman, or by both together.[46]

At the beginning of March she was denied a new trial by the New York Supreme Court. By that time she admitted her adultery and attempted to excuse it by reason of her husband's cruelty. On March 3, Mary was sentenced to be hanged on April 27, 1859, at Albany. Speculation was that no further attempt would be made to alter the outcome through the courts but that her supporters would direct their efforts to lobbying Governor Morgan for a commutation of the sentence.[47]

When Judge Harris passed sentence, Mary, said a reporter, "was dressed in a purple de laine dress, with a light plaid shawl, and wore a black velvet hat, a veil partially concealing her face. She looked pale and somewhat careworn, and when she took her seat behind the District Attorney, burst into tears." Before passing sentence Harris asked the prisoner if she had anything to say. "For a while there was no response. Mrs. Hartung sobbing and weeping most piteously, her face buried in her hands. In about one minute she responded as follows: 'All I have to say is, that I am not guilty of the murder of my husband. I have said so before, and I say it again. This man Rheinman, will confess it over my dead body!'" Harris went on to urge her to accept the fact there was virtually no hope she would escape the imposition of the death sentence he had passed. "Another thing I would have you feel. I fear, very much fear, from the strong sympathy in your behalf, and the great efforts of your counsel, that strong hopes may be exerted that you may escape," he said. "I entreat you to dismiss such hopes. There is but little chance, I assure you, for you to escape. This is dreadful — it is appalling to see one so young as you doomed to a certain and speedy death, and that, too, not by the allotment of Providence, but by the judgment of the law. Give up any hope you may entertain of escape." He told her that even if her sentence was commuted to life imprisonment, "What better would it be for you? In the gloomy retirement of a prison what would life be worth to you? Is it not as well to die?" Judge Harris next lectured Mary on religion. "It is not all of man to die; there is a life after death, and that life is unending. What a work you have to do in the short period left to you! You have a soul, that will not die on the gallows! It will live forever and let me assure you that man cannot save it," he intoned. "There is a Being who can save your soul. Go to the Savior — your Savior and my Savior; confess your guilt, and seek forgiveness of that Savior, whose mercies are boundless and who saved one and carried him into Paradise — a thief on the cross with him. Oh, do not neglect this advice. Seek forgiveness by repentance and faith." When Harris passed sentence on Hartung he used words similar to those used by judges throughout America in capital cases. Said Harris, "The judgment of the Court is, that you, Mary Hartung, be confined in the county jail until the 27th of April next, and on that day, between the hours of 10 o'clock in the morning and 2 o'clock in the afternoon, you be hung by the neck until you are dead! And may God, in the fullness of His mercy, save your soul."[48]

Early in April, New York State Governor Edwin Morgan wrote a letter to William Hadley, Hartung's lawyer, explaining why he would not grant executive clemency to Mary. He explained that he had given the case careful consideration "with a sincere desire to arrive at a just conclusion, and with that leaning in favor of mercy which forms part of our nature, especially when that mercy is sought in behalf of a woman." Morgan added that if she were guilty of her husband's murder "she is guilty of a cool, premeditated murder of the most revolting character. If guilty, she availed herself of the opportunities the marriage state gave her to administer poison to him coolly, deliberately, maliciously. Murder by poisoning is the worst sort of murder, and the most difficult of detection." And, he reasoned, if she was guilty "I cannot reconcile it to my ideas of duty to save her from the penalty the law imposes upon her crime.... I believe her to be guilty of the deliberate murder of her husband by poisoning." In his letter Morgan also dealt with the general issue of women and capital punishment. "It is urged upon me that even though she is guilty, public opinion demands that her punishment should be commuted to imprisonment for life; and that if this is not done, no woman will ever again be convicted of murder in this State," he wrote. "Even were this true, I should see it as no reason for my interference. It is not a matter to be decided by public feeling, by the impulses of those who have not had time or inclination to scan the evidence carefully, and many of whom are influenced by an objection to capital punishment in general, or by a horror of hanging a woman, or both." Concluded the governor, "Moreover, though there is, undoubtedly, a great repugnance in the public mind to the infliction of capital punishment upon a woman, I do not think that it is so general as is assumed, or that it interferes essentially with the course of public justice." Morgan joined Harris in urging Hartung to accept the fact there was no hope of escape from her sentence. He recommended she devote herself to preparing to stand before her Creator.[49]

In the wake of Morgan's denial of clemency the *New York Times*, in an editorial, stating in no uncertain terms its opposition to the capital punishment of women, but not of capital punishment in general, declared, "We repeat the expression of our hope that this woman will not be hung. We should say precisely the same thing if her guilt were as clear as noon-day, for we do not think hanging a decent or proper punishment for a woman under any circumstances." Admitting there was little logic in the position, the editor tried to explain: "It would be difficult, doubtless, to give any very cogent reasons why we should not hang a woman as well as a man if equally guilty of murder — but it would be equally difficult to give any good reason for not striking a woman, as well as a man, under equal provocation. The reason for the distinction lies in the feeling that it exists and should be observed. There are cases where feeling must take the place, and do the work of reason, and this is one of them." He went on to argue there could be no danger to society from sparing a woman's life and giving her a life sentence, while avoiding the mentioning of the obvious point that such an argument could be applied equally to a man. Then he tried to argue that Hartung's guilt had not been clearly proven, although he could cite nothing in support of such a contention. Still, he acknowledged a strong community support for the woman and said that behind the clemency appeal to the governor "has been a very general, and most influential concurrence of the citizens of Albany."[50]

Another manifestation of the strong community agitation to save Hartung from the gallows came in early April when a bill was introduced in the New York State Legislature by a Mr. Buffington, which provided for the sentence of death on Mary to be commuted to a term of 10 years at Sing Sing prison. As opposed as it was to the execution of women the *New York Times* opposed the bill not on the basis of content but on constitutional grounds. The newspaper understood such a law would have been struck down by a higher court. As well, the bill drew fire from other newspapers. "There is certainly something repugnant to one's feelings in the hanging of a woman, but if crime be a matter of sex the law should so declare and not leave the distinction to be drawn by the loose and vague sentimentality of the members of the Legislature," thundered the editor of the *Brooklyn Eagle*.[51]

Even more vehemently opposed to the Buffington bill, which went nowhere, was the *Evening Post* newspaper of New York City. "Let the Legislature consider that the question of Mrs. Hartung's guilt or innocence, and the question whether women should be hung or not, constitute no reason at all for the inauguration of such a monstrous and subversive principle as that implied in the bill," stated the paper's editor. As a compromise the editor of the *New York Times* suggested a general law on the subject that would also cover specifically the Hartung case. For example, a law enacted that prescribed imprisonment for life instead of hanging, in the case of every woman convicted of what had been capital murder. He speculated that public sentiment would favor such a law and that Governor Morgan would promptly and eagerly sign it.[52]

Another paper arguing against special clemency for Mary was New York's *Courier and Enquirer*, which argued, "There exists among a portion of our people an opposition to the hanging of women. On what tenable grounds such an opposition can be based, is somewhat difficult to imagine. If hanging is justifiable in the case of men, it certainly is so in that of women. There may be something particularly revolting to the feelings in seeing a woman hang, but that has nothing to do with the question." Because executions were held for the purpose of deterring people from committing crime, "therefore whether the person to be executed be a coarse, bloated, bull-necked rowdy, or a handsome, delicately-formed woman, with a swan-like neck, makes no difference. If both have been guilty of murder, both should suffer the same punishment. The feeling that would lead to the restricting of capital punishment to men only, is a morbid one, and springs from that false sympathy which has of late years so frequently been manifested for those whom the law has condemned." Following that outburst the editor of the *Times* looked around for those tenable grounds, and found them. He felt one had only to look around to see how deeply rooted that opposition to the execution of women was and that abhorrence was "in the instinctive tendencies of man towards that womanhood which incarnates for him all the dearest relations and most honorable responsibilities of life, and in the very modesty of nature itself. The same feelings which make civilized men shrink from the spectacle of womanhood unsexed by woman herself on the platform or in the field make them shudder at the thought of womanhood unsexed by man at the whipping-post, or on the gallows." In conclusion the editor declared, "Most devoutly, therefore, do we hope and trust that this State will never again exhibit to the world the abnormal spectacle of hanging a woman. It is as needless as it is brutal and inhuman." And when the people of the state had reached the same point as the *Courier and Enquirer* in feeling no opposition to the hanging of women and in finding no tenable grounds upon which such an opposition could be based "and can look with cold indifference on the spectacle of a mother, wife or sister put to death by the executioners of the law, they have gone backward whole centuries in civilization, and have become brutalized and insensible to the best feelings and the holiest instincts of humanity." Once again the editor urged that a general law be enacted by the Legislature that declared no woman would be hereafter executed in New York State.[53]

On April 18, 1859, a reporter visited Hartung in jail, almost exactly a year since the death of Emil. He found her reading the Bible. "She was dressed in a neat calico dress with a loose white muslin sack. She is really a very pretty German woman, quite tall, young, and pleasing in her way." According to the journalist, many of those agitating for a commutation or a reprieve of Mary's sentence did so because her paramour Rhineman was still in jail awaiting a trial. They thought her fate should await the outcome of his trial.[54]

Just two days before her slated execution, on April 25, Judge Wright of the State Supreme Court granted a stay of execution to allow time for more legal proceedings. But in December 1859, that same New York Supreme Court denied Hartung a new trial. It meant the case was referred back to the trial court to enforce the judgment — meaning she would be sentenced to a new death date in the January term of the court.[55]

Mary was much distressed when informed she would not receive a new trial and a reporter speculated she was greatly disappointed in her estimate of the character of her paramour Rhineman. From remarks she had made it was believed that she had long expected from William some admission whereby she would be saved from the gallows. But to that date Rhineman had maintained a silence. When told he had been apprised of the decision of the Supreme Court to not grant her a new trial, she enquired whether he had said anything. When told he had not, Mary wept bitterly and called him a "coward."[56]

On January 26, William Rhineman was acquitted on the charge of being a principal in the murder of Emil — reportedly the jury rendered its verdict without leaving their seats. However, he was taken back to jail to await his trial on other indictments, as accessory before the fact and accessory after the fact.[57]

Another thunderous editorial in favor of the execution of Hartung, and women in general for capital crimes, was issued in the middle of February 1860 by the *Courier and Enquirer* and signed by "Webb." Wrote Webb, "Accustomed always to regard the sex as the weaker, our first feeling is that

2. 1840s and 1850s

a woman is in danger, and our first impulse to interpose on her behalf. But the very consideration of the sex of the guilty party cannot but enhance the enormity of the crime, if the consideration is allowed any weight at all. The law, however, does not discriminate." Relax its strictness then, he worried, and the "terror" it was intended to inspire in the evildoers would be nil; "it will be useless and its existence any longer upon the statute book, but conducive to evil. Let it be allowed then to take its course, and let crime be lessened by the terrors it excites. ... let the majesty of that law she has violated be fully vindicated, and let her punishment be a warning, a just and terrible one, to those who offend against the peace and welfare of the community."[58]

New York State's legislature, however, was not finished with the Hartung case. The legislature of 1860 enacted a statute defining and punishing capital crimes that, said a reporter, "has created no little embarrassment in the administration of justice, and under which at least one criminal escaped the full vigor of the law." Under the common and statue law prior to 1860, the crime of murder in the first degree was punishable by death; the law defining that death should be inflicted by hanging the criminal by the neck until he was dead. That 1860 law (it applied to everybody in a capital case) declared that murder in the first degree should be punishable by death, but failed to say by what method death should be inflicted. Under that law all who were convicted of murder in the first degree—or who at the time of its passage were under sentence of death—should be confined for one year in state prison at hard labor, and thereafter executed if the governor should so direct, by the issuing of a death warrant. But with no method specified, observers of the time said it meant, in effect, there was no ability to implement a death sentence. But there was no punishment for murder in the first degree except execution. On that point judges refused to shoulder the burden and thus, district attorneys in one or more cases asked for a verdict of murder in the second degree so the crime might not go unpunished. So poorly framed was the 1860 law that, although the legislature of 1861 ignored it, the legislature of 1862 swiftly repealed the 1860 measure, thus leaving in full effect the common law and the statute previously in existence. As to the indirect influence of Mary Hartung in causing that bill to be enacted, the *Brooklyn Eagle* had no doubt. "She was young, good looking, and it was believed instigated to commit the crime by a paramour whom the law failed to reach. Mrs. Hartung elicited the sympathy of some of the ablest lawyers in Albany, and it is said that her sex, her misfortune, her youth, her interesting face and person, secured for her the sympathy of some of the leading members of the Legislature of 1860," said the paper. "At all events it was rumored and believed by many that to meet the case of Mrs. Hartung the law of 1860 was enacted."[59]

Whatever the reasons for that 1860 law, it worked, by raising various legal issues, to Mary's advantage. On December 12, 1861, she was released from prison after some 3.5 years of incarceration, by Judge Wright of the State Supreme Court, on a proceeding brought before him by her counsel. On December 20, 1861, she was rearrested on a bench warrant issued by the district attorney. On March 25, 1863, the New York Court of Appeals issued an order discharging Mary Hartung from custody. And that ended legal proceedings against the woman, in respect of the death of Emil Hartung.[60]

When she was released finally a reporter observed, "During all those years of imprisonment she has amused herself, and earned not a little spending money by working at fine needle work, and she has at all times received friendly attention at the hands of many of the first ladies of the city. The horror created by the idea of hanging a woman 'in these days of advanced civilization,' has had much to do with saving her."[61]

A few months later a news account wondered what had worked to save Mary, since she was poor and unknown at the time of the murder. "Without money and without fame, her case was fought with greater persistence, adroitness, and extravagance of resource than have been shown in any other before or after. During her trial Mrs. Hartung won sympathizers by her youth and bearing and friends by her personal charms," speculated the account. "There was nothing adventitious about her beauty, nothing that was manufactured as an effective foil to her grim surroundings. Hers was the loveliness of a rose, her own liveliness because she was herself. Those who saw her still speak of the wondrous coloring of her cheek and the soft fires of her glance. Without any apparent effort on intention she fascinated her lawyer...." And, apparently, as well, the nameless reporter who wrote that account, even though he admitted her defense at her trial "was a weak attempt to shift the guilt onto Reimann." It was said, in 1895, that shortly after her release from prison in 1863, Mary "married a worthy farmer and continued prosperous and contented."[62]

2. 1840s and 1850s

Ann Bilansky

A tall, childless, 32-year-old woman by the name of Ann came to St. Paul, Minnesota, from Pleasant Hill, Illinois, in April 1858. She came in response to a request from her ill nephew John Walker to come and care for him. After arriving in the state's bustling capital of 10,000 people, Ann first lived in a shanty with Walker. Soon, though, she married Stanislaus Bilansky, an early pioneer of the area. Her new husband, then on his third marriage, was a short, heavyset bar owner in his 50s. He lived in a three-room house, drank heavily and was abusive. His second wife had left him after nine years of marriage, leaving three children aged six, eight, and 10 in the custody of Stanislaus after their divorce. Ann dutifully took care of those children and the aging and frequently ill Stanislaus, who often complained he was near death. A poor man, Stanislaus owned little more than a small cabin that doubled as his bar and small grocery store, plus a two-room shanty behind it. At the urging of Stanislaus, Walker had built and then resided in that shanty.[63]

Death came to Stanislaus in March 1859 after 10 days of violent sickness. He died on March 11, at 4 A.M. After a doctor examined the body a hastily assembled coroner's jury heard testimony from various people, including neighbor Lucinda Kilpatrick, live-in housekeeper Rosa Scharf, and John Walker. The jury concluded death was from natural causes but was critical of Ann for failing to summon the doctor in her husband's final hours. Stanislaus was buried on Saturday, March 12, at 5 P.M. That evening Kilpatrick decided to change her testimony. She went to the St. Paul police and told the chief that on February 28 she had been out shopping with Ann and saw her purchase arsenic from a druggist. In light of that new revelation the body of Stanislaus was exhumed. A second coroner's jury found the man had died of arsenic poisoning, despite what was at best shaky evidence from the experts. Ann was indicted for murder. By that time rumors had spread that she and Walker had been "on very intimate terms" prior to her marriage.[64]

At her trial in the spring of 1859 the argument was made that Ann's motivation in committing murder had been her adulterous affair and a desire to get rid of a disagreeable husband. No testimony was introduced to show the couple quarreled or fought; death by arsenic poisoning was not well proved; and Kilpatrick, a prime spreader of the adultery rumor, had had an affair with Walker herself, a liaison that had ended only a little earlier. The family doctor testified Stanislaus had been long treated by him, had a "gloomy disposition" and "often complained of ills, came to see him up to 20 times a year," and, the doctor said, had "hypochondria." Deliberations were started by the jurors on June 3 and in less than six hours they returned a verdict of guilty of murder in the first degree against Ann. Moves for a new trial failed and the state's highest court affirmed Ann's conviction on July 23, 1859. Two days later, an inattentive jailor left her alone in a hallway after dinner. While the jailor was away she escaped through a basement window. After hiding in tall grass she eventually made contact with Walker. He gave her some men's clothing but their plans to flee the state were foiled by the police after handbills offering a $500 reward for her capture were distributed by the county sheriff. Those flyers told of the escape of a murderess who was described as "tall in stature," "very talkative," with a "masculine" voice and who had "lapped" teeth, "grey eyes, light hair" and a "Roman nose." Police arrested the pair one week after her escape. Walker was jailed for over a month but a Ramsey County grand jury refused to indict him on September 13. In court on December 2, 1859, Judge Edward Palmer sentenced Ann to be hanged by the neck until dead and directed the sheriff to select the execution site. Minnesota Governor Henry Sibley had the legal responsibility of fixing the execution date.[65]

On that July day when Ann's conviction was affirmed by the Supreme Court, Justice Flandrau wrote a personal letter to Sibley asking for clemency. Although he was convinced of her guilt, and noting the sentence would be death, Flandrau wrote, "It is my firm conviction that a strict adherence to the penal code will have a salutary influence in checking crime in the State, but it rather shocks my private sense of humanity to commence by inflicting the extreme penalty on a woman." Unwilling to set an execution date, Sibley, a Democrat, let his term expire on December 31, 1859, taking no action in the Bilansky case, leaving the political problem to his Republican successor Alexander Ramsey. During the same time, after a sentence of death had been passed, efforts were made by the Minnesota legislature to abolish capital punishment. A resolution was passed instructing the legislature's judiciary committee to "inquire into the propriety of abolishing capital punishment." However, the committee returned with a recommendation to keep capital punishment. On January 18, 1860, a bill was introduced by Representative G.W. Sweet to prohibit the execution of females, substituting life imprisonment. On the same day, a bill to abolish capital punishment altogether was introduced in the Minnesota Senate, while still another bill introduced in the House sought to mandate that executions be conducted in private in jails. Governor Ramsey was lobbied intensely by those trying to save Ann's life but at the end of January 1860, he instructed Ramsey County's sheriff to carry out the sentence between 10 A.M. and 2 P.M. on Friday, March 23, 1860.[66]

Sweet's bill was defeated (after "woman or girl" in the text was changed to "person"—thus rendering the measure as one to abolish capital punishment completely) by a vote of 33 to 22 on January 31, 1860. On the next day Representative Acker introduced a bill to commute Ann's sentence to life imprisonment at the state prison. After a fight it was passed by the House 41 to 32. Acker's bill was referred on to the Senate, where Senator Thomas Cowan argued that "it was an outrage on public sentiment to make a poor, friendless woman the first victim in the State to the death penalty." But Senator J.H. Steward opposed commuting her sentence, feeling she had a "full, fair and impartial trial," and saying he wanted the law to take its course because she was "a devil incarnate." Ultimately the Senate passed the bill by a vote of 19 to 13. It had been amended very slightly but it was repassed by the House. Thus, both houses of the legislature had approved the bill to commute Ann's sentence. Senator J.S. Winn caustically suggested Acker's bill be retitled "A bill for the encouragement of prostitution and murder." The object Ann had in disposing of her husband, Winn contended, "was that she might live with her paramour, with whom she had for a long time been associated on terms of disgraceful intimacy, during the time her husband was living." That bizarre attempt to amend the bill was voted on and defeated 30 to 2. On March 8, Ramsey vetoed Acker's bill, calling the proposed commutation contrary to public policy. Said Ramsey, "She sat by the bedside of her husband not to foster, but to slay." And: "She watched without emotion the tortures she caused and by and by, administered no healing medicine, no cooling draught, but ever under guise of love and tender care, renewed her cup of death." A husband, added Ramey, "will not suspect that she who has sworn to love and cherish will betray and destroy; and it shocks the moral sense of the whole community to believe it." Acker's last-ditch efforts to override the governor's veto failed to garner the required two-thirds vote of House members.[67]

Clemency petitions continued to pour into Ramsey's office but to no effect. The *Pioneer and Democrat* newspaper wanted Ann hanged but called upon Ramsey "to make the execution as private as executions usually are in States where public executions are prohibited." Ramsey, though, refused to do even that. The movement to make executions non-public events was then well underway. By 1835, five northeastern states had enacted laws forbidding public executions "out of a growing sense that public executions were brutalizing and demoralizing to society and in response to America's anti-gallows movement, which had gained strength in the mid–1830s," said an observer. As of 1860 a total of 19 states (including Illinois, Indiana, Iowa, Kansas, Michigan, and Ohio) had outlawed pubic executions. Ann's execution was described as "semiprivate," not because of a law or action by Ramsey, but because Sheriff Tullis (the person in charge of the execution) decided to exclude the general public — county sheriffs appeared to have a fair amount of discretion, in the absence of specific laws, in determining just how public an execution became.[68]

Early on the morning of March 23 a crowd assembled and soon the streets around the jail compound in St. Paul held an estimated 1,500 to 2,000 people. Ann wore a black robe and a veil over her head. Before leaving the jail she said to her escort, "Don't let a crowd see me. I am willing to meet my God, but I don't want to have a crowd see me die." But it was too late for that, as she had to walk across the street to the gallows. Although a fence surrounded the gallows it was not very high and people could easily find a spot to see over it. People in the street watched from the tops of buildings and from carriages and hay wagons. Besides that, about 100 people were admitted to the enclosure, including some 25 to 30 women, a few of those carrying infants. She proclaimed her innocence from the scaffold. The crowd, described as "solemn," was said to have quickly dispersed. According to this account, "From colonial times to the present, only a very small percentage — about 3 percent of all American executions — have been of women."[69]

At the time of her execution one reporter commented, "The hanging of a female in this country is so unusual a thing that we publish below an account of the execution, contrary to our usual custom. We do not recollect but two or three cases of the execution of white women in this country of late years." When the trap was sprung "the fall was about four feet, and machinery was so nicely adjusted that the noise was scarcely heard outside the enclosure. There was scarcely any movement in the body after it dropped, a slight convulsive motion, and a heaving of the chest, was all that was observed." According to the journalist, "Her demeanor on the scaffold was excellent. She was not defiant or stoical, neither did she shed a tear. It is the opinion of many that she expected a pardon or reprieve to the last moment."[70]

Executions of Women in the 1840s and 1850s[71]

(All were executed by hanging and all for murder, except as noted.)

1840, February 5, (Jones), black slave, Scott County, Kentucky.
1840, September 5, Betsy (Wilson), black slave, Fauquier, Virginia.
1843, February 11, Mary Smith, black slave, Alabama.
1844, April 26, Rosan Keen, black servant, Cumberland, New Jersey.
1844, February 9, Esther Foster, black convict, Franklin, Ohio.
1844, March, Nancy (Beasley), black slave (attempted), Montgomery, Alabama.
1845, May 10, Emaline, black slave, Marion, Georgia.
1845, May 23, Elizabeth Reed, 40, white housewife, Lawrence, Illinois.
1845, November 8, Lavinia Burnett, white, Washington, Arkansas.
1846, December 11, Lucy, black slave, St. James, Louisiana.
1846, February 24, Elizabeth Van Valkenburgh, 47, white housewife, Fulton, New York.
1846, March 28, Pauline (Rabbeneck), black slave (attempted), New Orleans, Louisiana.
1847, November 9, Mary Runkle, white housewife, Oneida, New York.
1848, May, Lucy (Hamilton), black slave, Meade, Kentucky.
1849, December 11, Pherebe (Shepherd), 25, black slave, Fayette, Alabama.
1849, January 12, Eliza (Griffin), black slave (poisoning), Brunswick, Virginia.
1849, January 12, Roberta (Ezell), black slave (poisoning), Brunswick, Virginia.
1849, May 25, Margarette, black slave, Caswell, North Carolina.
1850, May 22, Cicily, black slave, Tippah, Mississippi.
1851, July, Juanita, Hispanic, Sierra, California.
1851, July, Mily Fox, black slave (poisoning), Louisiana.

1852, July 30, Ann Hoag, white housewife, 31, Dutchess, New York.

1852, May 14, Mahalia (Mason), black slave, Giles, Virginia.

1852, September 10, Molly (Champion), black slave (attempted), Sussex, Virginia.

1852, September 10, Jane (Depp), black slave, Powhatan, Virginia.

1852, September 10, Jane Williams, black slave, Richmond City, Virginia. Jane and her husband John (both black slaves) were hanged side by side for killing their master's wife and child. The execution drew an estimated crowd of 6,000. Authorities offered to pay Jane's owner $500 in compensation for taking away his property through execution.[72]

1853, August 12, Margaret Buckner, black slave, Culpeper, Virginia.

1854, Jane Elkins, black slave, Dallas, Texas.

1855, December 21, Celia (Newsome), black slave, Greene, Missouri.

1855, February 26, Melvanie (Frilvox), black slave, St. Charles, Louisiana.

1855, March, Martha (McKeller), black slave (arson), Dallas, Alabama.

1856, February 9, Minerva, black slave (arson), Trigg, Kentucky.

1856, June 20, Anna (Wilson), black slave (arson), Charles City, Virginia.

1856, September 12, Amelia (Clarke), black slave, Caroline, Virginia.

1857, August 21, Catharine (Thompson), black slave, Louisa, Virginia.

1857, February 13, (Green), black slave, 65, Prince William, Virginia.

1857, February 13, (Green), black slave, Prince William, Virginia.

1857, May 8, Massy (Norwood), black slave, Granville, North Carolina.

1857, November 20, Nancy (Brothers), black slave (attempted), Nansemond, Virginia.

1858, February 12, Charlotte Jones, white, 35, Allegheny, Pennsylvania.

1858, February 26, Jenny (Hall), black slave, 30, Arlington, Virginia.

1858, October 22, Mary Twigg, white, Montour, Pennsylvania.

1858, March 5, Lucy (Dougherty), black slave, 40, Galveston, Texas.

1858, September 10, Jane (Musgrove), black slave, Bedford, Virginia.

1859, November 25, Nancy, black slave, Pike, Alabama.

1859, September 30, Angelina, black slave (arson), Culpeper, Virginia.

3

1860s

Martha Grinder

Martha Grinder came to the city of Pittsburgh around the summer of 1859, arriving with her husband from Louisville. At the time of their arrival they were a very poor family but their circumstances improved over time and they moved to a better house. They began to exhibit a better style of living, new furniture was bought, and their wardrobe replenished. By August 1865 they had lived in about four different houses in Pittsburgh. At the end of August Martha found herself in jail on suspicion of poisoning a neighbor by the name of Mary C. Caruthers to death. Because of that arrest an old case against her came to light and became the first of what would be a growing, and often hysterical, list of allegations aimed at Grinder. A young Irish girl named Miss Jane P. Buchanan had been for years in the employ of Mrs. Kirkpatrick, a widow who kept a boarding house. Finding the work too hard she got a position working as a servant for Martha Grinder. Accordingly, on Wednesday, February 24, 1864, Buchanan had her trunk removed from Kirkpatrick's house to the residence of a friend, and then Jane went to Martha's place. She did not take all her effects with her as she viewed the first week or so of her new job as a trial period. On Thursday, she became suddenly ill and got worse on Friday and Saturday. Martha tried to convey the impression to visitors that Buchanan's sickness was the result of too close an intimacy with a young man named Roberts, but as Mrs. Kirkpatrick and her daughter (visiting their ailing former servant) knew her character was "irreproachable" they did not believe the story. On Saturday night Mr. Grinder called at the house of Jane's friend and took her trunk home with him. It contained a quantity of good clothing, $45 to $50 in cash, and $11 in gold. Buchanan continued to grow worse and died on Sunday morning. Suspicion was aroused but nothing incriminating was found and the inquest jury returned a verdict of "death from natural causes." However, the trunk of the deceased was found to contain nothing of value when opened after her death, and Jane's friends had to take up a collection so Buchanan could be buried. When Martha was arrested on August 30 on suspicion of murdering Caruthers, the body of Buchanan was ordered exhumed. Grinder was confined in one of the cells in the female ward of the county jail. Her little daughter was in the cell with her. Observed a reporter, "An effort has been made by some charitable persons to induce Mrs. Grinder to consent to the removal of her child, but she refuses to permit her to leave." And, "She appears to be well supplied with money, and her meals are furnished from the Warden's table."[1]

Typical of the hyperbole and exaggerated charges leveled at Grinder was the editorial in the *Chicago Tribune* of August 31, 1865, wherein the editor declared Martha Grinder "appears to have attempted the murder of nearly every man, woman and child that came her way for the past ten years, having succeeded in the murder of six persons, and very nearly succeeded in the murder of as many more." In most of those cases, remarked the editor, there appeared to have been no motive whatever and no temptation except that she had the opportunity. Her practice seemed to him to have been "to poison every person she had the opportunity to poison, and if any advantage followed, it was purely secondary or incidental." Worried even then that Grinder would successfully invoke an insanity defense, the editor fretted, "She will, with all her cunning and duplicity, be either remanded to a comfortable home in some private asylum till the medical director pronounces her 'cured,' or possibly she will be acquitted altogether."[2]

Grinder's alleged poisoning of so many people was said to have mostly taken place at her home, wherein she served up poison-laced food or drink to guests and visitors. "Her kindness of heart and remarkable conversational abilities soon rendered her a favorite among the residents of the neighborhood in which she resided and always made her a welcome visitor," said a reporter. As to the sudden increase in wealth that came the Grinders' way, Martha explained that she had inherited money. When Buchanan's trunk was opened after Jane's death, all of the money, a set of jewelry, and nearly all of the clothing were found to be gone. Among the few remaining items there could not be found enough clothing to dress the body. Mrs. Grinder kindly donated some of her clothing. Friends of the dead servant knew precisely the contents of Jane's trunk because a friend had counted the money and did an inventory of the trunk on the Wednesday Jane had moved it, as part of the preparation for her new job.[3]

By the middle of September 1865, allegations about Grinder were being delivered at a fever pitch, as a news mania appeared to take hold. An account in the *Brooklyn Eagle* accused her of having murdered several more people, including her brother-in-law, a returned soldier named Grinder, who died suddenly in her home; a Mrs. Hancock, wife of a hack driver; and an old lady named Carr, who died after one day's illness. In the latter case, for no reason other than Grinder had access to Carr at the time, the newspaper declared, "There is no doubt that she caused her death." As well, she was accused of poisoning two children to death. They were children of a German woman Martha had visited, and after the children were buried, Grinder visited the house and supposedly succeeded in giving a dose of poison to the mother, but she survived. Also said to have been nearly murdered was Annie Gold, who was alleged to have received a cup of poisoned coffee from Grinder.[4]

A couple of days later a shocked *Chicago Tribune* editorial stated, "During the past two weeks the evidence against Mrs. Martha Grinder, the American Lucretia Borgia, has been fast accumulating and scarcely a day passes that we do not hear of some new fact, illustrating her utter heartlessness and fiendish desire to destroy life.... It reveals nothing less than a settled determination on her part to destroy the entire family of her husband, and it is almost certain she succeeded in killing at least two of her husband's brothers." Samuel Grinder, 25, died on December 4, 1864, while Jeremiah Grinder, 21, died on November 15, 1864. Both were soldiers. According to this account about half a dozen others in the Grinder family were said to have been poisoned by Martha but recovered. Generally, each person poisoned would get sick — including violent vomiting and purging — when at Martha's house on a visit. When many of these alleged victims recovered, they inexplicably returned to the same house to be poisoned again. After the *Chicago Tribune* gave her the nickname of the new Lucretia Borgia, it was widely adopted by other newspapers.[5]

Finally, on October 15, 1865, the grand jury indicted Martha Grinder for the murder of Mrs. Mary C. Caruthers by the administration of poison — specifically by mixing arsenic and antimony in certain food, drink, and medicines, administered to the victim between June 27 and August 1, 1865.[6]

A few days later more sensationalism came in a report originally published in the *Pittsburgh Dispatch* and reprinted verbatim by the *Brooklyn Eagle*. "Never, perhaps, since the days of the Borgias, has the world heard of a more atrocious and bloodthirsty woman than Martha Grinder, now confined in our jail awaiting trial. For days and even weeks the city press has been filled with startling narratives of her hellish deeds, and each it would seem were more atrocious than the former." The latest addition to the list of victims came from the Tressel family. Reportedly, Mrs. Tressel befriended Martha back in February or March 1862 only to have Grinder poison her two children to death and to make two unsuccessful attempts to murder Mrs. Tressel, one before the death of her two children and one after. Tressel's two-year-old child and four-month-old infant had died within a week of each other.[7]

On October 28, 1865, the jury returned a verdict of guilty of murder in the first degree against Martha. Surprisingly to many, the jury took several hours to reach a verdict, with the first vote having stood at six for conviction and six for acquittal. Apparently the stumbling point was the sanity of the accused. Some of the jury considered her to be insane and had to be persuaded otherwise. Just before she was sentenced, on December 2, 1865, Grinder still had two murder indictments outstanding against her; one was for Jane Buchanan and one was for Samuel Urlander, her brother-in-law. However, she was not tried on either count.[8]

When she appeared in court for sentencing she was described as follows: "She appeared to be in a feeble condition, and totally unprepared for the terrible ordeal. Her face was pale, and indicated that she was laboring under great mental suffering. She wore a dark merino dress, dark bonnet, and was heavily veiled. Grinder was sentenced to be executed on January 19, 1866. After expressing agreement with the verdict and summarizing the "diabolical cruelty" of her crime, Judge Sterrett declared, "It is scarcely necessary to say to you that the crime of which you stand convicted, calls for the highest penalty of the law ... a fearful crime — one from which human nature instinctively shrinks with feelings of horror, but when it is planned by one of your sex, and executed by means of deadly poisons, against which helpless infancy and the mature vigor of manhood

3. 1860s

are alike powerless, it assumes the most horrible and detestable features." Pointing out there were no mitigating circumstances, the judge advised Grinder to hold out no hope for a successful appeal for mercy and that she should prepare herself to die. "We kindly entreat you, therefore, to humble yourself before God, and earnestly implore His mercy and forgiveness through the merits of a crucified Savior. In this way, and in this alone, can you be prepared for the awful change that shortly awaits you in the execution of the sentence...."[9]

Just before she was executed on January 19, Martha made a confession, admitting to the murders of Caruthers and Buchanan, but denying all the other charges of poisoning brought against her. During the approximately five weeks she systematically dosed Caruthers with poison it was noted Martha "was unremitting in her attention to the sufferer, and exhibited so much apparent kindness and sympathy as to completely disarm suspicion." The body of Caruthers was buried shortly after her August 1, 1865, death but then exhumed on August 30. Caruthers first took sick on the evening of June 27 with vomiting, purging, throat problems, pains in the stomach, dizziness, and nausea. Martha lived next door to the woman and was foremost among those who tended to the ailing woman. At the trial James Caruthers testified that immediately after taking food sent by Martha, he and anyone else who partook was affected in the same manner as his wife at the time of her first becoming sick. When the illness of Mrs. Caruthers continued the family doctor advised the couple to leave their residence for a time and go to the country. They did, and both rapidly recovered their health. Upon their return to the city the attentions of Martha recommenced and again the strange sickness manifested itself. When the mother of Mrs. Caruthers arrived on July 28 she ate some of Grinder's food and immediately became ill with the same symptoms as the others.

Martha was born in 1833 and was twice married. The first marriage took place in Harrodsburg, Indiana, when she was just 14 years old. She had two children by her first husband and none by her second, Grinder. Her general health was good and she had never used morphine or anything of that kind. Those few facts about her background had been elicited by a group of three doctors who came to visit her in prison to assess her sanity. Reportedly it was done incognito so Martha never knew the reason for their visit until they had concluded their clandestine examination on January 18, whereupon they told her who they really were, that they had concluded she was perfectly sane, and that there was certainly no hope she would escape her sentence. According to this account Grinder was just the third woman to be executed in Pennsylvania, preceded by Charlotte Jones and Mary Twigg.[10]

Grinder was executed at 1:15 P.M. on January 19 in the southern courtyard of the jailhouse in a ceremony witnessed by about 100 people. The windows of the courthouse, which overlooked the jail yard, were filled with faces. "Mrs. Grinder was dressed in a brown alpaca dress, trimmed around the neck and down the front with white lace, lightly made kid slippers and white stockings. She took a seat provided for her on the scaffold and remained entirely unmoved while a prayer was being offered in her behalf," observed a reporter. "Her features wore a pleasant smile from the time she left her cell until the fatal white cap was drawn over her face. Not a muscle quivered; not an expression of the countenance escaped her that could by any possibility be construed into either remorse or fear of death, mental agitation or any kindred emotion. There was nothing like a forced determination to appear clam and composed; it was evidently natural and entirely unaffected." On several occasions the morning of the execution she stated emphatically that she had not the slightest fear of death, as she knew she would be saved, but only expressed her regret at being made a public spectacle of, and that the manner of her death displeased her. Her calmness in the face of death was said to have amazed people. "There is something inexplicable in the entire conduct of the woman. Something more than courage, physical strength, or even faith has conduced to enable her to bear herself with such astonishing, not only fortitude but meekness, gentleness and childlike cheerfulness," said a journalist. "She has been a marvel and a wonder to all who have had association with her since her conviction."[11]

The execution itself did not go well. When Sheriff Steward sprang the trap, at "the next instant Mrs. Grinder was suspended in the air struggling convulsively with death. Owing to the damp weather the noose did not work as smoothly as it otherwise would have done, and the neck was not broken by the fall. She struggled violently for several minutes, and at one time her right hand caught hold of the platform where it fitted to the drop, in spasmodic efforts to relieve herself." Grinder's confession, dated January 18, was given to the press immediately after she was hanged. It

3. 1860s

read, "In view of my departure in a few hours, from earth, I want to say that I acknowledge my guilt in the case of Mrs. Caruthers, and also in the case of Miss Buchanan, but I am innocent of all other charges made against me in the papers, for poisoning people. But, bad as I have been, I feel that God, for Christ's sake, has forgiven me, and through his mercy I hope to find an entrance into Heaven. I die without hard feelings to any one, forgiving all as I hope to be forgiven." And that was all she wrote, except for a short second paragraph that thanked various people for their kindnesses to her, such as Sheriff Stewart.[12]

The execution of Grinder caused the *New York Times* to editorialize, "It is true enough that in themselves, Mrs. Grinder's crimes merited the gallows, if any human crimes can merit it. But the rule in this country has been that, no matter how atrocious might be the crimes perpetrated by a woman, it was impossible to have any one of them brought to suffer the ordinary penalties of the law." According to the editor, "It has been thought a favor and an honor to the sex to permit murderesses to assume a position among them equal to the best; and we have even seen them feted in public, applauded in court-rooms, and borne away in triumph from the scene of their crimes or from the bar of justice." He believed that no less than 1,000 men had gone to the gallows in the 19th century to that point but only about two women (prior to both Grinder and Mary Surratt) and that constituted "the entire number of female executions since our country gained its independence." At the same time, he argued, something like 10 percent of all capital crimes had been committed by women. "If depravity impels women to the most awful violations of the Divine law, we know of no sanction for their release from the Divine penalty," he concluded.[13]

Nine months after Martha was executed it was reported that James Caruthers had gone mad and been taken from his home to an asylum, declared "a hopeless lunatic." That prompted the editor of the *Chicago Tribune* to note that it was not the usual practice to speak ill of the dead. However, he promptly did just that by editorializing, "None of us will every forget or will ever cease to shudder at the monstrous deeds of Martha Grinder. No woman that ever lived in that community — perhaps no woman that every lived in the nation — roused such universal abhorrence by the deeds of horrid cruelty she wrought, or caused such a sense of relief and renewed safety by her death. No criminal of modern times has terminated so fearful a career of crime by so just a doom." Even after her death the editorial fashioned a charge against her not previously mentioned: "While she lived she was a terror and a monster, who dealt in death as a pastime and poisoned babes in order that she might judge the effect her drugs would have on adults."[14]

Mary Surratt

After the assassination of U.S. President Abraham Lincoln on April 14, 1865, a great effort was made, understandably, to bring all those involved to justice. By May 4, 1865, some 15 people were being held in custody for their alleged parts in the plot, and a few others were still being sought. One of those held was Mrs. Mary Surratt; one of those still being sought was her son John Surratt. The main figure in the plot was John Wilkes Booth, who shot Lincoln. He remained on the run until the authorities ran him to ground on April 26, and killed him in the attempt to capture him.[15]

Evidence against Mary Surratt ranged from slim to nonexistent. However, the whole matter was more a political issue than it was a justice issue. Even then the media played up the role and influence of Surratt to something it never was in fact. According to a report in the *Brooklyn Eagle*, "Mrs. Surratt, whose son John has thus far eluded the vigilance of the detectives who are on his track, bears no small part in this plot. She has long been a secret agent of the Confederacy, in the secret mail service, and has ever been known as a bold, masculine rebel sympathizer." It was also reported, "Young Surratt does not appear to have been a puissant spirit in the scheme; indeed, all design and influence therein was absorbed by Mrs. Surratt and Booth. The latter was the head and heart of the plot; Mrs. Surratt was his anchor, and the rest of the boys were disciples to Iscariot and Jezebel." And it was said John Surratt knew of the murder and connived at it while the others in the plot "all relied upon Mrs. Surratt, and took their cues from Wilkes Booth."[16]

On May 11, 1865, eight people were charged and arraigned in Washington, D.C., in the plot to assassinate Lincoln and others, and to overthrow the U.S. government. All faced possible death sentences. Mary was the only woman. Three of the men arraigned that day would go on to be executed with her: David Herold (who assisted Booth in the short period he was on the run); Lewis Paine (who attempted to murder Secretary of State William Seward on the same night Lincoln was shot. Seward recovered and continued to serve as Secretary of State under President Andrew Johnson); and George Atzerodt (who planned to assassinate Vice President Andrew Johnson but failed to put his plan into action). At her arraignment Mary was described as follows: "Mrs. Surratt evinced this morning the first manifestations of fear and seemed very much broken down and humbled. She weighs about two hundred pounds and was very slovenly dressed."[17]

Civilian legal procedures were not used in the trial as the eight were tried by a military court containing nine members with the initial sessions held in secret. Up to about May 13, all applications by reporters for admission to the court had been rejected. However, the military tribunal had declared that such portions of the testimony as might not result in injury to justice would be published from time to time before the trial ended. But a sudden change in policy meant the press was admitted to the court, for the first time, on May 14. Thereafter the press was admitted, apparently, to at least some of the court's sessions. A description of Mary in court on May 14 went as follows: "This wretched woman is dressed in full mourning. She wears her bonnet and veil during the sessions of the court. Her age is probably fifty. She is a large Amazonian class of woman, square built, masculine hands, full face, dark grey lifeless eyes, hair not decidedly dark, complexion swarthy." And, continued the account, "Altogether her face denotes more than usual intelligence.... Her eyes are rather soft in expression, and strangely at variance with the general harshness of the other features.... This unfortunate, like the others, is in irons. A bar of ten inches in length, passes from one ankle to the other, and is attached to an iron bar that encircles each of her hands."[18]

A couple of weeks later a quite different description of the woman in court was given, along with a speculation that she clearly must have been an integral part of the conspiracy. "There, now, you see the face perfectly; and between us, it is a fine one. Indeed, if there were nothing the matter, and we were called on at this distance of ten feet to give an opinion, we should pronounce her, for a woman of her age, handsome. She is tall and large, without being fat, weighing perhaps a hundred and eighty pounds. Her hair, seen in the shade of her bonnet, reveals no grey, and is a beautiful dark brown, well polished with the brush. Her face, as befits such a form, is broad but not coarse — just the reverse. It is fair, the cheek slightly tinged by the interest of the circumstances; and her eye is bright, clear, calm, resolute, but not unkind." And, with regard to her cunning: "Immersed as she is in crime, she does not forget a woman's art. She is doing her best to make a favorable impression, by dress and aspect, upon her judges. She was the very person to mould the material [the plotters] which fell into her hands. She no doubt ruled them like a queen. But the court, fortunately is made of quite another metal."[19]

Toward the end of the trial, the *Brooklyn Eagle* scored the military court proceedings in an editorial wherein it declared that since the trial was in the hands of a court unknown to the laws of the land and its sessions were secret whenever it pleased the military court, all credibility for the proceedings was lost. "This is due solely to the fact that the public have no faith in military commissions, and no confidence in proceedings which are published or withheld just as it pleases the authorities," said the editor. He urged the military court to admit it had made a mistake and let the accused be handed over to civilian authorities.[20]

On July 5, 1865, President Johnson (elevated to that office after Lincoln's death) approved the findings and sentences of the military commission. Four of those charged were to be hanged; three others were to be imprisoned for life; one was sentenced to six years at hard labor in the penitentiary. Thus, all eight who were tried were convicted. When Johnson approved the sentences on the 5th the accused were still unaware of the verdicts and sentences; all four executions were set for July 7. Surratt's guilt was likely limited to knowing in advance of a plot to kidnap Lincoln. When that long-standing plan was put into effect it became broader, more grandiose and more lethal, with the plan being to murder a number of high-level government officials and eventually topple the federal government. Mary ran a boarding house in Washington, D.C., and one or another of the conspirators had boarded there. They perhaps held some planning sessions there, but nothing implicated Mary directly. All, of course, were Southerners, dedicated to the cause of the Confederacy.[21]

On July 6 the prisoners were visited one by one by Generals Hancock and Hartranft, who announced the final doom to each of the conspirators in their separate cells. It was the first time they heard they were to be executed in about 24 hours. Mary uttered a few words, "I had no hand in the murder of the President," and begged the officers to extend the time as she was not prepared to die in so short a time. She asked finally for four more days. Reportedly, strenuous efforts were made on the 6th by the friends and counsels of Surratt and Herold to have a reprieve granted in their cases, and in the case of Surratt to commute the sentence of death. It was said that four members of the military commission had signed a petition to President Johnson favoring the commutation. Mary's daughter visited her mother and then went straightaway to the president to plead for mercy. A reporter speculated, "There is no reason to believe that the President will pardon or commute the sentence of any, unless it may be in the case of Mrs. Surratt. During yesterday afternoon her excitement and nervousness became alarming, and she was likely to be completely prostrated in consequence." The executions were to be held in the small yard adjoining the military prison in Washington, D.C. With respect to her guilt, the *Brooklyn Eagle* declared, "Her crime was that of harboring the conspirators and in suffering them to make her house a sort of rendezvous."[22]

Editorializing about the sentences on July 7, the *Brooklyn Eagle* thought there was a "wide distinction" in degree of guilt of the four sentenced to death, arguing that Paine and Atzerodt were guiltier, with more sympathy for the other two. "The evidence against Mrs. Surratt was compatible with the theory that the plot was limited in the first place to the abduction of the President and his chief advisors," the editor felt. "It is possible that the darker crime, which Booth in all probability contemplated, was kept from his less resolute associates. That it should be kept from one whose direct aid was not looked for — of a sex proverbially incontinent of secrets, and naturally disposed to shrink from crime inspired by passions which seldom move women to atrocity, is more than probable." Concluded the editor, with respect to Mary, "Deep and dark as was the crime which is today to be expiated on the gallows, we do not believe that the public will look with any favor on the spectacle of the execution of one whose sex in distress appeals to the best feelings of every manly heart."[23]

Mary's daughter Anna Surratt remained with her mother all night before the execution. During that same evening Paine informed Colonel Dodd, who had charge of the prisoners, that as far as he was aware Mary knew nothing about the assassination. She had never said a word to him on the subject, nor had any of the conspirators mentioned her in connection with the matter. A procession to the scaffold took place at 1:15 P.M. on July 7, led by Surratt, who was described as "a middle-aged woman dressed in black, bonneted and veiled, walking between two bare-headed priests." Limbs of the four were pinioned and caps (hoods) were drawn over their heads. At 1:25 the drop fell and all four bodies were simultaneously suspended in the air. The only comment made about the manner of death was for one observer to say, "Payne died hard." Medical examinations held after 30 minutes when the bodies were cut down revealed none of the four had their necks broken except Surratt. Apparently most people had expected some sort of reprieve or commutation for the woman because, said a reporter, "In every part of the country except Washington the impression was universal that her sentence would be commuted into imprisonment for life."[24]

Surratt was described as a married woman about 45 years old at the time of her death and as one who occupied a good position in society, owning a tavern and farm at Surrattsville, near Washington. For some time Mary had resided on H Street in Washington, in a "respectable" four-story brick house owned by her. Her household consisted of herself, her daughter, and three boarders, Miss Honora Fitzpatrick, Mr. Holman, and Louis Weichmann.[25]

Soon after the execution a man named John P. Brophy signed an affidavit in which it was stated that the chief witness against Mary, Louis Weichmann, had confessed to Brophy that Surratt was innocent and that Weichmann was induced to give his evidence because authorities pressured and threatened him unless he lied on the stand against his landlady. Weichmann was employed as a clerk in the War Department, boarded with Mary, and was treated as a member of the family. That led to his arrest as a possible accomplice in the murder, and to his subsequent disclosure of things he had supposedly heard and seen while a boarder at the house. Brophy's affidavit was made on the day of the execution but there was no time to get it to President Johnson. In the wake of Paine's exoneration of Surratt, General Hartranft said, "I believe that Payne has told the truth in this matter." Weichmann had said of Mary, "She may possibly have been cognizant only of the capture and of the parties in it. Yet even that deserved death. It was treasonable and criminal to lay hands on the person of the President in aid of the enemy, and as such it ought to be punished." He added, "Mrs. Surratt is to be much blamed. She would have exercised a woman's influence and a mother's love, and then she could have prevented all. But no, she was too infatuated. She loved the South too much.... Now, who is there, after all these facts, that will not say that Mrs. Surratt knew what was in Booth's mind? God grant that he may have spoken to her only of capture; but I believe what Judge Bingham said, and what every true Union-loving man will say, 'Capture meant murder.'"[26]

Weichmann, of course, denied all Brophy's allegations. Not every member of the media was on Mary's side, though. Said the *Chicago Tribune*, "A concerted effort is being made by that portion of the Northern press which declared the war to be a failure, to make a martyr out of Mrs. Surratt." To that end they had adopted the tactic of attacking the credibility of a witness. According to this account, that Surratt conspired and combined to do the murder and attempted murders was "clear."[27]

By August 1867 it was reported that the military court's recommendation for mercy for Surratt was a part of the original court record — a fact said to have been in dispute. President Johnson denied having seen such a recommendation before the execution. Said the editor of the *Chicago Tribune*, "Andrew Johnson is directly and almost solely responsible for the hanging of Mrs. Surratt. It is true his Cabinet approved the sentence, but it was he who signed the death sentence. It was he who, with the recommendation of the Court to mercy before his eyes, refused at the last to exercise the clemency with which the law had clothed him." That recommendation for mercy from the military court was not due to any doubt as to her guilt but "in consideration of the sex and age of said Mary E. Surratt."[28]

About a year later a rumor circulated to the effect that General Hunter was the only member of the nine-man military court who refused to sign the recommendation for clemency for Surratt. However, he stepped forward to say he had signed it, "and that I have always looked with utter contempt on the execution of the poor woman, excusing at the same time, thousands of rebel men who so much more richly deserved hanging."[29]

For decades a controversy swirled over whether or not President Johnson saw the recommendation for mercy attached to the court record when he reviewed the material with only Judge Advocate Holt, of the military court, present. Johnson always insisted no mercy recommendation was present with the documents; Holt always insisted it was there. As the issue came down to one man's word against another's, the issue was never resolved. By the early 1870s it was reported that all those in the Johnson administration that had a hand in the affair then believed that Surratt had not been proved guilty of being aware of Booth's plan to kill Lincoln, but that her knowledge extended only to the long-previously-planned abduction of Lincoln plot.[30]

In a late 1873 response to Judge Advocate Holt's continued insistence that a mercy recommendation was in the report at the July 5 meeting, the by-then ex–President Johnson said he and Holt were alone on July 5 and discussed all four death cases and that no recommendation for mercy was seen by him or was among the papers Holt brought to that meeting. According to Johnson only the question of Surratt's sex was discussed by the two men, with Holt having urged that just because the criminal was a woman was no excuse in itself for leniency, and that when a woman "unsexed" herself and entered the arena of crime "it was rather an aggravation than a mitigation" of the offense. To discriminate in favor of Mary Surratt, Holt was said to have argued, at the expense of the three men, "would be to offer a premium to the female sex to engage in crime, and to become the principal actors in its commission." Thus, when the meeting ended the four death sentences were confirmed.[31]

Media articles continued to raise the Surratt story for decades. A brief mention of her in a newspaper in 1881, in regard to something else, remarked briefly on her trial, "She being a Southern woman and a Catholic, the court martial was organized to convict, and she was hung for keeping boarders."[32]

For some 30 years the man who had been Surratt's counsel at the trial, John W. Clampitt of Chicago, had reportedly been gathering documentary evidence with the aim of establishing the innocence of his late client. Supposedly he had enough such evidence to refute Mary's guilt and was ready to publish the evidence when a fire in early 1895 destroyed his home in Chicago, along with all the evidence he had assembled.[33]

Bridget Durgan

On Monday, February 25, 1867, a terrible murder took place at the little town of Newmarket, New Jersey, about three miles west of Plainfield, with the victim being the wife of Doctor Lester Coriell. Around midnight

3. 1860s

the servant of the household ran to a neighbor's house and banged frantically for admission, carrying the Coriell's two-year-old child. She explained something terrible had happened. Neighbors accompanied her back home and raised the general alarm. At the house (Dr. Coriell was out on house calls) neighbors found the body of Mary Ellen Coriell, stabbed to death from multiple stab wounds. There was blood all over the place and signs of a struggle that had ranged over several rooms of the house. Servant Bridget Durgan told the following story as to the events of the evening. At 8:30 P.M. two men called and asked to see Dr. Coriell. When told he was out, they left. At 10:30 they called again and went into the lounge with Mrs. Coriell. Soon thereafter Mrs. Coriell screamed and yelled to Durgan in another room to take the child and run away to the neighbors for help. She did. However, her story was full of holes and inconsistencies and she was not believed. Within a few days she was charged with the murder of Coriell. When she appeared at an inquest she was described by a journalist as follows: "Bridget Durgan, the alleged murderess, is a stout Irish girl of about twenty-three years of age. She has an evil look that strikes a person forcibly on beholding her. Her manner throughout the inquest yesterday betokened that she was either a cunning evil-doer, hiding her moral ugliness under a simulated appearance of a half idiot, or was a half-witted creature in the full sense of the word."[34]

Bridget's trial began on May 20, 1867, at New Brunswick, New Jersey. Said a reporter, "She is an ordinary looking Irish girl, with plain features that are not very expressive. She was plainly clad. Beyond a little nervousness during the reading of the indictment and the District Attorney's address, there was nothing in her demeanor to indicate how deeply she was interested in the proceedings." In his opening address to the jury, District Attorney Charles Herbert explained that his was "no common case of homicide.... A lovely woman, adorned with all the virtues of a wife and mother, in her own house is butchered by a fiend." The knife by which the murder was committed belonged to the family and was found afterward in an outhouse to which the prisoner was seen to go at 4 A.M. on the morning after the murder. There was blood on her skirt when she went to the neighbors for help. There were three cuts on the inside of the forefinger of her right hand, made by clasping the knife. Dr. Coriell left home around 5 P.M. on that fateful day and returned home to find his wife dead. Durgan started to work for the family on October 22, 1866, and lived with them every day up to the murder, except for a couple days when she was away over Christmas. Still, Dr. Coriell had told his wife to discharge her at the end of February (no reason seemed to have been printed by the press for such an action). Bridget was said to have preferred to stay on with the family, even for $1 or $2 less salary per month, but she also displayed no animosity over her pending discharge. At the trial Dr. Coriell agreed things were normal in his household on that last Monday. Bridget was doing her work, the physician explained, and "she did not complain to us about being discharged. Mrs. Coriell and I had had perfect confidence in Bridget up to this occurrence; we thought Bridget an honest woman; we frequently left her in charge of the house, sometimes with the child, while we were out, she seemed fond of my child and the child usually fond of her."[35]

On Friday, May 31, 1867, Bridget Durgan was found guilty of murder in the first degree. The jury retired at 4 P.M. and reached their verdict at 5 P.M.[36]

Among the many holes and inconsistencies in her story was the fact she did not run for help to the closest neighbor but some two miles farther along to bang on the door of one of the remoter neighbors. No evidence was found anywhere that two strangers had visited the house of the night of the murder — for example, there were no footprints in the snow that lay everywhere. Imprints of teeth marks that were found on the neck of the murdered woman corresponded exactly to the teeth marks of Durgan. When the story of two strangers failed to work, Bridget afterward accused three different people, by name, of the murder — one at a time. However, all of them had alibis. The case caused the *New York Times* to editorialize, "The investigation of this case has excited unusual interest. To every household where servants are employed it has brought a sense of insecurity. Especially in the country where husbands and fathers are compelled to leave their families in isolated locations alone with their servants." Usually this newspaper was vigorously and vociferously opposed to the capital punishment of women but in this case it limited itself to remarking, "In New Jersey a strong determination is expressed that the perpetrator of this brutal and inhuman deed shall suffer the extreme penalty of the law, and that no considerations of sex or circumstances shall intervene to shield her." Apparently, in this instance class trumped sex.[37]

As Durgan waited in jail to be sentenced, various people visited her in hopes of getting a confession out of her. None succeeded. One of those visitors was a *New York Times* reporter who told his readers, "The cell in which Bridget Durgan is confined is commodious, neatly whitewashed, and furnished only with a bed and bedding, on which she sits by day and reclines at night." He went on to explain, "She is not so hideous as some have painted her in appearance. Still she is by no means attractive. She is a rather ordinary-looking Irish servant girl. Her head is large, her forehead broad and low, her face full and not expressive, her eyes, owing, it is said, to their being diseased, are rather sunken and the lids are habitually partly closed. She is of medium height and rather fleshy." She was also described as having that bloated look that persons accustomed to labor were apt to assume after being confined for some time without exercise and sunshine. Durgan was 22 years old, had been in the United States for about two years, and had never lived-out in New York, having come to live in New Jersey soon after landing in America.[38]

On June 17, 1867, she appeared in court before Judge Vandenburgh, who sentenced her to be executed by hanging on Friday, August 30, 1867 between the hours of 10 A.M. and 2 P.M. As the judge concluded, it was reported "there was some applause" from the spectators and "the prisoner sat down as soon as the sentence was pronounced and commenced to cry aloud, rocking herself to and fro and uttering screams that could be heard far beyond the Court-house. After some delay she was removed, still screaming, from the Court-house and carried to the jail, where for some time she continued to utter screams that were heard by the crowd without."[39]

A lengthy letter to the editor of the *New York Times* from Mrs. Elizabeth Oakes Smith appeared in August 1867. She said she had for many years visited prisons in many parts of the country to see female prisoners, "the better to understand my own sex." Smith was a well-known feminist writer of the 19th century. She visited Durgan about one week before the execution and reported, "In the scale of human intelligence I find Bridget Durgan on the very lowest level. She has cunning and ability to conceal her real actions; and so have the fox, the panther, and many inferior animals, whose instincts are not more clearly defined than are those of Bridget Durgan." With respect to her head, Smith reported, "She is large in the base of the brain, and swells out over the ears, where destructiveness and secretiveness are located by phrenologists, while the whole region of intellect, ideality and moral sentiment is small." And, more generally, "The whole person is heavy, inclined to fullness, and the hands are large, coarse, and somehow have a dangerous look, for hands, as well as faces, have expression." Continuing on in her description, Smith described the servant's face thusly: "There is not one character of beauty, even in the lowest degree, about the girl; not one ray of sentiment, nothing genuine, hardly human, except a weak, sometimes a bitter, smile. The wonder is that any housekeeper should be willing to engage such a servant. I have an idea that this same girl was offered to me in an intelligence office in Brooklyn, and that I refused to even talk with one so repulsive in appearance." However, she concluded, "I have looked upon Bridget Durgan without prejudice, and I describe her without exaggeration.... That she is dangerous to a community, might have been easily seen before she steeped her hands in blood." Smith was ambivalent, though, as to whether Bridget should be executed, being opposed to capital punishment in principle but perhaps ready to make an exception. "In this case I observe that women are unanimous in the feeling (for it is hardly an opinion) that she ought to hang.... There is little doubt that the law will have its course in regard to her, and perhaps in most cases of crime it is better to let it do so," stated Smith. While visiting Durgan, according to Smith, Bridget remarked to her, "Ladies don't often talk kind to me; they say I ought to be hung, and they are glad I am going to be hung."[40]

With just three days to go before her execution all the last-minute efforts to postpone it had failed. Her health was reported to be unimpaired, her appetite good, and her sleep regular. Morbid curiosity had reached a high pitch and there was a rush of visitors trying to see the condemned woman. Contradictory statements were made in the press, ranging from a report Durgan had revealed nothing to one that claimed she had made three separate confessions.[41]

The sheriff, in charge of the execution, was said to have been "beset" with applicants for tickets of admission (no charge) to the jail yard to witness the hanging. Between 400 and 500 tickets had already been issued. "The jail is daily visited by a great many persons most of them ladies, anxious to see Bridget," said a newsman. "The turnkey informs me that today [August 27] he turned away as many as 200 persons from the jail door." Some supporters of Durgan had circulated the story Bridget had become pregnant since being incarcerated. (The State always postponed the execution of a woman confirmed to be pregnant.) But three doctors who were called in to examine her all declared she was not pregnant. By this time Durgan had confessed to murdering Coriell. Her motive was not robbery, as many had supposed, but a desire to supplant her mistress in the affections of her husband.[42]

Reporting on Durgan's execution, a reporter noted first that Mary Ellen Coriell was 31 and had been married about nine years; Dr. Coriell was about 40. Said the journalist, with respect to Durgan, "No one seemed to have any sympathy for her. The universal expression was, 'If any one should be hung, she should.'" Sheriff Clarkson was in charge of the execution. Journalists arrived in New Brunswick early in the morning of August 30 to find the streets swarming with people and that "best clothes" were being worn. Once those reporters entered the jail compound, noting, "We found ourselves immediately in the midst of a crowd of a thousand rough and jostling men, and were it not for the gallows that stood before us, could have thought that the gathering was for the purpose of witnessing a race or a prize fight. The men were literally pushed together. The officials, with clubs, acted quite as rudely as the spectators, and many a private row and scrimmage were indulged in while the wretched woman was mumbling her prayers in the murderer's cell." There had been a noisy and riotous night in the streets around the jail on the 29th, made up of equal measures of religion, whiskey, rowdies, and so on, that kept Bridget awake until 1 A.M. The method used to hang the servant was the "upward jerk" gallows; a method that regularly failed to break the neck of its victim and thus guaranteed that death was not quick and painless, when it failed. As the condemned woman was led to the gallows at 10:10 A.M., "the crowd surged to and fro. Every man pushed for position. Oaths and profane ejaculations of the most outrageous nature, mingling with cries and calls, such as one may hear at a circus. For five minutes we stood in the midst of these brutes, and wondered of what stuff and refuse they were made," wrote a thoroughly disgusted reporter. Bridget was dressed "in a plain brown suit, and wore a white collar and white gloves. ... she was as steady as a ship's mast, and quite as devoid of emotion." As the noose was affixed cries of "Down in front" and "Hats off in front" were heard from the crowd. "Up she went with a jerk and the knot twisted to the back of her neck as her huge body fell to the length of the noose with a heavy thud. The strain was tremendous and her half-pinioned arms flew up.

Officious officials seized her hands and pulled them down, holding them while the contortions of her muscular frame afforded ample gratification to the noisy 'gentlemen' in front.... Her neck was not broken; she died slowly of strangulation...." One of the reasons for the "difficult" execution may have rested with the fact that the usual executioner, a Mr. Isaacs, declined the job, saying he "hung men, not women," with the result that a last-minute replacement had to be found. Yet Isaacs was in the jail yard as a spectator. In the words of the *New York Times*, Bridget Durgan "was jerked into eternity." As well, several "confessions" were hawked about, offered for sale. The recorder of the city, David Jeffries, proposed to sell a Durgan confession to the *New York Times* for $1,000. A jailer under Sheriff Clarkson was offering his Durgan confession for $250. An evening newspaper paid $50 for yet another, one described as "not worth the paper it is written on." Bridget's lawyer offered yet another. Every person offering such a document claimed all were bogus except his own; but no two were alike.[43]

A different reporter on another paper noted, "A great many more than five hundred people were so anxious to be included in the list of witnesses that some of them suggested excellent bargains to the fortunate holders of tickets, which bargains were in every instance refused." People with admission tickets lined up as much as 90 minutes before the gates opened. "It was disgraceful enough, shameful enough, that the crowd should have been let in at all to witness such a scene," he wrote. "Really, this was very like a scene at a fair." People without tickets searched frantically for vantage spots outside the yard, such as on top of sheds, at elevated windows and so on. This equally disgusted reporter did not describe or even allude to the final horror, that of one or more of the "officers of the court" having to come forward, hold the struggling woman's semi-free and flailing arms, and exerting downward pressure themselves on her body to help her on the road to "eternity." Perhaps he was just too sickened.[44]

While the *New York Times* had always opposed the capital punishment of women it made an exception this time, in no uncertain terms, in an editorial on August 31. "All we do know is that the world is well rid of a monster. It is unfortunate that our civilization does not permit us to be relieved of such without the disgraceful accompaniments of a levee in the condemned cell, and passport to Paradise written and sealed on the scaffold. More abominable curiosity, more mawkish sentimentality, than we remember in the case of almost any other modern criminal," he fumed. But even the horror of the end gave him pause: "The atrocious spectacle of the hanging was properly concluded when the filthy jailor who had charge of Durgan rushed into her embrace. The final tableau was a satire upon the forms of justice, and an insult to the poor lady who lies cold in her grave."[45]

Bridget Durgan was 22 at the time of her death. She was born in Cloogh, County Sligo, Ireland. Her father, then dead, had been a grocery man. Durgan had two brothers and two sisters. She said her father did not approve of her boyfriend, who also worked for him. To split the couple up he fired the man, who promptly disappeared. Unhappy at home, Bridget determined to leave home and go to America. Because she had no money at all she helped herself to 20 pounds sterling from her father's hiding place and used nine pounds sterling of that amount to pay her passage to the New World. She had a couple of short-term live-in jobs as a domestic in New York City, but did not care for either. Then she got a similar job in Piscataway, Middlesex County, New Jersey. Dr. Coriell treated her once or twice when she was ill and Bridget chanced to hear of a job opening in that household and took it.[46]

According to Durgan's confession she had come to be determined to get rid of Mrs. Coriell and take her place in the household. Learning Doctor Coriell would be away for a long period of time, on that Monday she secreted the butcher knife in a convenient spot and conversed with the wife for a spell. After a time the mistress fell asleep, whereupon Bridget hit her over the head with a small chair. Mrs. Coriell got up to defend herself and the struggle went back and forth to other rooms. Finally, Durgan got the knife and stabbed her. Immediately she left the room to change her bloodied clothes, but before she could do that she heard Mrs. Coriell stagger up and struggle to open the window and get out. Bridget attacked her again, finally killing her, and then grabbed the child and fled the house, still wearing the bloodied clothing.[47]

Lucy Parnell

On Friday, February 28, 1868, Lucy Parnell, a black woman, was executed by hanging at Snow Hill, Maryland, for the murder of Hanson

Robbins. The scaffold was erected in an open field. Lucy shook hands with all those admitted to the execution area, and expressed herself as loving everyone, as having made her peace with God, and being ready to go home to him. Reportedly, Parnell died "with but little apparent suffering." In her confession Parnell said on the night of the murder she had retired to her bed while Robbins was lying on his plank by the fire. Between midnight and dawn Robbins approached her bed, woke her up, and demanded to have sex with her. She refused but he insisted, using violent language. When she continued to refuse he finally ordered her to get up and leave the premises or he would throw her and her belongings out into the road. Robbins then retired to his plank/bed by the fire and Parnell fell into a doze, supposing the deceased had abandoned his intentions of throwing her out. But again she was awakened by an angry Robbins who was dragging a table belonging to her towards the door with the intention of throwing it outside. Parnell got angry, grabbed a large tool used in cider making, snuck up behind Robbins and struck him a heavy blow on the head that knocked him senseless. Then she struck him a second time as he lay prostrate. At that stage her two daughters woke up. The three took the body across the road and laid it down. Robbins was then alive, as he was heard groaning. Lucy sent her daughters back home, dug a hole in the ground herself, and placed Robbins, still alive, into the hole. Finally, she covered him up and did her best to conceal the spot.[48]

Sarah Victor

In February 1867 a young soldier in the U.S. Army by the name of William Parquet sickened and soon died. No suspicious circumstances seemed to exist and the body was quickly buried. But suspicions were later raised and the body was exhumed almost a year after his death. Upon examination of the body a large quantity of arsenic was found in the remains. William's sister, Mrs. Sarah Victor, was arrested and brought to trial in June 1868 in Cleveland on a charge of murdering her brother by poisoning him. Victor had a life insurance policy for $3,600 on her brother William at the time of his death; she was the sole beneficiary.[49]

Early in 1867, Parquet went to Cleveland from Euclid, Ohio, where he had been stationed, and stayed with his sister for a while. Soon he was taken sick, and died on February 4, 1867. At the end of June 1868 Victor was found guilty of murder in the first degree. The father of the two was described as "an ignorant Frenchman named Parquet, usually called 'Old Pocket.' The daughter was early taken into the service of respectable families, but, though possessing considerable talent, became very extravagant and finally vicious, driving her husband to drinking, and leading an abandoned life, though she took great pains to conceal the fact." The jury deliberated for five hours before returning its verdict. During some of the trial Victor talked out loud to herself, calling upon an absent sister to do various things, and making sundry promises to herself.[50]

On Friday, July 3, 1868, Sarah Victor was sentenced to be put to death by hanging on August 20, 1868. When she was brought into court that day before Judge Foote for sentencing she had in her hands a fan and an orange with a string around it "and commenced to play with them in a childish manner.... After playing for a time, she hung the orange on her chin by the string and opened her mouth like an idiot. Occasionally she would mutter to herself and once said, 'I don't want to hear Mr. Jones [prosecutor] talk so hard against me any more.'" She also sang parts of hymns while in court. Before pronouncing sentence Foote asked her if she had anything to say, either herself or through her counsel. Her lawyer, Mr. Castle, said it was obvious that in her condition Victor could not speak for herself and that he had nothing to say. Said Foote, "The law has fixed the judgment in such a case, and I have nothing more to do than pronounce the sentence in accordance with the judgment. Sarah M. Victor, you are to be taken to the jail, to be kept in close confinement until your execution, and on the 20th day of August, 1868, between the hours of ten o'clock in the morning and two o'clock in the afternoon, you are to be hung by the neck until dead; and may God have mercy on your soul. The Sheriff will see that the sentence is executed." According to a reporter, "During the pronouncing of the sentence Mrs. Victor maintained her stupid actions and appearance," including singing and humming. He added, "It may seem to some hard that a woman in such a condition should be thus sentenced, but the court previously had medical advice to the effect that all her insanity is assumed."[51]

Over the two weeks following her conviction Victor persistently refused the food sent to her, reportedly taking nothing but wine. The wine was given to her, mixed with water, by the spoonful and "Sometimes the nurse is obliged to almost force it down her throat." A reporter who visited her in her cell found her still strange and deranged, talking out loud to herself about her brother and sister, singing and humming, and taking no notice of visitors. According to this journalist it was the opinion of those who had charge of her and her physicians that at first her insanity was faked, "but now, from the effects of her pretensions, her excitement, and her abstinence from nutriment, that she has really become deranged." In accordance with that belief Felix Nicola, sheriff of Cuyahoga County, Ohio, wrote a letter to Ohio Governor Rutherford Hayes (later U.S. president). It said in part, "Prior to the rendition of the verdict, symptoms of mental derangement manifested themselves. But upon the rendition of the verdict, they became to all appearances, marked and permanent. Sentence was delayed for days, in the hope that this condition of things was but temporary. It, however, continued, and it was deemed best to have the sentence pronounced, as by the peculiar phraseology of the law on the subject, it was doubtful whether your Excellency could interfere until after sentence. It is now very evident that Mrs. Victor's mind is shattered." Nicola was clearly looking for a change in sentence, in the form of some type of executive clemency from the state governor.[52]

Twenty-one days after conviction it was reported that Sarah had still taken "not one mouthful of food." Some doubted the truth of that statement, believing she was eating on the sly. Meanwhile several letters had passed back and forth between Sheriff Nicola and Governor Hayes in regard to Victor's mental status. The latest, from Hayes, requested Nicola to collect and forward to Hayes "sworn evidence of the woman's condition."[53]

Governor Hayes, on July 16, reprieved Victor, moving the execution date from August 20 to November 20, and ordered her to be removed to the Northern Ohio Lunatic Asylum at Newbury. Later in 1868 Hayes commuted her sentence to one of life imprisonment.[54]

When her sentence was commuted to life she was incarcerated in the Ohio penitentiary, where she reportedly spent the hours, many of them in solitary confinement, in constant weeping. In January 1876, she made an application to the court in Columbus, Ohio, to have the original death sentence carried out, on the ground she had never consented to the commutation. After weighing the matter for 18 months or so, the court dropped the matter.[55]

3. 1860s

Ohio Governor Foraker granted a pardon to Sarah Victor on December 25, 1886, after Sarah had been incarcerated for close to 20 years. The revised story of the death of William Parquet was related as follows. In 1867 Sarah was living in Cleveland while her brother was stationed in the regular army at Elmira, New York. He wrote to her that his army comrades were all getting their lives insured for their families and friends, and that he was going to get his insured with her as the beneficiary. He came to visit her in Cleveland and had his life insured with a company represented by Mr. Charlton, a friend of Victor's. William then returned to his company at Elmira, but soon after went back to Cleveland on another visit, where he took sick and died on February 4. Although he was a young man, Parquet was said to have been not very healthy. At the inquest it was introduced into evidence that he had been in feeble health for years and that in his periods of depression he had sometimes threatened to kill himself. Victor collected the insurance money from William's policy. Another sister of the pair, a Mrs. Gray, demanded the money or at least a share of it. When she did not get it she began to put the story about here and there that her brother had been foully dealt with, tales that led to the exhumation of William's remains even though almost a year had passed since his death. The chemist employed by the state, Professor Cassels, found arsenic in the stomach and other parts of the body, "probably in sufficient quantities to destroy life," said his report. However, a reporter noted some of the problems with arsenic in the body, especially after a body had passed through the hands of an undertaker. "But at the time the only deodorizing substance used by undertakers was arsenic, and though it was not brought out in the evidence, some of the arsenic found by the chemist might have been injected into the stomach by the undertaker employed. It was in evidence that while in the army the supposed victim had contracted a disease for which he was in the habit of taking this deadly poison." (At that time arsenic was a popular treatment for venereal disease, from which Parquet suffered.) However, Victor was arrested and placed on trial, and found guilty on circumstantial evidence only. Despite that, there was always doubt expressed in some quarters as to the guilt of Victor, with many people believing that the chemical analysis was imperfect. Reportedly, Sarah's "reason" had been restored to her by the late 1870s and repeated efforts had thereafter been made to secure a pardon for the woman. But a "strong opposition" from Cleveland was said to have prevented various governors from acting. All along Victor maintained her innocence. Some time earlier Governor Foraker began looking over the evidence in the case and eventually decided a pardon was warranted.[56]

Hester Vaughn

At the November 1868 meeting in New York City of the Working Women's National Association, the large audience was reportedly "aroused to a high degree of enthusiastic sympathy" by an appeal from Eleanor Kirk on behalf of the "friendless girl" then imprisoned in Philadelphia under sentence of death for the crime of infanticide. Said Kirk, "Inasmuch, as we have reason to suppose that Gov. Geary believes her innocent, because of the absence of direct proof, and feeling confident that a united appeal to him will secure her pardon and release, we earnestly entreat your sympathy and assistance, as far as may be, in the good work of giving liberty and life to one whose death is unjustly determined." Kirk added, "The extenuating circumstances of the case are, that the mother was, in midwinter, driven, forlorn and destitute to a barren attic room where, freezing and starving she gave birth to a child. The mystery is, not that the child died, but that the mother lived." Further mass meetings to lobby for the condemned woman's release were scheduled.[57]

At the next meeting, held December 1, 1868, at the Cooper Institute in New York City, again under the auspices of the Working Women's National Association, a large audience was present, "principally composed of ladies." Susan B. Anthony called the meeting to order and nominated Horace Greeley to be chairman. Speakers spoke in favor of abolishing capital punishment, and advocated women's rights, among other topics. Another who spoke in support of Hester Vaughn, besides Anthony and Greeley, was Elizabeth Cady Stanton. A delegation was appointed to lobby Pennsylvania Governor Geary for clemency, and a collection for Vaughn raised $500.[58]

What particularly outraged the influential women's group was that Hester had been convicted on a lack of evidence and had an inadequate defense. Vaughn's case illustrated the plight of a poor woman up against a legal system that always sided with the rich, the ruling elites, and with "the man." Hester was born in Gloucestershire, England, was well brought up, married, and came to the U.S.A. After arriving here she learned her husband — who had preceded her to the New World — had another wife. He abandoned Hester. Vaughn went to work as a dairy maid at a farm in Jenkintown, Pennsylvania, and, explained the women's group — a delegation from which had visited her in prison on Thanksgiving Day — "There misfortune befell her. She fell a victim to the lust of a bad man. She went to Philadelphia, and there in a cold garret her child was born." The child was found dead lying by the side of its mother. A shyster lawyer took her last $30 but never visited her once in prison, next seeing her again only when she was led into court. There was no evidence introduced to show that the child, born prematurely, had been born alive, or that it had not expired almost immediately in the freezing cold of a Philadelphia winter day. When the judge sentenced Hester he remarked the crime of infanticide was becoming so common that an example had to be made. And so Hester Vaughn was sentenced to death.[59]

All of the pressure brought to bear by such an influential group as the Working Women's National Association, and many others who lobbied for the woman, apparently bore fruit because on May 20, 1869, four words in a brief newspaper paragraph declared, "Hester Vaughn is out."[60]

Later that year, in December, a report noted briefly that Hester Vaughn was in England "sick and in distress." Apparently she was ill during the entire voyage home across the ocean and the limited amount of money given her was exhausted in the purchase of necessities during the voyage. A fund was then being raised in Philadelphia for her relief.[61]

Harriet Grier (Crittenden)

Governor Bullock of Georgia reprieved Harriet Grier, alias Harriet Crittenden, a black woman, who was condemned to be executed at Macon on Friday, July 23, 1869, for the murder of Nancy Wright, a white girl who was about 17 years old, near Macon on March 16, 1869. A reprieve was granted until August 20 so that she "might have full opportunity for prayer and penitence." Just two days before her slated execution, and before the reprieve was granted, she made a written confession. In it she said her real name was Crittenden and not Grier as she was called in Macon. When she was a slave she belonged to Oliver Crittenden at Americus, Georgia.

Her father, a slave at the same place, was called Joy Crittenden. Harriet came to Macon from Americus about three weeks before she committed the murder. She met Nancy Wright on the streets of Macon the evening of March 15, went home with her and stayed the night. Nancy showed her new friend some money that night that she had earned earlier in the day from selling some wood. The next morning Harriet went to a nearby store where she had a few drinks before returning to Nancy's house and agreeing to go into the woods with her and join her in chopping up some wood that they could then sell. They took the axe and started off. After chopping for a time Nancy gave the axe to Harriet to chop for a spell as she wanted to rest. Suddenly, wrote Harriet, she got the idea she could easily kill Nancy and take the money. Harriet struck Nancy on the head with the edge of the axe and then struck her twice more when she was down and struggling. Then she took the money from Nancy's pocket and ran off. Counting the money she found a total of $3.20. Going into downtown Macon she used the money to buy some "toys, cakes and candy." As to her motivation, she wrote, "Don't know what made me kill Nancy, unless it was whisky and the devil. I never committed a crime before. I know the murder was a mighty bad crime, the worst I could commit, but I did not think of it at the time." And, "When Judge Cole passed sentence on me I was much frightened, and felt like I was choking. I could not pray or sleep when I returned to jail, but the good people came and prayed for me, and learned me how to pray to God for forgiveness, and I feel now that he has forgiven me and that I will go to Heaven. I have no fears of death; have seen people hung, and know what is to be done, but I am not afraid." No media record existed of her execution and her sentence was perhaps commuted.[62]

Executions of Women in the 1860s[63]

(All were executed by hanging and all for murder, except as noted.)
1860, July 13, June (Jones), black slave, Montgomery, Alabama.
1860, March 23, Ann Bilansky, 34, white housewife, Waseca, Minnesota.
1860, March 23, Ann (Croxton), black slave, Essex, Virginia.
1860, March 23, Eliza (Croxton), black slave, Essex, Virginia.
1860, September 7, Frances (Berry), black slave (poisoning), Franklin, Kentucky.

3. 1860s

1861, April 26, Paula Angel, Hispanic, San Miguel, New Mexico.

>Nineteen-year-old Angel was executed for the murder of her married boyfriend, whom she had stabbed to death when he would not leave his wife for her.

1861, January, Rhodie (Witherspoon), black slave, Darlington, South Carolina.

1861, January, Silvy (Witherspoon), black slave, Darlington, South Carolina.

1861, June 18, Lizzie (Jones), black slave, Montgomery, Alabama.

1863, Mary Naylor, black slave, Anne Arundel, Maryland.

1863, January 9, Margaret (Butt), black slave, Richmond City, Virginia.

1863, May, Bet (Dillard), black slave, Amherst, Virginia.

1863, May, Jane (Dillard), black slave, Amherst, Virginia.

1863, May, Sarah (Dillard), black slave, Amherst, Virginia.

1863, November 13, Chipita Rodriguez, Hispanic innkeeper, San Patricio, Texas.

>Chipita was hanged from a tree in Texas for the axe murder of horse trader John Savage. She was taken to the execution site sitting sidesaddle on a horse. Her final words were that she was not guilty, after which the horse was led away from under her.

1864, February 17, Eliza (Bantling), black slave, Marengo, Alabama.

1865, Delores Moore, Pima, Arizona.

1865, July 7, Mary Surratt, white landlady (conspiracy), Washington, D.C.

1865, March 10, Amy Spain, 17, black slave (unknown), Darlington, South Carolina.

>Amy was hanged from a tree for treason and conduct unbecoming a slave. When she heard the Union Army was nearby and would soon occupy the town she expressed her pleasure by exclaiming, "Bless the Lord, the Yankees have come!" For that she was put to death.

1866, January 19, Martha Grinder, white housewife, Allegheny, Pennsylvania.

1867, August 30, Bridget Durgan, 22, white servant, Middlesex, New Jersey.

1867, November 13, Lena Miller, 40, white housewife, Clearfield, Pennsylvania.

>Lena was hanged in Pittsburgh for having poisoned her husband to death in July 1867.

1868, February 7, Susan, 13, black, Henry, Kentucky.
>	Aged just 13, Susan was hanged for murder. She was a babysitter who reportedly killed one of her charges. It was said that many "solid citizens" of the town asked for a piece of the rope used to hang her as a souvenir after they cut her body down.

1868, February 28, Lucy Parnell, black, Worcester, Maryland.

1869, December 14, Sarah Bradley, black, Sussex, Delaware.

4

1870s

Mary Wallis

Mary Wallis, a black servant, was hanged to death at Upper Marlboro, Prince George's, Maryland, on February 10, 1871. She was convicted of poisoning a nine-month-old infant that belonged to the family of Albert M. Read, a clerk in the Treasury Department of the U.S. government, at Washington, D.C. In the summer of 1870 Read moved his family from Washington to the residence of B.D. Fabian, near Beltsville, Maryland. On Saturday, July 2, 1870, Mary Wallis, employed as a domestic servant in the Fabian household, was caught in the act of stealing some clothes belonging to Mrs. Read's child's nurse. Being confronted in the act Wallis became sullen and threatening in her manner. Mrs. Fabian was informed of the facts and told Mary she would have to leave the house and her employ on the following day. Mary's dislike of the nurse was said to have intensified as the day wore on. In the evening she was directed to boil some milk with which to feed the child during the coming night. A small boy who was employed about the place saw her take some powder from a bottle and add it to the milk. Advanced at the trial was that Wallis thought the nurse would first test the milk by drinking a bit herself and thus perhaps die, and if not, when the baby died from the milk it would be the nurse that got the blame. About 1 A.M. on Sunday the baby awoke and was given the milk but took only a little. Mrs. Read and Mrs. Fabian each tested the milk then and found it to be very bitter. But the baby died in agony within half an hour. Mrs. Read also was taken with violent pains, but recovered. The doctor who arrived examined the milk and at once detected strychnine in it. When the boy declared what he had seen, Mary Wallis was taken into custody. Subsequently she admitted to poisoning the milk as part of a plan to get even with the nurse. Her trial was held on August 24 and 25 and resulted in a verdict of guilty of murder in the first degree. In December, Maryland Governor Bowie signed the death warrant for Wallis, selecting February 10, 1871, as the execution date.[1]

Wallis was formerly a slave, belonging to Richard D. Hall, on whose place near Good Luck, about five miles east of Beltsville, she was raised. Her life was spent in the country, most of it in the neighborhood where the murder was committed. After the war she was employed as a house servant at various residences in the area of Beltsville. As a child she was said to have been given to fits of sullenness. When she grew up they were not so frequent but were "more threatening in their character." Said a reporter, "Her conduct in the court room and seeming indifference to her fate led to the belief that she was either an imbecile or was insane, and hence a recommendation for mercy which was presented by the jury." The belief that she was insane grew rapidly and resulted in a petition being circulated and signed by numbers of "the best citizens" of the county and presented to Governor Bowie at the beginning of February. It asked that her sentence be commuted to life imprisonment on the ground the jury had recommended mercy, due to her possible insanity. However, Bowie declared she was just the reverse of insane, "being bright and intelligent, but maliciously wicked, and he was therefore satisfied that the ends of justice demanded the enforcement of the sentence." The execution took place in the jail yard, enclosed by a board fence some 12 feet high. Crowds of men and boys had climbed on the fence and on the tops of wagons and carts placed outside the enclosure to watch the hanging. At 12:20 P.M. the trap fell. "She twitched her arms a little and there was a slight shrug of the shoulders, but beyond that there was no visible struggle. A few gasps for breath and all was over." After being left hanging for 20 minutes the body of Mary Wallis was cut down, placed in a "respectable pine coffin" and immediately buried in a pre-dug hole.[2]

Laura Fair

In San Francisco on April 26, 1871, the jury in the case of Laura D. Fair, charged with having murdered A.R. Crittenden, remained out for just 40 minutes before returning a verdict of guilty of murder in the first degree. According to the article, "Nine-tenths of the community regards the verdict as just...."[3]

An editorial in a Colorado newspaper praised the verdict and the response to it, commenting, "The unanimous approval which the press has given to the conviction of Mrs. Fair is one of the encouraging signs of the times. Not a journal of any importance has expressed a dissenting vote. Only one so far has protested against her being hanged, while on the other hand several have demanded that she suffer the extreme penalty of the law." This editor wondered why she should not be hanged, musing, "Can any objection be urged against it save the fact that she is a woman, and is this a valid one? She is a criminal, and one of the worst kind, and no false sentimentality should save her from the punishment she so justly merits." As far as he was concerned there were no mitigating circumstances involved. She shot her paramour dead because he would not cast off his lawful wife and fill her place with "a mistress and an adventuress. The shot was not fired in defense of virtue or injured reputation, for Mrs. Fair had neither. It was a deliberate murder, and added the highest crime known to God or man to her already long catalogue of sins."[4]

Some years earlier Mrs. Fair, "handsome, fascinating and accomplished," went to live in California, where she renewed her acquaintance with Judge Alexander P. Crittenden of San Francisco. According to a report, "Him she enticed to desert home and family, and she for several years lived in splendid style at the expense of her paramour. Having acquired a large sum of money, she went to the Eastern States, creating a sensation wherever she stayed by her extravagance." After she spent all the money Crittenden had given her when they broke up, Fair returned to San Francisco, with the reported intent of filling up her purse once more, again at the judge's expense. But he, having been induced to return to the family he had briefly abandoned to liaise with Laura, refused to see her. She swore to take the life of the judge, or Mrs. Crittenden, a threat she carried out by shooting the judge to death on the street while he was walking with his wife. During the trial it was revealed that Fair had been married four times. As well, "the prisoner was unmistakably supported by the free love portion of the community, who more than once made their feelings in favor of the shocking life of the prisoner, as revealed in the course of the trial, audible in court." With respect to the guilty verdict, this newspaper declared, "Society will have its due if the law takes its course, and Laura D. Fair ends her miserable life on the gallows."⁵

On June 5 in court Laura Fair was sentenced to be executed by hanging on July 18, 1871. "A number of ladies seated about the prisoner burst into tears as the court announced the painful sentence," noted an observer. "Indeed it was an ordeal for all who were in the court — none had ever witnessed the passing of the death penalty on a woman; though the verdict was just, all felt sympathy for her, and on all sides there were heard expressions of sorrow."⁶

A New Orleans writer who claimed to have known Fair in the prime of her power and beauty described her as follows, in exaggerated fashion that fed a media frenzy for more gossip in a much-publicized case. "Mrs. Laura D. Fair is said to be one of the most fascinating women that ever destroyed the peace of a family. She is above the ordinary height of women, symmetrical in form, graceful in carriage, and infatuating in manner and magnetism.... With the exception of her liaison with Crittenden, she was always wary and cunning and the terror of married women wherever she went. It was evident to men of the world that, although she never did anything which could call for rebuke, she was a smoldering volcano, and not averse to a warm flirtation. Men thronged around her wherever she went, and women hated her with inexpressible virulence." Adding to her legend and establishing the idea of the vamp before the word arrived in the lexicon, he continued, "when she entered a salon or a ball-room the gentlemen would desert other ladies to gather around her and compete for her smiles and recognition. She never allowed herself to be under any pecuniary obligation to men, but always delighted in taking their husbands away from young married women." And, "In short, she is a beautiful, heartless, fearless, terrible tigress, who loves and hates like a wild beast, and is always ready to murder anybody who crosses her passions."⁷

Laura's first divorce was granted in 1855 in New Orleans, from William Stone, her husband. From the court records of that case it was revealed that she left her husband on November 18, 1854. She accused him of mental and physical cruelty, of being regularly drunk, and so on. He denied all her allegations and claimed she behaved "improperly" with men. At the divorce trial in July 1855 each of the two, and their respective supporting witnesses, struck to their original complaints and stories. All except for Laura's sister, Mary Jane Payne, who testified she had stopped visiting

Laura because of her improper conduct with men. Margaret Burns, the Stone family servant at the time, said that one day Mrs. Stone picked up a knife from a table and threatened to cut her husband's head off.[8]

When an editor of the *New York Times* discussed, in September 1871, the lies and deceitful tactics a newspaper reporter had used to get an interview out of her, he declared, "Mrs. Fair is guilty enough to merit the severest punishment but the codes of civilized nations have long since abolished torture, and even so wicked a woman as she, lying in her cell awaiting execution, might have been spared the infliction of heartless impertinence."[9]

Fair's execution was stayed while legal procedures were undertaken, with an appeal to the Supreme Court resulting in a new trial being granted, scheduled for June 1872. She remained incarcerated as she had from the day of her arrest and a few weeks before the new trial she was visited in jail by a reporter from St. Louis, who was in San Francisco for a convention. Laura would not discuss the crime with the journalist but did discuss her early life with him, much of which had been spent in Mississippi, where she was born, and in Alabama. Said the reporter, "She has, perhaps, been a handsome woman — certainly a fascinating one — but confinement is telling on her. She was dressed, as most San Francisco ladies are at this time of the year, in a white pique dress, with an over-skirt and plait trimmings." And, "Whatever else she may be, she is a clever woman, and hanging, to speak harshly, would be about the worst use she could possibly be put to. Public sentiment here is, however, set against her, and unless she obtains a change of venue to some more favorable county, it will require the brightest wits of the legal profession to procure her release."[10]

However, on September 30, 1872, Laura Fair was acquitted by the jury in the second trial. It was a result that baffled and infuriated many observers. The editor of the *Colorado Daily Chieftain* fumed sarcastically, "Of course not. Mrs. Laura Fair is not a murderess; she is a blue-eyed angelic, seraphic saint and should be permitted to wander up and down the land and shoot whoever she likes. So thought the susceptible, tender hearted, addle pated jurymen, and so thinking, we have a verdict of 'not guilty.'" He added, "We can hang Mrs. Surratt on purely circumstantial evidence to carry out political ends, but when it comes to turning off a strumpet to carry out the demands of justice that is another thing. Out, we say, upon this sickly, damnable humanitarianism which leaks through the brains of jurymen, who never read the papers, and which is ready on the flimsiest pretext to throw the mantle of charity and mercy over the most atrocious crimes and blood stained murderers."[11]

Equally outraged over the verdict was an editor on the *New York Times*, although his language was not so much over the top. "Mrs. Laura Fair is a very remarkable woman — very remarkable people are becoming scarce, therefore it would be a pity to hang Mrs. Fair." That, he felt, was the line of argument that must have been used by "a marvelously ignorant San Francisco jury" to reach its verdict and that "turns loose upon society a woman who has outraged nearly all the fundamental principles on which society rests." According to this account Laura, a woman of "indifferent antecedents," and three times divorced, had attempted to shoot her partner in a boarding house that she ran in Virginia City in 1864. She was tried for that crime and acquitted. The lawyer who defended her in that case was A.P. Crittenden, a middle-aged San Francisco lawyer of "some eminence." Their acquaintance turned into "criminal intercourse" and in 1870 Fair was known to San Francisco society as the mistress of Crittenden. By that time, though, Crittenden (married with a family) was beginning to tire of his paramour and tried to get shed of her. Laura resisted. Then she quietly waited for him on board a passenger steamer, waited till he was quietly seated between his wife and daughter, put a pistol to his breast and shot him. (Earlier accounts said she shot him dead in the street.) At neither trial was the shooting denied, nor was any evidence ever introduced to claim self-defense. At the first trial in April 1871 Fair's defense rested upon Fair's alleged susceptibility to "spasmodic fits of insanity." According to the editor that trial was remarkable for several reasons. One was the strange defense and "Partly also for the morbid enthusiasm in favor of Mrs. Fair, which was professed by certain women who persisted in thinking that she was somehow a martyr to the cause of equal rights." After a new trial was granted, concluded the editor, it meant she had "been spared to be tried by the most ignorant jury of her countrymen that could be obtained, and to be finally acquitted. Whatever were the grounds on which this verdict was arrived at, the result is nothing less than a most ridiculous and shameful miscarriage of justice." One thing that enraged many observers was the fact that the second trial was virtually identical to the first. The evidence, the witnesses, and so on, were the same; nothing new was introduced. Yet the verdicts could not have been more dissimilar.[12]

A month after Fair was acquitted and released, great excitement was generated in Truckee, California, by the report that Laura Fair was in town. A large crowd gathered in front of the hotel to look at the name of "Mrs. Fair" on the hotel register. The Truckee band was reportedly preparing for a serenade when the hotel manager told them it was a different person with the same name. Thereupon the crowd dispersed.[13]

Just a week or so later a report surfaced that Laura was to take to the lecture circuit in the upcoming season, but a newspaper sarcastically observed that she could make more money by teaching pistol shooting.[14]

Nevertheless, Laura did launch herself on the lecture circuit that fall. On November 21, 1872, in San Francisco, at the hour she was to appear to lecture on "Wolves in the Field," about 2,000 people congregated in front of Platt's Hall on Montgomery Street and almost as many more were congregated before her residence on Kearney Street. At both places the crowd was boisterous and threatening at 8 P.M. Fair asked the city chief of police for an escort of officers to the lecture hall. However, the police chief advised her it was not safe to appear on the street or at the hall and therefore he declined to furnish an escort. He did, though, send men to keep the streets clear and to preserve the peace. A carriage arrived for Laura to take her to the hall but she decided to stay in her apartment with friends. "The crowd hooted and yelled, and men tried to force their way up stairs, but were driven back. After about two hours but few remained, and all is quiet now," said a newsman.[15]

Early in February 1873 Laura delivered her lecture "Wolves in the Field" (mostly an attack on her critics, especially the media and the clergy) in Sacramento. According to an account, "She denied having attacked the press and clergy generally. She spoke against them only as individuals, who had persecuted her. The audience was small."[16]

Phoebe Campbell

Phoebe Campbell was executed by hanging at 8:27 A.M. on June 20, 1872, in London, Ontario, for the murder of her husband George Campbell. She was reported to have met her fate with calmness and composure, evincing no emotion. Her paramour and supposed accomplice, Thomas Coyle, was then in prison awaiting trial for his part in the affair. In her confession Phoebe accused him of committing the murder, but admitted she was his accomplice. The murder took place in the Ontario township of Nissouri, near London, in July 1871. It was a private execution at which, said a reporter, "The condemned woman walked from her cell to the scaffold, pinioned, and without assistance, her step firm, her countenance ruddy and healthful, and her whole demeanor that of a person in good spirits, satisfied with herself and all around her." Phoebe's neck was instantly broken at the end of the seven-foot drop.[17]

On the night of July 14, 1871, George Campbell, a "respectable and passably well-to-do farmer" of the township of Nissouri — a little village in the County of Oxford — was found murdered in his house. Great excitement and fear was aroused and pickets were placed around the village (population about 100) to see that no one should escape. George's head had been beaten to a pulp. Soon suspicion centered on his wife Phoebe, who, as was well known in the village, had not been living on the best of terms with him, mainly because of "having given him the gravest cause for hatred and contempt which a wife can give a husband." That was a reference to her affair with Coyle. When questioned, Phoebe first gave the story that in the middle of the night while sleeping beside her husband she had been awakened by a hoarse voice whispering, "We want your money." She saw two strange men in the room bending over George. The three struggled; he yelled to Phoebe to go and get the axe. She did so, came back to the room, and was just about to use it on the robbers when one grabbed it off her and used it on George. After killing her husband the thieves ransacked the house but found no money and fled. Or so Phoebe's story went. A coroner's jury believed none of it and fixed the blame on Phoebe and her paramour Coyle. On the next morning she told the county attorney her first story was false. It was Coyle who committed the murder and had instructed her to give the earlier false account she had related, or so the second story went. Soon thereafter she delivered yet another different tale, that a cousin named John McWain had killed George. All the evidence, though, was clearly against the woman, such as her clothes being saturated with blood when she was found on the morning after the murder. From July 15, 1871, to April 1872, Phoebe remained in jail and then her trial was held in London in April. Unfortunately for her, she had written several letters to Coyle while incarcerated that were incriminating, intercepted, and used against her at the trial. Phoebe was convicted of murder in the first degree on April 6 with the jury returning a verdict in 80 minutes. Her execution date was set for June 20. The judge told her to hold out no hope that the sentence of the court would be altered, for "the case was as clear as the murder had been wantonly atrocious." Said an American reporter, "At the time the murder was committed, Mrs. Campbell was a rather tall and finely formed woman, in perfect health. Even had Canadian juries been as favorably inclined to listen to pleas of insanity in all cases of murder as our own juries are and had counsel been so inclined to utter such a plea in this case, it would have been of no service to the woman for it would evidently have been a preposterous one. She was in perfect physical, and, therefore, presumably, in perfect mental health." The reporter also noted, "Her brain was very large, much larger than that of the average woman; her will was indomitable, and her combativeness strong."[18]

A reporter who visited her in her cell on the day before the execution observed, "Mrs. Campbell kept up her spirits most wonderfully, and yesterday when your reporter visited her she chatted about various matters, and laughed heartily several times, looking and acting very unlike a person on the verge of eternity.... She lay down for about an hour but did not sleep" during her last night on earth. He added, "She was perfectly resigned, and even anxious to meet her fate, alluding to the scaffold as being the gate to heaven. She prayed earnestly for Coyle, hoping that he might make a full confession of his share in the crime. While all around her were people weeping there was not the slightest sign of emotion to be detected on her face, nor did her demeanor betray any nervousness." As she stood on the scaffold and last-minute adjustments were made, a statement Phoebe had written was read out by a clergyman accompanying her. In it she thanked various people for their kindnesses and observed, "I say it would have been wrong to let me free after that dreadful crime. I deserve more than I am getting, to think my poor husband was launched into eternity without a moment's warning, while God has spared me to repent and prepare for death. Oh my dear friends, I hope you will take warning by what you see and hear. It is a solemn thing to die if not prepared." The execution itself was not quite private as about 50 people were present, because "the Sheriff very properly limited the number of tickets he issued to the members of the press." Although the banks of the river near the jail were crowded with people, the scaffold was so situated within the jail compound as to prevent anyone outside the walls of the jail compound from seeing the execution.[19]

Susan Eberhart

Susan Eberhart (sometimes Eberhardt) was convicted of murder on May 29, 1872, as the accomplice of Enoch F. Spann in the murder of his wife on May 4, 1872. Spann was executed in April 1873, and then on May 2, 1873, at 11:30 A.M., Susan was executed; she was 19 years old. Her last words were reportedly, "I am ready and willing." She was said to have been perfectly composed and unmoved, and to have no dread of death. A reporter summarized her attitude when he wrote, "She had no fears, and hoped to meet all in a better world." Susan was executed in Preston, Webster County, Georgia, on a day one account described as "the saddest day ever witnessed in Georgia."[20]

At her request a statement of what she did in connection with the murder was written by her on May 1 and given to reporters for publication immediately after her death. It was entirely self-serving, painted her as an innocent victim, and contradicted a confession she made when first taken into custody. According to her account she did nothing with respect to the crime except to be present and to hand Spann a handkerchief when he called for it, to use as a gag on his wife's mouth. Susan said she was awakened in the night by Spann, who held her tightly by the hand and was commanded to accompany him and aid in his plans to kill his wife. All the while, she said she begged and pleaded with him not to kill the woman but it had no effect. After the woman was murdered, Eberhart claimed Spann forced her to take flight with him even though she begged him to leave her behind, but he said, "If you don't go, I will pick you up and tote you off." As well, she denied making any confession at all to her captors when she was first arrested and that if only the truth had been given in the testimony, whatever might have been her punishment, it would not be hanging. After being incarcerated, and some six months earlier, Eberhart found God and thus attained inner peace and what she believed to be God's forgiveness. At 11 A.M. on May 2 the sheriff took the prisoner, surrounded by a guard, on a buggy ride from the jail to the gallows in a grove of pine trees about a quarter of a mile from the jail. "She had on a white, small-figured cambric-finished dress, neatly arranged and trimmed at the expense of the Sheriff. Her hair was plainly combed in two long braids, one on each side, the ends tied together at the back. She wore a calico sun–bonnet." When the trap dropped at 11:30, said a reporter, "She fell five feet, and struggled but slightly. She was pronounced dead in eleven minutes, cut down in nineteen minutes, placed in a coffin and carried for the night to her father's house to be buried from the church at Preston tomorrow." Eberhart was hanged on the same gallows and with the same rope that had been used for Spann. Said an account, "About seven hundred persons were present, half Negroes. There were a dozen white women. Her neck was not broken.... None of her kindred were present. She was the second woman ever hanged in Georgia."[21]

Libby Garrabrant

Ransom F. Burroughs was found dead at Paterson, New Jersey, on December 27, 1871. When the Paterson coroner's jury held an inquest into the man's death it returned a verdict, on January 4, 1872, that the deceased came to his death from the effects of arsenic poison administered to him by Libby (Libbie) Garrabrant, his young mistress, who was 18 or 19 years old.[22]

At that inquest Libby acknowledged that she had bought the arsenic and went on to describe the manner of Burroughs' death. She added Ransom took the poison in her presence, mixed with Laudanum, Jamaica rum, and sugar, but that he lived on for three days. He had been dead a week or so when he was found. Libby insisted she told nobody of the death because Burroughs had asked her not to. "Her testimony was a mass of absurd contradictions. It was given in a careless manner, and frequently convulses the audience with laughter, in which she joined," said an observer. "She seemingly viewed the inquest as a great joke, except when the Coroner sought to implicate her lover Bogert Van Winkle (Wink); then she was always on her guard." A roomful of goods owned by Burroughs turned up concealed in the house of Gilbert Riley, a friend of Libby and Bogert. He had been arrested. One speculation was that she was merely a tool in the hands of the two men. Revealed at the inquest was the young woman's background. Her eldest sister Almira had married a Mr. Graham. Two months later he was stricken with typhoid fever. His wife nursed him for eight months until he became paralyzed and an "imbecile." She was by then destitute. A mechanic named Steele, who had often done Almira favors, persuaded her to elope and marry him. By that time the relatives of Graham were looking after him. Later Steele and Almira returned to Paterson and opened a store. However, all of Almira's relatives repudiated her, except Libby. Steele seduced Libby, an act that precipitated a quarrel between himself and Almira. Soon thereafter Steele died from poison; subsequently Almira poisoned herself to death. Libby then went "from bad to worse" until taken to jail on the murder charge. A cousin of the family, John Garrabrant, was accused of poisoning his first wife. He escaped punishment and married a second woman, who was afterward arrested for poisoning John. She also escaped punishment.[23]

A day or so later Libby told another story. In this story Bogert, to whom she said she was engaged, poisoned Burroughs by putting arsenic in some pudding and then hanging around in the evening to see that he ate it. Libby claimed she was present when her paramour died, that she wrote the suicide note found on Burroughs, and that she liked Wink so much she decided to take the blame herself. After Libby told her new story, Wink was arrested. He denied all the charges.[24]

Under orders from Wink, Libby elaborated, she purchased the arsenic, buying the particular brand he described, and she then gave it to Bogert without knowing to what use he intended to put it. Libby told many different tales after the death of her paramour. Bogert was a suspect, at least of being complicit, even before he was arrested. As to the motive, it was speculated that Ransom had been murdered so as to obtain possession of his furniture and household effects. Burroughs had kept a beer saloon.[25]

At her murder trial Libby's father, Peter J. Garrabrant, testified "he looked upon his child, and had always done so, as being very weak in intellect, easily led astray, and had always considered her as having less intelligence than other children." Testifying in her own behalf, Libby said she went to Burroughs in 1871, and that he kept a "disreputable" house and girls who were there gave him the money they received from men. Wink used to come to the house and she became engaged to him. Both, she said, were in the house when Ransom was taken ill. She explained Bogert had previously asked her to buy arsenic for him and she had refused. But afterward she got it because Wink said he wanted to take it to his brother. After Wink gave her the money, Libby bought 15 cents' worth from Mr. Smith, the druggist — she told Smith she wanted it to kill rats. She bought it on the Monday after Thanksgiving and Ransom took sick that same night, but did not die. On Wednesday evening Bogert told her he had given Burroughs poison. Bogert stayed overnight, leaving the house on Thursday; Ransom died on Sunday. Libby said she wrote the suicide note found on Burroughs on the Wednesday after the man died; Wink told her what to write and she did so. Some time after that the body was found. In the meantime, after the death but before the body was discovered, much of the furniture and goods belonging to Ransom had been removed to Gilbert Riley's house.[26]

On May 5, 1872, the jury delivered a verdict of guilty of murder in the first degree against her. Deliberations by the jury had lasted less than 50 minutes. An editor with the *New York Times* called her an "inhuman murderess" and noted that since her trial had ended two weeks earlier "she spent her time idly gossiping with other prisoners and with the occasional visitors who dropped in to see her. She showed hardly any sensibility, and did not seem to fear a sentence of death. Destitute as she had shown herself to be of all moral feeling, the few persons who had volunteered to be her friends could scarcely believe that she could be so indifferent to her fate." When she was brought into court on May 19 for sentencing the courtroom was jammed, standing room only. Libby "was neatly attired in a brown dress, black shawl and black velvet hat," and she was said to have betrayed more emotion than in past court appearances. Judge Bedle expressed satisfaction with the verdict and said, "It is enough to say that in the judgment of the Court your crime was deliberate and most wicked. Your moral sense has been much debased, and you have fallen very low, and no doubt are both legally and morally responsible for your act." Bedle added, "When once the female character is debased, and she allows herself to become a prey to the most vicious passions of her nature, terrible consequences may be the result." Libby (real first name Elizabeth) was sentenced to be executed by hanging on July 19, 1872.[27]

No sooner had the death penalty been assessed than a petition was in circulation to commute her sentence to life imprisonment. It was felt by a reporter that a strong pressure would be brought to bear to have her sentence commuted to life imprisonment because there was a growing sentiment in the community against hanging any person, and especially a woman. A month after the sentence was passed nearly 5,000 people had reportedly signed the commutation petition to the New Jersey Court of Pardons. Shortly thereafter Libby Garrabrant's death sentence was commuted to life imprisonment, to be served at the New Jersey State Prison.[28]

Much later, in the spring of 1886, legal proceedings involving a bill of impeachment were undertaken at Trenton, New Jersey, against State Prison Keeper [Warden] Mr. Laverty. Among other things he was charged with having "undue intimacy" with several of the female prisoners under his charge — one of whom was Libby. Said a reporter; Libby "has the reputation in prison circles of being incorrigibly bad. She was an unusually pretty girl when she was first put into prison. She has grown stout and tall since, but is a very handsome woman still."[29]

The first woman summoned to testify at the impeachment trial of Keeper Laverty was Libby. She had then been in jail 14 years and was the only female life convict in the prison. For some time she had served in the keeper's household. (In this period, throughout America, it was common, and usually legal, for the warden of a prison to take prisoners in his charge into his own household, normally within the prison compound, to function as unpaid domestics, cooks, gardeners, and so on. So much abuse resulted from such a system that it was soon outlawed by state after state.) On the stand Libby was reluctant to testify, fearing retaliation if she did. However, the court declared it would protect her and so Garrabrant testified. Laverty had "betrayed" her in a promise of using his influence to secure her pardon — in exchange for sex. She also testified she had seen Laverty and Eva Steele (another prisoner accusing the Keeper of intimacy) in a compromising position. At one time Libby wrote a letter to Mary Biner, telling the latter of Laverty's relations with her. For that she said she was placed in a cell, and between Thanksgiving and Christmas was in solitary confinement. Libby had been taken as a witness before the state prison inspectors in 1883 when inmate Gertie Meyers made charges of immorality against the keeper. But she, Libby, said such charges were false when she testified in that case — because she was afraid of being put in the dungeon if she told the truth. She admitted that Meyer's charges were based on fact.[30]

Many more years passed. Late in 1901 it was reported that members of the Woman's Christian Temperance Union (WCTU) at Paterson, New Jersey, were at the head of a movement to secure the pardon of Libby Garrabrant, who had then been incarcerated at the New Jersey State Prison at Trenton for 29 years. During the previous 15 years repeated efforts had been made to have her pardoned. Every such request had been ignored. For this effort the WCTU expected to have at least 10,000 names affixed to its petition that it planned to present soon to the New Jersey Board of Pardons. In its brief summary of the case, the WCTU declared, "She lived with Burroughs in Paterson, and among the visitors to her home was Bogert Van Winkle, a young man about town. Van Winkle believed the old man had considerable money and influenced Libbie to take his life by poisoning his food." Mrs. N.H. Schall, who had been the WCTU visitor to the state prison for 14 years, and many other people all asserted that without a doubt, "Libbie has thoroughly reformed."[31]

Elizabeth Workman

In Sarnia, Ontario, on June 19, 1873, Elizabeth Workman was hanged to death in the jail yard for the murder of her husband in February 1873. Apparently the couple had been drinking heavily on the day of the murder and became involved in a physical fight that left the husband dead. Right up to the time of her execution Elizabeth declared she did not intend to kill her husband and that his death was the result of a drunken brawl. According to a news account, "She ascended the scaffold with a firm step, and manifested fortitude and nerve which astonished all present. After the preparations were finished, she expressed a hope that her case should be a warning to wives who have drunken husbands, and to husbands who have drunken wives. She died almost instantly."[32]

A large portion of the community of Mooretown (where the murder occurred) regarded the death of Mr. Workman as more the result of a drunken quarrel than a premeditated murder. Thus, a good deal of sympathy was expressed for Elizabeth and strong efforts were made to have her death sentence commuted. Various petitions were signed and submitted to officials in Ottawa, asking for a commutation, including one from the local County Council. However, all such efforts failed. A reporter observed the drop fall at 8:10 A.M. "and the wretched woman was launched into eternity. The drop was about six feet into a pit which had been dug for the purpose and her neck appeared to have been broken by the fall, as she died without a struggle or a groan." After hanging for about one hour the remains of Workman were cut down and the woman was officially pronounced dead.[33]

Lodecea Fredenburg

The conviction on November 27, 1875, of Lodecea (sometimes Lodicia) Fredenburg (sometimes Fredenberg) and her son Albert Fredenburg for the murder of their relative Orly Davis at Herkimer, Herkimer County, New York, was followed by the immediate sentencing of the pair to death. Both were sentenced to be executed by hanging on Friday, December 31, 1875, between the hours of 10 A.M. and 4 P.M. After sentence was passed a reporter visited Albert in his cell, where he protested his innocence and said he believed his mother and his daughter were the guilty parties. It was upon the testimony of Albert's 12-year-old daughter that Lodecea and Albert were convicted.[34]

For a number of years prior to the murder Lodecea had been a resident of the town of Herkimer in a household consisting of herself, her married son Albert and his family, and Davis, the brother-in-law of her deceased husband. Apparently she and her kin were held in low esteem in the community because, remarked a newsman, "She had lived there for many years throughout all of which she and her family were shunned and avoided by all except the vicious and depraved community who always found congenial associates beneath her roof." Davis was said to have been a paralytic and viewed as an increasing encumbrance to Lodecea. She determined to get rid of him. To accomplish that she took her son Albert as an accomplice and between the two of them they murdered Davis. Lodecea first knocked him down with an almost fatal blow; then she lifted his helpless body, laid his head on a block, and held him in that position while her son chopped off his head with an axe. At least those were the major facts disclosed at the trial by the 12-year-old daughter of Albert, who witnessed it all. In both cases the death sentence was commuted to life imprisonment by New York Governor Tilden. Albert was sent to the state prison at Auburn, while Lodecea was sent to Sing Sing. In 1876, she was transferred to Kings County Penitentiary.[35]

An 1880 article that looked at life in the state prison commented briefly on Lodecea, saying, "She is very quiet and says but little. All the work she does is to patch up old garments."[36]

Around July 15, 1884, Lodecea Fredenburg died of natural causes while still incarcerated and was buried at the penitentiary. She was about 80 years of age when she died, making her around 70 at the time of the murder. "Of late years she has been weak of intellect and her mind wandered, but neither to keeper, fellow prisoner or confidante did she ever confess the crime," said a reporter. Always she had maintained her innocence and denied all knowledge of the murder until after its commission. Albert remained in prison at the time of his mother's death.[37]

Anna Hollenschied

For years Henry and Anna Hollenschied (sometimes Hallenschied) and their grown daughter Wilhelmina had lived in a small log cabin in the Hermann, Missouri, area. In due course the daughter married a man named Christian Alband, who had spent the ten years he had been in America wandering around as a "tramp." Early in 1875 he showed up in Hermann, poverty-stricken and owning little more than the clothes on his back. After a short courtship he married Wilhelmina and moved into the Hollenschied home. Right from the start the two men did not get along. Quarrels between the two became the subject of gossip and it was understood in the vicinity that Henry wanted to get rid of Alband, but refused to let his daughter leave home to accompany him. Henry intimated to acquaintances that he would soon be rid of Alband and that the younger man would never take his wife away from the farm. At the time of his death in June 1875, Alband was 28 years old and had been married four months. On June 16 the pair came to blows again and each used farm implements as clubs but were separated before serious harm could be done. On June 18 Henry traveled to Hermann on business and remarked the pair had a fight—he even showed his bruises about. "Now Alband will not come back," he added mysteriously. Suspicion was aroused by that statement and the fact Alband was no longer seen by anyone. During a subsequent investigation Anna was queried and immediately burst into tears, sobbing, "Oh, my man, dey will kill him." Asked what she meant she merely pointed to a spot on the riverbank 150 yards from the house, and added, "Oh, there is his body." When the area was dug up the horribly mutilated and battered remains of Alband were discovered. Confronted with the facts, Henry admitted the crime. Later, in jail, both husband and wife confessed to the crime. On the morning of June 17 Alband had a quarrel with his wife. On learning of that, Henry confronted Alband, and the latter attacked him. Then the two women stepped in to pull him off Henry. They wrestled Alband to the floor and held him there while Henry battered him for 15 minutes with a club. On July 27 all three were indicted for murder in the first degree. Mrs. Alband was found guilty in the July term of the Circuit Court of Gasconade County of murder in the second degree and sentenced to 13 years in the penitentiary. Wilhelmina died of natural causes in prison on September 13, 1875. Anna and Henry were tried in the November term of the court and found guilty of murder in the first degree. Both were sentenced to be executed on December 17, 1875.[38]

Agitation began for commuting the sentence of Anna to life imprisonment. One argument advanced to justify a change in sentence was that the then legal subjection of a wife to her husband rendered a wife incapable of incurring such a responsibility. With respect to such an argument, the editor of the *St. Louis Globe Democrat* argued, "If Mrs. Hollenschied has no stronger claim to Executive clemency than the one now under notice, her execution cannot be called legal murder, nor can any one blame his Excellency if, reviewing the case and finding that her only plea is one that would annul the law, he should, however reluctantly, allow the law to take its course."[39]

Yet just 10 days later, a couple of days before the execution, the same newspaper editorialized that it hoped Missouri Governor Hardin would commute Anna's sentence. "Without undertaking to define its cause or reason, we can at least say that there is in the public mind a moral sense which revolts at the spectacle of a woman undergoing the penalty of death by hanging. We believe it has not been witnessed in this country since the execution of Mrs. Surratt." The editor added, "At any rate, it has been very rare, and we hope Missouri will not be the scene of its next presentation. Let the Governor send Mrs. Hallenschied to the Penitentiary for life, even though he should find it an imperative necessity to hang Mr. Hallenschied, her husband and accomplice."[40]

In Hermann on December 16, excitement began to mount with the double execution just one day away. A gallows had been erected on the banks of the Mississippi River but at the highest point (150 feet) above the bank. It meant that while only a selected few were to be allowed inside the gallows compound, the execution (due to its elevation) would be visible from every street in town and for miles around. People were then beginning to arrive from as far away as 50 and 75 miles to watch the double execution. Two coffins had been prepared and were side by side under the gallows. In an interview given to the press on the 16th, Henry acknowledged he murdered his son-in-law but claimed it was the result of a "fair" fistfight that was started by the younger man and that no person's death was intended. He insisted that his wife and daughter had nothing whatever to do with it, with Wilhelmina being absent throughout the altercation and Anna arriving only at its conclusion. When Henry realized Alband was dead he took the body to a spot on the riverbank, stripped it of its clothing, and so on, and buried it. In her press interview Anna said she had no hand in killing Alband and arrived only when the fistfight between the two was ending. A reporter described her as follows: "She is a very small woman, thin and dried up in appearance, and a type of the ignorant low German. She is sixty-two years of age. She spends her entire time in knitting socks." Anna and Henry had been married some 40 years. According to a reporter, "The sentiment of the community is that death would be well merited in the cases of both man and wife. A petition for the commutation of her sentence got only thirty signers, and one for the old man but five. This is a town of fourteen hundred inhabitants. The crime which they were convicted of is regarded as the most horrible ever committed in this community." Late in the afternoon of the 16th the sheriff received official notification from Governor Hardin that the sentence of Anna Hollenschied had been commuted to life imprisonment. At least 100 wagons had arrived in Hermann from the country by then, filled with people who had come to see the hanging.[41]

As scheduled, Henry was hanged the next day, December 17, in a monstrous display of barbarity, both from the aspect of the crowd, and the technical aspects of the execution. It was just such execution spectacles that shamed jurisdictions one after the other to make executions non–public events, and ultimately to find a method of capital punishment other than hanging. By 11:00 A.M. on December 17 at least 250 wagons had arrived and, said a reporter, "From sunrise to sunset it was a day of boisterous reverie, coarse oaths and unfeeling jests were freely and loudly indulged in at the expense of the famed felon." And, "Many women mingled with the turbulent multitude, and expressed their indignation that Mrs. Hollenschied, commuted by the Governor, was going to escape." The crowd, well lubricated with alcohol, was said to have responded to Henry on the gallows in "blood thirsty" fashion: "He was made the object not only of laughter, but ridicule and abuse.... Among the crowd were two hundred women, who laughed at him as if he had been a clown, but of these he took no notice. Some of them said aloud that his wife ought to be up there with him, but this he did not seem to hear. Fifty-eight year old Henry did die instantly but he was almost decapitated as blood spurted from a gash across his windpipe almost from ear to ear. The black cap [hood] had flipped up enough so all of the neck could be seen by the spectators. Nor did Henry's death put an end to the spectacle as, reportedly, there was much carousing, boozing, and brawling on the streets of Hermann after the hanging, with an observer remarking, "It looked as if the peaceful village was overrun by a horde of barbarians."[42]

Johanna Turbin

Near the end of October 1876 in Washington, D. C., a black woman named Johanna Turbin was convicted of murder in the first degree with regard to her husband. Along with the conviction was a recommendation from the jury that executive clemency be granted. On October 31 Judge McArthur sentenced her to be executed by hanging on Friday, December 29 — a necessary step before clemency could be granted. In passing sentence the court said, "I do not know that it has ever fallen to the lot of a judicial officer in this district to pronounce sentence of death on one of your sex. This may be accounted for by the fact that women observe the law better than men." McArthur added, "The crime of which you have been convicted is a most atrocious and revolting one, and perhaps there never was one committed by either sex which surpasses it in atrocity. The victim was your husband, and after inflicting the fatal blow you mutilated the body in the most dreadful manner. If there ever was a case where capital punishment is deserved, this is the case." Then he stated that the jury had a repulsion to the execution of a woman and had petitioned for the intervention of executive clemency and after passing sentence he acknowledged he would sign a paper that would save her life. However, McArthur advised Turbin that she would never get out of jail. And soon thereafter her sentence was commuted officially to life imprisonment.[43]

Recapping the Turbin case, an editor with the *New York Times* said, cynically and sarcastically, "Thus we are spared the disgrace of hanging a woman merely because she had committed an atrocious crime, and the sacred right of women to kill their husbands is established more firmly than ever." No details of the murder were given except to say the couple quarreled; she killed him, and cut his body up into pieces. The editor went on to say, with respect to women, capital punishment, and insanity, "Hitherto women who have been tried for murder have been acquitted on a plea of insanity. Of course, this was merely a legal fiction, invented in order to remedy the failure of the law to exempt the sex from capital punishment. Every one knows that Mrs. Harris, Mrs. Fair, and other female homicides, were perfectly sane, and were acquitted solely because of their sex. Still, no lawyer has so far ventured to claim an acquittal for a female homicide on the solitary plea that she was a woman." To end his diatribe the editor discussed the interaction of race and insanity in capital cases, noting no plea of insanity had been entered on Turbin's behalf because she was black. "It is universally recognized by our courts that colored criminals are never insane," he wrote. "As a rule, the colored murderer has neither money, friends, nor political influence, and hence she is hanged with great promptness and the inexorable impartiality of the law is thus justified." If Turbin had been a white woman the editor was certain the jury would have quickly found her insane and thus acquitted her. In a conclusion dripping with venom he said, "Now that it is settled that no woman can be hanged for murder, we should also exempt the sex from punishment for lesser crimes."[44]

Jennie Smith

The murder of Officer Richard Harrison Smith of the Jersey City, New Jersey, police force while sleeping at his home at 133 Pacific Avenue, Jersey City, early on the morning of August 1, 1878, created a sensation in the town. Crowds of people milled about the area in front of the house over the following days. Two murder weapons were quickly found; one was an eight-inch carving knife, the other was a sash weight (an 18-inch long weight of lead about as large around as a man's wrist) that had formerly been attached to the gate at the front of the house for the purpose of swinging it shut. Both items belonged to Smith. On August 2, by order of the coroner, the victim's widow Mrs. Jennie Smith was taken into custody on suspicion of either having committed the murder herself or of being an accessory. "Mrs. Smith, who is subject to hysteria, had several attacks during the night," declared a reporter, who went on to describe her thusly: "The widow is a woman about 22 years of age. In appearance she is not beautiful, but she is rather attractive and has a good figure, brown hair and blue eyes ... and bears herself while free from hysteria like a woman of nerve and determination."[45]

Smith had been stabbed some 15 times and then had his head bashed in by the sash weight. Suspicion was said to have attached itself to Jennie right away because the "atrocious manner" in which the murder was committed led many to believe that she did it. "It seems hardly probable that any but the cruelest or maddest of minds could have led a person to plunge the knife fifteen times into the victim's body and then to bash his brains out with a bludgeon," said a reporter. "The argument that Mrs. Smith is too delicate to have accomplished the work unaided is looked upon by the authorities as absurd, yet they do not doubt that she had an accomplice." For some time past, as it was revealed, neighbors had talked of a scandal in which the name of Jennie Smith had been frequently connected with that of Covert Bennett, a young man who formerly resided in the neighborhood. Previous to Richard's appointment to the police force a few months earlier, the Smiths kept a boarding house at 110 Pacific in which Bennett boarded. It was said Smith's discovery of the affair led to the couple's abruptly moving to 133 Pacific. After he became a member of the Jersey City Police Department, Smith was detailed to night duty but at his own request he was placed on day patrol. In making that request he told his captain that he had domestic difficulties and wanted to be home at nights. Two weeks before he was murdered, Smith returned home unexpectedly one day and found Bennett in the house. Words followed and Smith ordered Bennett to leave the premises immediately, which he did in the view of several neighbors. Richard Smith had been divorced by his first wife in 1871 with the cause being "undue familiarity with downtown women"; the divorced wife soon afterwards married Richard's brother. With respect to Jennie one observer commented that her reputation was "somewhat doubtful" when he married her. Smith had a reputation as something of a ladies' man and that led to a secondary theory of the murder being that a man associated with one of Smith's many female conquests may have killed him.[46]

4. 1870s

Investigations by reporters led to the conclusion that even before his first marriage Smith was noted for his attention to the fair sex. All the evidence that had been gathered from those investigations, said a journalist, "goes to prove that the attractions of wedded life did not wean him from his evil ways. While he persisted in his own act of infidelity, he emphatically objected to any action on the part of his wife that aroused the slightest suspicion of immorality. On more than one occasion he abused and assaulted her because of her intimacy with young Bennett." Most people continued to believe Jennie was the murderer if for no other reason than the amount of damage inflicted on the victim, signifying emotions out of control: "They believe the murder to have been the work of a desperate woman, frenzied by jealousy or the disappointment resulting from the interruption of an unholy intimacy." Jennie denied all such allegations. She had been reared from girlhood, it was reported, surrounded by "vicious influences." Her mother, Mrs. Wooley, had long been a noted character in Jersey City. With her daughter she formerly kept a house of ill repute on Grand Street. Later she kept an equally disreputable place called the Right Bower on Twelfth Street, and after leaving there she went to Hoboken. Officer Smith frequently visited Jennie Wooley, even before his first marriage, and he was said to have been very fond of her. He was 30 when he died.[47]

Living upstairs from the Smiths were the McGregors, who described the Smiths and their relationship to reporters. "There is no doubt that they hated each other heartily; that Smith was fully aware of her criminal intimacy with several men; that he not only upbraided her, but half-starved her at times, and frequently beat her," they claimed. "The report that he had threatened to kill his wife does not seem to be well established; but those who knew the man say he was rough, even brutal, in his manner, and that it is entirely probable that he may have made the assertion when angry." Police were still searching for Bennett — who had not been seen since before the murder — but said they did not regard him as a suspect. Dr. Sampson, who had been treating Jennie for some months, said there was no doubt the young woman was predisposed to hysterical attacks and that she frequently had "paroxysmal" attacks of the disorder. Sometimes they were of such a violent character as to resemble epilepsy. Once she had lain on the floor in the grip of one of those spasms for 26 hours; on another occasion the paroxysm prostrated her for 18 hours. He said he could scarcely credit the theory she could have committed the murder in a normal condition. Nevertheless, since the evidence against her was so strong he was forced to conclude she was guilty and that in a frenzy of hate or jealousy she had committed the deed.[48]

On August 6, 1878, Jennie Smith was formally charged with murder. According to an account, "The Police have, it is frankly stated by some of them, been endeavoring systematically to force a confession from Mrs. Smith, and have not succeeded." By this time Cove Bennett had voluntarily stepped forward to be questioned by the police. Asked why he had not surrendered earlier, Bennett said he had not heard about the murder for a time and that he had "waited until the Police had got the real murderer in custody." He said he was 19 years old.[49]

Finally, though, the two were charged with the murder and went to trial in Jersey City in February 1879. Throughout the trial the courtroom was jammed. According to Jennie's version of events at the trial, on the morning of August 1, Jennie called the McGregors upstairs and said her husband had been murdered and that she had been chloroformed by the murderer. A small bottle of chloroform was found in the room; the knife and sash weight were discovered in the cellar.[50]

A couple of weeks into the trial the session slated for February 17 did not start on time. After a delay of 90 minutes the judge appeared in court to cancel the trial and order a new one. One of the jurors, Herman Duben, was unable to continue. He had been examined by three physicians, separately, and declared to be "insane." Duben did not know how many children he had, thought two plus one equaled four, and gave the impression he was the one on trial for murder, insisting he was innocent of the crime. Those behaviors were displayed on Saturday and Sunday, February 15 and 16. While options such as continuing with a jury of 11 men or bringing in an alternate were considered, they were dismissed as unacceptable and a new trial, slated for May 1879, was ordered.[51]

When the defense presented its case in May, lawyer Fleming said that eight or nine years earlier, Jennie Wooley, 16 at the time, conceived an affection for the dead officer. He was then a married man but was soon divorced and he and Jennie married. Jennie was described as a "volatile, gay creature" while Smith himself was said to have not been fond of labor. He would rather have earned a dollar or two at cards than in regular and steady employment. His associates were gamblers and women of even lower repute than his male associates. When they went into Smith's house he had no other employment than that which he found in assisting his wife at her household duties. And so, to make ends meet, the couple took in boarders. Bennett was among them. According to the defense it was undeniable that Bennett visited the house after the couple had moved and Smith had become a member of the police department. But those visits were purely for business reasons as Bennett had a debt due him from Smith. "Unholy love there was," said Fleming, "but it was on the part of Smith for other women."[52]

On the night before the murder Smith retired at his usual hour. Between 2:00 and 3:00 A.M. on the morning of August 1 he awoke and asked for a glass of water. Jennie got him one. At the time the house was quiet. She went back to sleep but was later awakened by a pressure on her side. A tall man stood by the bed and administered to her something that left her senseless. When she regained consciousness her husband lay dead with 15 stab wounds and a crushed skull. The bedclothes were covered with blood and an empty vial exuding the odor of chloroform lay upon the floor. And that was the story Jennie presented at her second trial.

Late in May the pair were convicted. Each was placed on a suicide watch in their respective cells. Jennie had her scissors taken away form her. Mrs. Mary Phillips, who had been in jail for around seven months, placed there by the sheriff to spy on Jennie, was released from confinement when the conviction was lodged. Sheriff Toffey paid her $200 in witness fees, at a rate of $1 per day.[53]

A jammed courtroom greeted the pair on June 9 when they appeared for sentencing. Their executions were set for July 25. As to the courtroom on the day of sentencing, it was reported, "In the gallery were several hundred women, some of whom were young and of respectable appearance, all seemingly quite as anxious as the men on the floor below." And, "Mrs. Smith was dressed in deep mourning. A stylish bonnet crowned her head, and from it a voluminous crepe veil swept to her feet." After the death sentence was delivered "Mrs. Smith never opened her eyes as the sentence was pronounced and did not shed a tear nor change the expression on her face." And, "The women in the gallery wept violently, and one sympathetic creature shrieked and then fell to the floor in a fainting fit." A movement to secure a new trial began almost immediately with a subscription fund set up by ex–Congressman Hardenbergh.[54]

The financial obstacle to a new trial for the pair — $1,000 — was overcome in a few days and on June 13 it was announced enough money had been raised. At first a benefit concert was to be held, by famed American opera singer Emma Abbott, but since time was of the essence and it would take too long to organize such a concert, Abbott simply approached and made personal appeals to some of her well-heeled friends. Contributors to the fund included Judge Hilton ($300) and robber baron Jay Gould ($300). "With the passing of the sentence of death upon the unfortunate woman came a revulsion of the public sentiment, and a feeling of public sympathy was aroused in her behalf," said an account.[55]

A day later an editor on the *Brooklyn Eagle* agreed that Smith and Bennett had been convicted on "insufficient testimony" and said, "There is no doubt that the excitement of popular sympathy and interest in this precious pair is due entirely to the fact that Mrs. Smith is a rather comely woman who has not been given perfectly fair play." If it had been Bennett alone, thought the editorial, no such groundswell of support would have been aroused; indifference would have been the only public response. Although he agreed the pair ought to have a new trial he also wrote: "That they should suddenly be transformed into a pair of martyrs on whose behalf the emotions of the public should be industriously stirred is to be regretted." Still, he thought there was little doubt the pair were guilty of the murder of Smith and that it was "one of the cruelest and foulest murders that ever shocked a community." Additionally, the editor reserved a great deal of bile for Emma Abbott, whom he regarded as a dupe. "She has personally visited the brokers of Wall Street and obtained subscriptions from them and from large merchants and others, gentlemen who contributed, we have no doubt, because Miss Abbott requested them to do so, and who would, in all probability, have subscribed to a fund to secure the execution of the criminals had that been the object of her zealous solicitation." He went on to say that the relationship between her "and the precious pair of self confessed adulterers, more than probably guilty of one of the foulest murders known to this generation," was firmly established, with Abbott having become the recipient of Smith's confidences "and now identify[ying] herself with the fortunes of one of her own sex whose shameful life her murdered husband endeavored to improve, and who, in spite of this endeavor, grossly deceived and murdered him in his sleep." Fumed the editor in his conclusion, "Miss Abbott's championship of the criminals may save them from the halter they have earned, but it will not save Miss Abbott from the judgment of indelicacy which she has merited."[56]

On July 20, 1879, a new trial was granted, which started on January 20, 1880. Eleven days later the jury retired to reach a verdict and 2.5 hours later the jury acquitted Smith and Bennett.[57]

Two weeks later a report surfaced that Jennie had announced that she was about to hit the lecture circuit with a speech entitled "At the Foot of the Gallows." No press accounts surfaced as to whether or not she actually did lecture.[58]

Kate Sothern

One calm night in the fall of the year 1876, the citizens of Pickens County in north Georgia were thrown into consternation by the murder of a young woman named Narcissa Cowart, at a dance, by another young woman, Mrs. Kate Sothern. Not long after the marriage of Robert Sothern, "a handsome but wild young fellow," said an account, to Kate Humbrick, "one of the most beautiful and fascinating young ladies in North Georgia," a dance was held at the home of her father, Mr. Humbrick. Most of the people from the neighborhood attended, one of whom was Cowart, "one of those handsome country girls who, knowing her charms, delighted in making conquests of men, but never dreaming that harm would in any way result." (This is one of many accounts that rendered the participants almost as upper-class members of polite society. Many other accounts rendered them as something quite different — in modern parlance, as low-life white trash.) During the course of the evening Cowart danced a time or two with Robert. That annoyed Kate, who informed her husband he should not dance with, or speak to, Narcissa any more that evening. Robert apparently agreed. Fueling the jealousy of Kate was the fact Narcissa and Robert had once been a couple. Around midnight Kate was furthered annoyed to see the pair dancing together again. Seething inside, Kate went to her father and asked to borrow his knife. When he asked why, she said she wanted it to cut a toothbrush (at this time small branches were often cut from trees and shaped, to be used as "toothbrushes"). Worried by the lateness of the hour to be cutting a toothbrush, the father nevertheless handed over his knife. Returning to the dance Kate attacked Narcissa and stabbed her to death (stabbing her one time, or several times; accounts varied), either after no brawl at all or after a physical fight in which the women knocked each other around for a time. Robert Sothern then got involved, grabbed his wife and fled the residence, perhaps by brandishing a gun, perhaps not. After the couple made good their escape, the Cowart family put up a reward of $250 for the capture of Kate; the governor of Georgia added $100. A year went by before any more was heard of the couple, at which time they were apprehended living in Franklin County, North Carolina. By this time the couple were the parents of an infant. In April 1878 Kate was tried and convicted of murder in the first degree and sentenced to be executed by hanging on June 21, 1878.[59]

At the trial the father of the murdered woman reportedly frequently shed tears of sympathy for the prisoner "and public sympathy, which had been decidedly against her, gradually turned to her side, until today there are probably few who desire the shedding of her blood." During the entire proceedings in court she sat with her infant in her lap. Not long after her sentencing, at a meeting of the Woman's Suffrage Society in New York, several prominent members spoke in Kate's behalf, urging a pardon, writing letters, and so on. Mrs. Matilda Fletcher said at the meeting, "It would be right for an army of women to go down there and take Mrs. Sothern forcibly from the jail."[60]

In the wake of the death sentence the *Atlanta Constitution* editorialized, "I do not believe that a woman should be hung under any circumstances, and I propose to do in my humble way, all that I can do to save this woman from the infamous death to which she has been condemned.... I do believe that the public sentiment of Georgia is overwhelmingly against the execution of a woman." Finding no fault with the jury, or the verdict, or the judge, the editor added, "But there is something above and beyond the judge and the jury that will raise a potent protest against the taking of this woman's life. Our civilization cries out against it; our social safety does not demand it; our best sentiment will condemn it. Surely the penitentiary is strong enough, and imprisonment therein punishment enough for the protection of society against the sins of women."[61]

Around May 23, 1878, Georgia Governor Colquitt commuted Kate's sentence to 10 years imprisonment. One factor behind the move, besides the formidable lobbying on her behalf, was that he was still smarting politically for not commuting the sentence of Susan Eberhart.[62]

More material rendering the women, or at least Kate, as something akin to demure flowers of Southern womanhood came from Kate's sister Amarilla Humbrick, who was interviewed in prison halfway through her two-year sentence for her part in assisting Kate in the murder. She had not been on the run and was tried and sentenced before Sothern resurfaced. Amarilla was 15 at the time of the murder; Kate had been 18 or 19. According to the sister, right after the marriage Kate had persuaded Robert to move 14 miles away from the old homestead to put some distance between themselves and Cowart, who still had eyes for her old flame. The evening of the dance marked the first return by the couple to visit the folks in some time and Amarilla said her sister would not have come on that day if she had known a dance was scheduled, especially one attended by Narcissa. As well, Kate was described as a member in good standing of the local Baptist church.[63]

By the beginning of June 1878, Kate was increasingly portrayed in the press as a heroine and a folk hero. Although her sentence had been commuted, a flood of letters and petitions continued to flow in to the governor; they all wanted Sothern to be pardoned. Expressing the sentiments of many were the remarks of one observer: "Every true husband in Georgia should admire Mrs. Kate Sothern — the woman who knew her rights and had the courage to maintain them." Photographs of the couple were then available for sale and said to be a hot item. When the train carrying her to the prison to which she had been assigned stopped briefly in Atlanta it was observed that "an immense crowd, including many ladies" was awaiting the arrival. An Atlanta newspaper editor sarcastically declared, "Women who feel disposed to kill their husband's paramours may now do so, feeling assured that they will obtain the sympathy of the world and to have their places in history beside Kate Sothern, the Georgia heroine." Then he noted, regarding the heroine label, "Of course no one can dispute the justice of her claim to this proud title. She was the successful rival of a mountain prostitute for the hand of a mountain rake. She married a man whose guilty connection with this woman was open and notorious — whose connection with her continued up to within two or three days of the wedding and which was resumed a very short time afterwards."[64]

Later in June the *Columbus* (Georgia) *Enquirer* claimed the "romantic" parts of the story, such as Robert's saving his wife gallantly, and so on, were all lies. The account noted the fight was between two women with a bunch of men looking on, all of whom did nothing to stop it because they were all "very ignorant people." No evidence existed, it said, to support the story that Robert saved Kate by somehow moving her through the crowd and out to an escape. "All that was the imagination of a fancy sketcher," said the newsman. As to the couple, "Kate Sothern is not pretty even. She is of medium height, about 20 years of age, and has dark brown hair, and the twang of a North Georgia cracker. She is very ignorant, can hardly read and write, and Bob is worse educated than she." She was then on the plantation of Colonel Smith in Washington County and was employed in the household, cooking and washing for the convicts who worked on the plantation. (At the time convicts were regularly "leased" out to individuals to be used as cheap labor. Such systems, of course, were rife with abuse.) Sister Amarilla was employed in Smith's household as a servant. Kate spent a lot of her time tending to her six-month-old baby. Nor had Robert been left out. "Bob Sothern is nothing but a strong, good-looking animal — a common, ignorant boor. He is now a guard to convicts on the same plantation. The woman Kate killed was on a par with the rest," commented an account. Reportedly the couple had turned themselves in after the one year on the run to get the reward. A reporter disgusted with the principles involved and the media coverage observed, "On reading this evidence one feels utterly disgusted with the amount of sentimental twaddle that has been expended on this case." And, with respect to the facts, "We do not believe there is a single woman, no matter how warm and sympathetic her heart may be, who, after reading this sworn testimony will sign a petition for Kate Sothern's pardon.... If such an act were pardoned the doing so would be a mockery of law."[65]

So notorious was Kate that she became the butt of a joke in July 1878. Originally published in the *Buffalo Express*, it went as follows: "Kate Sothern, the Georgia murderess has been put to work in a convict camp as a cook, and now she wishes she had been hung — and so do the convicts."[66]

Despite the above remarks from the disgusted reporter, petitions for a pardon continued to be signed. And women from Maine to California flooded Governor Alfred H. Colquitt with pleas for a pardon. In March 1882 Colquitt granted Kate Sothern a pardon and she was immediately released.[67]

4. 1870s

During those three years Kate was supposedly incarcerated she gave birth to two children, one of whom was named Alfred H. Colquitt.[68]

Executions of Women in the 1870s[69]

(All were executed by hanging and all for murder, except as noted.)

1871, February 10, Mary Wallis, 17, black servant, Prince Georges, Maryland.

1873, May 2, Susan Eberhart, 21, white servant, Webster, Georgia.

1874, May 1, Ann Hunt, black, Elbert, Georgia.

1875, November 26, Alcee Harris, 24, black, Ouachita, Louisiana.

    Afraid that her husband Henry was going to kill her after they had been arguing, Alcee Harris persuaded a friend, Toney Nellum, to kill him with an axe. Both confessed their guilt and they were executed side by side on a gallows set up outside the courthouse before a crowd estimated at 5,000 people.

1878, December 19, Ellen Osgood, Liberty, Georgia.

5

1880s

Margaret Meierhofer

John Meierhofer was a German past middle age that lived in the Newark, New Jersey, area in 1879. His eccentric habits led his neighbors to think he was demented. "He was neglectful of personal appearance and very unsightly. His habit of life was of the barbarian order," noted a journalist. After serving as a private in the Union Army he returned to his old house, a shack not far from the city of Orange, where he scratched out a living at farming in a small way. Reportedly, "His queer ways were for years the talk of the neighborhood. He was so cross, unkempt and wild in his ways that grown people avoided him and little children feared him." In early life he married Margaret. Before her marriage she had worked as a servant in a farmhouse near the Meierhofer place. Her reputation was said to have been "always a little cloudy." To make both ends meet, Margaret took in boarders. She ruled her husband with an iron will, was unfaithful to him and flaunted her infidelity in his face. When he sought to remonstrate with her she often "clubbed him into submission." She had two children and it was reported of her that "the woman was unintelligent and had few social relations." One afternoon in September 1879 a Dutchman by the name of Frank Lammens called at the farmhouse to get a light for his pipe. He wore the garb and had the appearance of a tramp. Little was ever known about his life except that much of it had been devoted to vagrancy and crime. He had served several terms in prison for robbery. During one term of imprisonment in 1864 in Auburn, New York, he was transferred to the lunatic asylum. When Lammens stopped at the farm that day he carried a satchel containing the proceeds of robberies he had lately committed and a loaded revolver. Margaret took to him from the start. She offered him a job doing chores around the place and an "illicit intimacy" developed quickly between them. While all that was going on, John continued to pass his nights in the barn.[1]

Among Margaret's boarders was John C. Pearson, a West Orange schoolteacher. At 6:00 A.M. on October 9, 1879, Margaret knocked on his door and asked for his help. She appeared agitated and asked him to write a letter to the justice of the peace at Orange, asking him to protect her against a man in the house who, she said, had threatened to burn the buildings and murder her husband unless she promised to leave home and go with him. Pearson wrote the letter to Justice Jacquit. Margaret signed it and sent it to Jacquit by her son Theodore, one of the pupils at Pearson's school. When Pearson returned home at suppertime he did not see John and asked about him. At first Margaret was reluctant to talk but finally said that Lammens had killed her husband and concealed the body in the cellar. Lammens, who had been in residence at the place for three weeks, had earlier explained John's absence by saying he had gone to Newark to buy clothes. Pearson raced off for help and returned later that night with the law. Lammens was awakened from sleep and arrested. In the cellar John's body was found, shot through the head. Margaret was questioned by the police and denounced Frank as the murderer. Lammens claimed innocence and denounced Margaret as the killer.[2]

One reporter was baffled as to how Margaret could have had lovers, saying, "Mrs. Meierhofer was a coarse, ignorant and shockingly depraved woman. That she should have stirred the emotions of any man seems almost inexplicable."[3]

At the trial Lammens said he was not at home at the time of the murder — but at a bar getting a drink at 11:30 A.M. However, the barkeeper said he was in the bar at 6:30 A.M., and not later. Lammens insisted Margaret must have shot John when he was out at noon. Margaret said she dared not report the crime or leave the house all day, as she was afraid of Lammens, who she insisted had killed John. Yet when a woman called at the home later that day to visit Margaret the latter said nothing. And when three hunters dropped in for a visit, Margaret said nothing to them either. Both were convicted of murder in the first degree and sentenced to be hanged on January 6, 1881.[4]

On the day of the execution, the district attorney stood by the gallows with two reprieves in his pocket: one for the woman, in case the man confessed and declared her innocence; the other for the man, to be used if the woman confessed and declared him innocent. Margaret was hanged first, followed by Frank. To the end each maintained his and her own innocence and each blamed the other. Up until the end doubt remained in official quarters that both were guilty; it was always thought only one of them was guilty. Despite the strong belief that one of them was innocent, both were hanged.[5]

The executions took place in Newark in that city's Essex County Prison. As required by law it was a private execution with those admitted limited to 12 deputies appointed by the sheriff, two clergymen, three "experts" (that is, medical personnel), and 12 witnesses, ordinary citizens appointed by the court. Margaret was said to have "exhibited the greatest fortitude and went to her doom without a tremor." At 10:32 A.M. on January 6, the sheriff raised his hand and the 650-pound weight of the upward jerk gallows fell. "The body of Mrs. Meierhofer went up very sharply. Her hands, which were clasped in an attitude of supplication fell slowly apart, but beyond that there was no movement of the body. Her head turned slightly to the left, and as the strain of the recoil came upon the rope the body turned once around." Those three doctors on hand checked the pulse after the body had been hanging for nine minutes and found it to be 160 beats per minute; a minute later the dying woman gasped faintly. Within 12 minutes after the execution the pulse had fallen to 80; in 14 minutes to 64, in 15 minutes to 50, and in 16 minutes the beats of the heart were so indistinct they could not be counted. Upon examination it was found the neck had not been broken and death was due to strangulation. Sheriff Van Renaselear said after the execution that it was the expectation that death would result from strangulation and that he believed the condemned suffered less that way than by having the neck broken.[6]

Lucinda Fowlkes

On the morning of January 15, 1881, the village of Keysville, Charlotte County, Virginia, was thrown into a frenzy of excitement when the story spread that Wilson Fowlkes, who lived about two miles distant in the adjoining county of Lunenburg, had been accidentally killed by falling into a well on his premises. He was a well-liked black man and soon a crowd, white and black, had gathered at his place to learn the facts. Upon investigation it was discovered that blood and brains were found on the ground between the door of his house and the well, and also on his bed and in other places in the room where he slept. Evidence of an attempt at a cover-up was apparent. When his body was retrieved from the well it was found that the forehead was completely crushed in. Suspicion focused on his wife Lucinda, who was taken into custody. Lucinda was said to be infatuated with a man named Isaac Deans and in his company went "to the extreme of wifely depravity." Wilson was not unaware of the connection and had frequently admonished Lucinda about her conduct with Deans, and on the Sunday before his death, having found words not enough, beat her severely. Additionally, he had threatened to shoot her to death if Deans ever came on the property again. On the morning of the murder Deans again visited the property and Lucinda resolved to kill her husband. Later she went to his bedroom while he was asleep and with one blow from a club killed him. Then she dragged the lifeless body to the well, threw it in and tried to make it look like an accident. Four children of the couple (one a grown daughter) were all asleep in the house during those events. When she was arrested Lucinda confessed to the crime. At her trial she was without counsel until after she had pled guilty to the indictment, when the court appointed an attorney for her defense. She then changed her plea to not guilty but was convicted of murder in the first degree.[7]

Another observer remarked about her, "The woman was very ignorant, and insisted that she was compelled to kill her husband in order to save her life. It is a very rare occurrence for a woman to be hung in the South. This is the first hanging of a woman which has taken place in Virginia for twenty-five years."[8] (The reporter's statement is incorrect: Virginia had executed three female slaves in 1863.)

One week before the execution Virginia Governor Holliday declined to interfere in the sentence of Lucinda Fowlkes, slated to be executed at Meherrin, Virginia, on April 22, 1881. On that day she was put to death at the Lunenburg courthouse within an enclosure erected for the purpose at the rear of the jail. State law required all hanging to be done privately and only the necessary number of officers of the court was present, along with one preacher and three citizens, who functioned as official witnesses; outside a crowd of 100 gathered, white and black. They could see nothing, though, and no disorder was reported. Fowlkes had slept well her last night and on the day of the execution she was reportedly calm, quiet and apparently unconcerned. She did not fear death, she said, and trusted in the forgiveness of God. On her final day she acknowledged that she had murdered her husband with no accomplices. While admitting her husband was jealous of Deans she insisted her husband had no cause to be jealous. Lucinda reiterated she had killed Wilson because he was mean to her, constantly beating and abusing her. The trap dropped at 11:35 A.M. "There was no struggling and few muscular contractions. The pulse had ceased beating in 8 minutes," and after hanging another 12 minutes the body was cut down.[9]

Catherine Miller

At Jersey Shore, Pennsylvania, on March 18, 1880, the body of Andrew Miller was discovered hanging from a beam in his barn with his skull crushed in. After an investigation the coroner's jury found that he met his death at the hands of George Smith, and that Catherine Miller, wife of Andrew and paramour of Smith, was an accessory both before and after the act. Both subsequently confessed, but even up to the last moment each accused the other of having planned the murder. On February 3, 1881, at Williamsport, Pennsylvania, the two of them were hanged. The night before was spent by both prisoners in "religious exercises, and they were much perturbed in mind this morning." Smith said, on his execution day, that Catherine was as much to blame as he was, and that he murdered Andrew at her solicitation. The drop came at 11:20 A.M. and, said a reporter, "There was scarcely any perceptible struggle by either, and no mishap occurred of any kind. Several hundred persons were assembled in the jail yard to witness the execution."[10]

Mary Booth

Mary Booth was the cook in the family of R.C. Gray, who, with his wife, had moved to Surrey County, Virginia. Virginia Booth (sister of Mary) and Martha Jones were the other domestics in the Gray household;

all were black. Apparently the father of R.C. Gray had a problem son whom he dealt with by buying him a farm worth $8,000 in a distant place and sending the son there from the family home in Chicago. R.C. Gray, said a reporter, "on account of reckless dissipation elsewhere, was located by his father in Surrey County, in this State...." Employed by Gray as overseer on his farm was a young Virginian named Travis Jones, who lived in the main house with the Grays. Rumors of domestic infidelity by the Grays were in common circulation. On April 8, 1882, Mrs. Gray and Travis were struck by the classic symptoms of arsenic poisoning after eating breakfast and in a few hours they were dead. Being indisposed that morning, R.C. Gray did not leave his bed and did not eat breakfast. Suspicion attached itself to the three servant girls and they were arrested.[11]

On April 11 it was reported that Mary Booth had confessed to poisoning Mrs. Gray and Travis by putting arsenic in their coffee. She implicated Martha Jones and others. Mary was just 14 years old. According to a reporter, "The feeling against Mary Booth is so strong that threats have been made of lynching her."[12]

At Petersburg, Virginia, on July 1, 1882, Mary Booth was convicted of murder in the first degree and sentenced to be executed by hanging on November 17, 1882. A petition, which had been signed by the jury, recommended executive clemency and was submitted to the governor. The other two servants were exonerated of any role in the crime. No reason had ever been uncovered and the motive for the crime was put down to "plunder."[13]

According to one account, "Gray employed eminent counsel to prosecute the accused and succeeded in convicting Mary Booth on purely circumstantial evidence and the other girls were discharged." As well, it was said it was not revealed at the trial that R.C. Gray had gotten up early on the morning of the murder and gone down to the kitchen and to an outhouse, where he had a jar of arsenic. Soon after the conviction and sentence of death were registered against Mary, Gray took to drink even more and became more "dissipated" than ever. He went to live with his wife's sister and continued to drink heavily. Then on August 25 he attempted suicide by revolver, shooting himself five times. Failing in that attempt he took a large dose of chloral from a vial in his pocket and soon after died. Speculation was that he was the victim "of a terrible remorse."[14]

Virginia's governor refused, on August 25, to commute the sentence of Mary Booth but changed his mind later and commuted the death sentence to one of life imprisonment, early in November. Reasons given for the commutation were the girl's age and the idea she "was only a tool in the hands of other unknown persons."[15]

Reportedly, the governor's action "meets with general approval. This is especially the case in Surrey County, where the murder was committed, and the Governor's action is warmly commended."[16]

Matilda Carter

Three blacks, Matilda Carter, Eldridge Scales, and Joe Hayes, were hanged at Wentworth, Rockingham County, North Carolina, on January 13, 1882, for the murder of Nash Carter (Matilda's husband) in December 1880. From the gallows all three made speeches declaring their innocence and that they were on the road to glory. Matilda spoke for 10 minutes and occasionally burst out into laughter.[17]

Ella Moore

Five black people were executed together by hanging at Eastman, Georgia, on October 20, 1882; one of them was Ella Moore. That mass hanging came just three months after a murder and was the result of a single trial and without appeal. It was a response to what was called the Eastman riots, for which an additional 17 black men were sentenced to life imprisonment. Located some 55 miles southeast of Macon, the town of Eastman was the site of what was called a "Negro camp-meeting" on August 6, 1882. It drew a large crowd, about 90 percent of which was black, and was apparently something like an amusement fair. Much drinking took place and after an altercation the police arrested a black man named Jake Tarrapin. As he was led away he attempted to escape and was shot to death by white marshal Pete Harrell. Soon the crowd went wild, convinced the white officer had killed Jake because he was black; revenge was demanded. Ella Moore recognized Jake as her nephew and pulled out a razor, urging the crowd on to avenge her sister's son. And they did, killing James Harvard, an innocent white bystander, whom they mistakenly believed to be Harrell. Somehow the crowd came to believe that in those few moments Harrell had changed his clothes and appearance. After Harvard was initially shot he was set upon by a crowd of angry black people and beaten to a pulp.[18]

Lucinda Teasdale

At Kingstree, South Carolina, on June 22, 1882, Lucinda Teasdale and Anderson Singleton were hanged to death for the murder of Phoebe Teasdale, wife of Anderson and half-sister of Lucinda. While Anderson maintained he was innocent, Lucinda admitted killing Phoebe but said it was self-defense.[19]

Emeline Meaker

There resided in the town of Duxbury, Vermont, in the early 1880s, a family by the name of Meaker that consisted of a father, mother, son, daughter, and a little nine-year-old girl called Alice, a relative of Mr. Meaker. Alice was removed from the poorhouse at Charlotte when she was about eight years old and had resided with the Meaker family for about a year before the murder. The town was to pay the Meakers $400 for her care and, in return, Alice was to live with the family until she came of age. According to one account Mrs. Meaker seemed from the start to despise the child, "often beating and whipping her brutally without adequate reason." On Friday morning, April 28, 1880, it was noticed by neighbors that Alice was missing and suspicion was aroused that all was not right. Authorities were notified and Emeline (sometimes Emiline) Meaker and her son Almon Meaker were questioned as to the girl's whereabouts. They denied any knowledge of her whereabouts but gave contradictory stories about where Alice had gone. Finally, though, Almon broke down and told the sheriff the facts. By his account he and his mother had taken the child to a nearby swamp and buried her, and the day before, he had purchased some strychnine, at his mother's direction, to poison the child. On April 30 he said the pair took Alice out in the wagon and while driving along they gave the poison to Alice in some sweetened water and in about 20 minutes

5. 1880s

convulsions began to wrack the girl's body. Emeline held her hand over the child's mouth to prevent noise. By the time they stopped at the swamp the girl was dead and they set about burying her. After Almon's confession the pair were immediately arrested and arraigned. Both pled not guilty but both were convicted of murder in the first degree and both were sentenced to be executed in February 1883. However, Almon's sentence was commuted to one of life imprisonment by the Vermont legislature. Emeline's execution date was later changed to March 30, 1883. Up until shortly before her execution, Emeline, who had been confined in the Windsor State Prison since June 1880, said an account, "feigned insanity, making the walls resound with her fearful screams and yells. She would attack her attendants and threaten them with fearful vengeance if they did not let her out."[20]

The Meakers were small farmers in the village wherein they resided and were said to be "noted for their limited intelligence." Horace Meaker was about 50 years old; Emeline, who had married Meaker when she was 18, was then 45, "sullen, morose, and a perfect virago." Louis Almon, the son, was 25 years old, "uncouth and uneducated," while daughter Nellie had grown up and moved out of the family home about a year before the slaying. Almon's first confession had it that he acted alone, committed the crime alone, and so on, to shield his mother. Independent witnesses had seen all three in the wagon that fateful day and Emeline had no alibi for the time. Next, he confessed as outlined above. Later, as he prepared for the gallows, he made another "full confession," throwing all the blame on his mother, and making many efforts to induce her to confess. As a result the legislature commuted his sentence on the ground that his weak mind was entirely overruled and controlled by his mother.[21]

During her final month on death row Emeline's behavior changed. "For several weeks past Mrs. Meaker seemed to comprehend that her attempt to feign insanity would be unsuccessful, and that she would have to stare death in the face, a watch having been placed over her night and day," said a reporter. "During the last few days she appeared calm and collected, and continued to knit with great vigor, eating and sleeping well and gaining in flesh." She had written to her husband and daughter a week or two before the execution, asking them to come and visit her before she was "murdered" by the state and asking to be buried at Barre, Vermont. Both requests were refused by them.[22]

During her final few days she sewed and knitted all the time. She was constantly under guard "but keeps her own counsel.... She evinces no sorrow for her past deeds and has no desire for religious consolation." Since Emeline was to be, reportedly, the first woman executed in New England there was "much interest" in the event and Sheriff Amsden was "besieged" by requests for passes to witness the execution.[23]

On March 29, one day before the execution, Emeline received a letter from her son Almon offering consolation and urging her to confess. Shortly after the delivery of the letter, Almon arrived, brought under guard from his prison, to visit his mother for an hour in her cell. She continued to deny guilt, to say the story was false and that Almon's lies had brought her to her present position. As well, she added, all the family hated Alice and had whipped her severely.[24]

Emeline Meaker was hanged on March 30, 1883, at 1:30 P.M. at Windsor, Vermont. Persisting in her innocence to the end, she had slept soundly the night before, retiring at 10:00 P.M. and rising at 6:00 A.M., whereupon she "combed her hair with great care, and put on her dress, made for the occasion, of black cambric, with white necktie and ruffles." As per her request from a day earlier, the sheriff took her out early to let her see the gallows. Inspecting it, she walked up the stairs, studied the mechanism and had the workings of the trap and the drop explained to her by the sheriff, in response to her queries. She died with "scarcely a struggle."[25]

Her execution was witnessed by about 100 people and, said the *Chicago Tribune*, "The murder for which Mrs. Meaker was hanged was so heartless and brutal that not a spark of sympathy was felt for her, and the only petition for commutation of sentence was based on the ground of sentiment against placing a female on the scaffold." And, "The wretched woman died friendless and alone, no kith nor kin being present to offer her consolation in her last hour. Her own husband and child were unwilling to have her dead body brought home, and so it was buried in the State Prison burial ground this afternoon." The drop was eight feet and she was pronounced dead after 12 minutes.[26]

In referring to her execution the newspaper the *Springfield Republican* commented that the firmness with which she met her fate was not a thing for admiration but an occasion for sorrow that New England could produce "women so far removed from all that is good in womanhood."[27]

5. 1880s

Barbara Miller

Around March 1, 1883, Barbara Miller and Charles Lee were arrested in Henrico County, Virginia, on suspicion of having murdered her husband Daniel Miller. All three were black. Within days Barbara confessed to a full knowledge of the manner of her husband's death, saying Lee killed him with an axe and then put his body on the railroad tracks to make it appear the man was killed by a passing train. She denied any complicity in the crime and claimed she would have told about the murder of her husband before except that she was afraid of Lee. The latter lived in the same house as the Millers and was believed to have been "criminally intimate" with Barbara, and for that reason killed the husband.[28]

Some years earlier Daniel was one of the suitors for the hand of Barbara Jones, and his main rival was Charles Lee. Daniel was old enough to be her father while Lee was a year younger than Barbara. "All the actors in the little romance were ignorant Virginia Negroes." Daniel was working for what was in Barbara's eyes the large sum of $5 a week while Lee made only $10 a month. She sacrificed her affection for the young man and took the "wealthy" older man for her husband. For the first three years the marriage was said to have gone along all right. After that, though, Daniel lost his job and became "shiftless," surviving only on odd jobs. Lee found that Barbara still cared for him and he proposed that he board with the couple. Daniel raised no objection and after that Lee supported the whole family. According to one account, "The new boarder and Barbara Miller soon began to live on terms of outrageous intimacy, and while their scandalous practices were apparent to their neighbors the husband did not seem to be aware of them. They lived on in this way for a year and Barbara Miller was known all over the neighborhood as Lee's paramour."[29]

Rumor had it that the couple began to talk about killing Daniel as far back as September 1882, but nothing came of it for a time. In November of that year Lee bought some poison, which he put in some ginger tea and gave to Daniel, but it had no effect. Subsequently Barbara was away in Richmond for a day, with Lee promising he would kill Daniel before she returned, but he lost his nerve. On the night of February 13, 1883, both firmly agreed Daniel must die. The next morning Daniel went outside; Lee followed him and killed him. Barbara was a tall, light-colored mulatto, about 29 years old at the time of the murder. She was born a slave, and was formerly owned by a well-known farmer of Henrico County. "She was more intelligent than most of her race, and early in life manifested a desire to gain knowledge. She attended school for several sessions and learned to read and could write a little," said a journalist. Daniel was at least 20 years older than his wife. In this account of the background it was said that before Lee had been living with the Millers a month the husband discovered he had good cause for jealousy "and in less than six months the man and woman took complete possession of the cottage. The husband was permitted to remain upon the implied condition that he did not interfere with the guilty pair. Miller was meek and rather indisposed to make trouble, so he submitted to the miserable terms dictated to him by his conjugal partner and her paramour." By February 1883 the married pair reportedly had frequent quarrels due to the wife's infidelity. Although Barbara's confession that Lee had wielded the axe that killed her husband had sealed Lee's doom, he remained very sympathetic to her and the pair visited each other daily in jail or communicated through notes. About three weeks before his execution Lee got religion and was baptized in his cell, in a bathtub brought in for that purpose. Barbara was present and assisted in the ceremony. The pair spent the night together in Lee's cell before his execution, which took place on August 3, 1883, although another account said her request to spend the last night with Lee had been refused. Miller had been convicted at a separate court session and was scheduled to be hanged on September 14, 1883, for being an accomplice in the murder.[30]

Several days before his execution Lee made a confession of his own. He said that before daylight on the morning of the murder Barbara had called him, handed him an axe and told him to do what he had promised to do. But his nerve failed him and Barbara stepped forward to deliver the deathblow. Then she prevailed upon Lee to take the body to the railroad tracks. When the body was discovered it was badly mutilated from the effects of several trains having run over it. At Richmond, Virginia, on September 14, as scheduled, Barbara Miller, the mother of six young children, was hanged to death in the jail yard of the Henrico County Courthouse before a crowd estimated at 100 people. Several thousand more people thronged the streets in the vicinity of the gallows compound. The trap fell at 12:12 P.M.[31]

On the morning of the execution date, Barbara's mother, sister, and some friends prayed all morning until she was called. At 12:12, said a reporter, "the trap was sprung and the body of the murderess fell nine feet. Probably owning to her light weight the fall did not break her neck. Her death was a fearful one. She lived thirteen minutes after the trap was sprung." Death was due to strangulation.[32]

Reflecting on the execution in an editorial the *Chicago Tribune* was unhappy because there was nothing in the execution itself that "made it a penalty to the miserable creature" (in a religious fervor she claimed to welcome death, and so on) and nothing in it to "terrify the class to which she belongs" (that being black women in Virginia on bad terms with their husbands). "Barbara Miller was as happy in taking her departure from society as any debutants just entering upon it.... There was nothing in the solemnity of the scene that made her forget the feminine weakness for dress, and her wants were gratified by providing her with a white Swiss muslin gown, a wreath of flowers about her neck, and a bouquet of huge dimensions to hold in her hand," he fumed. "Thus arrayed, the fantastic, miserable creature, all smiles and grimaces, was put out of the world."[33]

Another unhappy with the execution was the editor of a Trenton, New Jersey, newspaper, who said, "There was something peculiarly horrible and disquieting about the hanging of Barbara Miller in Richmond on Friday. Her religious fervor and her apparent desire for notoriety, which led her to relate stories of dreams about angels, were pieces of clap-trap that deserve the censure of common sense people." And, "The authorities should have had the execution in private, and not allowed hundreds of people, including women with babes in their arms, to witness the revolting spectacle. It is high time that the people demanded that hangings be conducted strictly in private, and not presented as public exhibitions."[34]

Margaret Harris

On Sunday night, August 19, 1883, after Mrs. Nancy Barnwell, a widow living near Fairmount, Georgia, and her two grandchildren had eaten supper, all became suddenly ill. After investigation it was found the family had been poisoned, from which effects one of the youngsters died. Margaret Harris (black), who had been bound over to Barnwell as an indentured servant when she was a child, was suspected of administering the poison and held for trial. In court it was developed that David Dukes wanted the girl to leave Barnwell and live with him. In order to free her from her indentures it was proposed to poison the whole family. A first attempt that involved putting poison in the family coffee pot nauseated the widow and the children but failed to kill them. A second attempt was made on August 19. Dukes gave her the poison and while she was alone in the kitchen, she poured the fluid over some rice that was boiling for supper and threw the bottle under the table. After being sentenced to death the girl, at someone's suggestion, as a ruse to gain time, said she had not told the truth on the stand, and charged Richard Barnes with being her accomplice instead of Dukes. When that did not work she confessed, a few days later, that her charges against Barnes were false. Dukes was sentenced to life imprisonment on the chain gang.[35]

According to another report, Margaret (18) wanted to marry Dukes (64) but Barnwell opposed the match. Margaret first said in court that Dukes induced her to try and "conjure" the old lady's life away by putting some white beans in a bottle with water in it and burying it with the neck of the bottle downward. She said he told her when the beans began to swell the old lady would get sick and when the beans burst so would the old lady. It did not work, she continued, and then Dukes gave her poison to put in the food. However, she went on later to make a sworn statement that Dukes was not guilty of giving her the poison or of knowing anything about the crime but fixed the guilt upon Barnes who, she said, gave her the poison and told her to put the blame on Dukes so that she and Barnes could get married at Christmas. The woman made many "confessions," all contradictory.[36]

Just days before the execution a petition was sent to the Georgia governor asking for a commutation of Harris' death sentence but, said a journalist, "as there has lately been a perfect avalanche of poisoning cases and an example was needed it proved of no avail.... Additional interest attached to it on account of the sex of the victim...." And so on October 19, 1883, at Calhoun, Georgia, just two months to the day since the crime was committed, said a reporter, "Margaret Harris, aged but 18 years, as black as ebony, short, plump, and disfigured by the loss of an eye, was hanged in an open field half a mile from the jail in this city at noon today in the presence of 5,000 spectators." She went from her cell to the scaffold guarded by 60 armed men and was accompanied by four preachers, two white and two black. Prayers were said, and at her request the clergymen sang "In the Sweet By-and-By," with the prisoner and some of the spectators joining in the chorus. The trap was sprung at 12:07 P.M. and the fall of eight feet broke her neck. Fourteen minutes after she mounted the scaffold she was pronounced dead. "Several of the women in the crowd are reported to have fainted when the drop fell, but the throng as a whole was orderly."[37]

A different account described her as follows, on her execution day, "Margaret Harris was about 18 years of age, coal black, five feet two inches in height, heavily built, and weighed 150 pounds. She had only one eye, the right one being put out, and altogether her face was not pleasant to look upon. Added to this she had very large hands and feet, which made her appearance even worse looking." During her last night Harris did not sleep at all and prayed all night. Part of her last statement, from the gallows, went as follows: "I have heard them say hanging was too good for me; I ought to be burned. I hope they will repent like me, and meet me in heaven, for there is no forgiveness here.... Farewell all! Goodbye! I must die! I hope this poor man [Dukes] will be released, as he is innocent, before God. He is innocent." Because of her last statement the sentence of Dukes was suspended pending a new trial, which he was granted.[38]

Angenette Haight

When George W. Haight was mortally wounded on February 27, 1883, in the town of De Ruyter, New York, his wife Angenette was soon arrested and charged with the crime. On the morning of March 27, 1883, before her trial had gotten underway, an effigy of Mrs. Haight was found at dawn dangling from the branch of a large pine tree in front of the Union Church. On a piece of paper attached to it was the warning, "Mrs. Haight, beware! Your turn comes next." Signed, "Vigilance committee." An illustration of Angenette shooting her husband that appeared in a New York paper was pinned between the warning and the signature. The effigy remained hanging for several hours.[39]

At 11:15 P.M. on the night of February 23, 1884, a verdict of guilty of murder in the first degree was pronounced at Morrisville in Madison County at the close of Angenette's murder trial. She was 62 years old.

When the verdict was given, it was reported, "The women in court sobbed and cried, and two of them went into hysterics and had to be carried out." As well, it was speculated that she caused the death of her two other husbands and her father, all of whom had made wills in her favor.

The dying statement of Mr. Haight was the only evidence introduced by the prosecutor. Soon after 3:00 A.M. on February 27, 1883, a bullet was fired into the brain of George Haight. He lived a few days in a dazed condition. Immediately after the shooting suspicion attached itself to the wife, mainly because of her extreme anxiety to have the insurance companies with which George had policies to be notified of his imminent death. He was her third husband and the other two were said to have died mysteriously after making wills in her favor. George had married Angenette in opposition to the wishes of his friends. Soon after their marriage she started to importune him to get some life insurance and he took out several policies. At the time of his death he had about $18,000 in life insurance, all with Angenette as beneficiary. About a year earlier he became somewhat worried over his wife's anxiety for more insurance so he allowed some of the premiums to go unpaid, but Angenette paid them herself. During the month of February 1883 he reportedly became more and more worried about his wife and even feared to drink his tea. Yet he continued to live with her.

On the fatal night, at about 3:00 A.M., their servant heard a pistol shot. She rushed to her employers' bedroom to find Angenette leaning over the bed and looking at a bullet hole in George's temple. She seemed a little alarmed and said George had committed suicide. Angenette did not want a doctor summoned but the servant went ahead and called one on her own initiative. George remained semi-conscious for three or four days and, at his request, was removed to the home of his uncle. In a statement he made before he died he said they retired as usual. Then at 3:00 A.M. he woke up to see Angenette coming toward him with a cloth in her hand. Before he had time to rouse himself she produced a revolver from under the cloth and fired a bullet into his brain.[40]

On February 25, 1884, Judge Murray sentenced Angenette to be executed by hanging on April 18. The courthouse was filled to capacity that day and when the prisoner entered the room she was attired in the same dark grey dress, black hat and widow's veil that she had worn all through the trial. After Murray expressed agreement with the jury's verdict and its

5. 1880s

justness he said, "It is painful to contemplate that such a crime was possible to be perpetrated by an aged female upon her own husband, while lying by his side in the dead hours of the night. To the credit of the female sex it can truthfully be said that such a crime is very rare indeed. You should not take any delusive hopes [of any future clemency], as we fully concur in the verdict, but should give yourself up to repentance." When the death sentence was pronounced, according to a news report, "There were cheers on one side and sobs on the others. Some of the women clapped their hands. The Justice immediately rapped for order, and directed the Sheriff to arrest the first person who should make any demonstration. The prisoner was hissed by the crowd as she was led back to her cell in the jail." And, "Mrs. Haight seems to feel that position she is in, but exhibits no outward emotion. She is still very proud, and has expressed a desire for a new black dress to be hanged in." At De Ruyter, where George had many friends, "the verdict was received Sunday morning, and there was an impromptu jollification. Mrs. Haight was hanged in effigy and there were other equally marked demonstrations.... The murderess has not a friend in the whole community, and all feel that the verdict is a just one." A reporter remarked, "The ability of the law to hang a woman still remains to be tested. Appeals have been begun, and with every one of them will be mixed the sentimental idea that a woman should not be punished with death for a crime, which would send a man to the gallows without any doubt. The only woman ever hanged in Madison County was Mary Antone, an Indian Princess who murdered her rival and was hanged in 1814."[41]

In the wake of Angenette's conviction an editorial in the *Decatur Weekly Republican* observed, "There is an unqualified spirit of murder about such a creature which removes her from sympathy even under the shadow of the gallows."[42]

On April 11 in Albany, New York, Governor Grover Cleveland commuted Angenette's sentence to one of imprisonment for the term of her natural life in the Onondaga County Penitentiary. He said he had examined the facts and had no doubt as to the justice of the conviction and that a sentence of death necessarily followed such a conviction under the provisions of the criminal law. "While there is naturally a feeling of repugnance against the execution of a woman, I am by no means satisfied that in the present condition of the law which prescribes the punishment of death for murder in the first degree females should be exempt from such punishment solely on account of their sex, but in this particular case, having made a full investigation of the condition of the condemned, I find that she is advanced in years, and the report of the medical examination made by my direction disclosed that her bodily ailments and infirmities are such that it is likely her life will not be of long duration in any event," said Cleveland.[43]

The next day, April 12, a reporter with the *New York Times* visited Angenette in her prison cell. She was found reading a newspaper article on the autographs of famous men. In reply to a question from the reporter, Angenette explained she had received many letters from people asking for her autograph but had answered none of them. Speaking of her trial, she said the people of De Ruyter had determined to convict her by lies or anything else. "Mrs. Haight is confined in a cell which is nearly filled by her bed, trunk, etc. There is a large mirror, and on it pasted a picture of her husband, with his death notice pinned on it. There was a Bible, a few other books and letters on the table," remarked the reporter, who concluded, "She evidently expects to go to prison for a short time only, to be treated well, and perhaps get some of her insurance money. She prides herself on her composure, and thinks she is quite a celebrity.... The general opinion throughout Madison County is that she should have been hanged."[44]

Roxalana Druse

William Druse, a middle-aged well-to-do farmer living a few miles from Richfield Springs, in the town of Warren, Herkimer County, mysteriously disappeared around the middle of December 1884. His wife seemed anxious to discover his whereabouts and the neighbors aided in the search by raking a pond in the vicinity and scouring the woods and fields for miles around. It was given out as the belief by his family that Druse had gone on a bender and would return home in due course. However, the larger community was suspicious, did not accept the drunken bender story, and rumors of foul play were whispered. Roxalana (sometimes Roxalina, and usually just Roxie) Druse was closely watched. Almost a month after the disappearance a bloodstained axe was discovered in a pond near the farm and was recognized as belonging to William. That caused the neighbors to bombard the other members of the household with questions. Those members were, besides Roxie, daughter Mary Druse, aged 20; George Druse, the 10-year-old son; and a 14-year-old nephew named Frank Gates. Those questions finally caused Frank to confess. According to the nephew, Druse and his wife had quarreled one day in the presence of himself and George. Roxie then sent the boys outdoors and shot Druse in the neck. She then put a rope around the man's neck and, calling Gates in, compelled him to fire another shot into Druse's body. Gates and Roxie then cut the body into pieces with knives and the axe, burned the flesh in the kitchen stove, and hid the bones in a swamp half a mile from the house. The boy and Mrs. Druse were arrested. The bones were recovered from the swamp and it was established that quarrels between William and Roxie had been frequent and took place over an extended period of time. Gates said the murder was committed on December 18 and that Mary had also been present and had assisted in the chopping up of her father's body. As well, portions of the body were fed to the family's hogs.[45]

At the inquest held in late January, Roxie swore that Charles Gates (father of Frank) was in her house when Druse was killed. She would answer no other questions. Charles Gates bought the revolver used in the murder (also buried in the swamp and later recovered) for Mary Druse. When the inquest finished at Utica on January 28 it concluded William Druse was shot and killed by Roxie (aged 40) and that Mary Druse, George Druse, and Frank Gates were feloniously present and gave aid to the woman.[46]

Later in that year Mrs. Druse was put on trial and on October 4, 1885, the jury returned a verdict of guilty of murder in the first degree against Roxie Druse. Two days later, on October 6, the Herkimer County Courthouse at Utica, New York, was crowded by people of all ages and both sexes to hear sentence pronounced on the prisoner. Judge Williams sentenced her to be executed by hanging on Wednesday, November 25, 1885. "Mrs. Druse never flinched nor showed any emotion until she was passing out of the courtroom, when she burst into tears."[47]

Among the jurors in the Druse trial was Adam Bellinger, a farmer living at Mannheim. "Mr. Bellinger is of a sensitive temperament, and the horrible details of the crime threw his mind out of balance," stated a reporter. "Symptoms of insanity have frequently been noticed in his actions since the trial, and he has finally been committed to the lunatic asylum" in Utica, as of the end of 1885.[48]

Legal maneuverings caused Roxie's execution date to be postponed to December 30, 1885, then to June 25, 1886, and then to December 27, 1886. When all legal avenues were exhausted New York State Governor Hill gave her another reprieve, a political one, to February 28, 1887. Hill came under great pressure to grant Roxie executive clemency and commute her death sentence. However, he did not want to deny clemency, or grant it, so he stalled for time with a reprieve and passed the buck, hoping to force the issue elsewhere. No such equivocation could be found in the editorial stance of the *New York Times*, which declared the answer of Hill to all the petitions sent in pleading for clemency "is of such a nature as to commend itself to the good sense of the great majority of the people of this State." That common sense could be found in the fact that Druse had "murdered her husband in the most brutal manner. The murder was deliberate, cold blooded and cruel and, unless women are hereafter to be wholly exempt from the extreme penalty of the law, there seems to be no reason why an exception should be made in the case of Mrs. Druse." This editor summarized her crime by saying that she, after some trivial quarrel with her husband at the breakfast table, with the aid of her daughter, got a rope around his neck, shot him once or twice with a revolver, finished him off with an axe, and then cut his head off. "Then the mother and daughter cut up the body and burnt it in the parlor stove while two other members of this interesting family, a son and a nephew who took a minor part in the tragedy, played checkers in the next room."[49]

When Governor Hill had granted the reprieve to February 28, argued the editor of the *Times*, he had "given her advocates an opportunity of making good their claim that public opinion is against the hanging of a woman who is convicted of willful and deliberate murder." Hill argued that if a distinction was to be made between the sexes the law should be changed and in the 60-day reprieve period the state legislature could, if so disposed, change the type of punishment for murders committed by women. That is, Governor Hill was ducking out of taking action himself, and passing responsibility to the legislators. Thus, the fate of Druse rested with the politicians of the state as a whole. An editor with the *Brooklyn Eagle* felt it unlikely the legislature would take any action, remarking, "Women of homicidal tendencies will have to put a curb on their desires and conform to the laws which have been made for the safety of all classes and of both sexes. The deliberate murder of a husband by a wife is just as revolting and unnatural as the murder of a wife by a husband. Both crimes when clearly proved should be punished to the full extent of the law." Also, the editor thought Hill had acted wisely as it afforded the elected representatives of the people "another opportunity of stamping their disapproval on the singular error that what would be a horrible crime if committed by a man is less heinous if the act of a woman."[50]

As far as he was concerned, said Hill, the case was closed and Druse must suffer her fate on the day selected unless in the meantime the law was changed. Hill said the situation was a clear case of murder and that he could find no reason for interference with the penalty except the sex of the condemned, which the law did not take into account. The governor summarized the murder as follows: a quarrel broke out between the couple at the breakfast table. While William was still at the table and during the war of words, Roxie went into another room and returned with a loaded revolver, concealed under her apron. She whispered to the two boys to go outside. When they complied there were just the three left in the room. Mary then placed a rope around her father's neck while he was at the table and Roxie fired the gun once or twice at him, wounding him. William fell sideways in his chair while Roxie, unable to make the gun fire again, called to Frank, whereupon both boys re-entered the house. Roxie gave the gun to Frank, telling him to shoot his uncle, threatening to kill the nephew if he did not comply. Frank fired two or three times and William, hit by the shots, rolled off the chair onto the floor. Then Roxie seized the axe and hit William on the head with it repeatedly until she chopped his head off. Over the rest of that day and evening the body was cut up into pieces and as much of it as possible was burned in the stove. Roxie threatened to kill the boys if they said anything. Roxie had previously made threats against William and boasted that she would be rid of him some day. After Roxie was convicted, daughter Mary pled guilty to murder in the second degree and was sentenced to life imprisonment in the state prison.[51]

After the murder and dismemberment Roxie burned all her husband's clothes and made every possible effort to conceal the crime. Telegrams were sent to friends in other places supposedly making inquiries as to William's whereabouts, and she compelled the boys to tell everyone that her husband had gone away from home for a time, as she herself told neighbors various and contradictory stories about William's absence. During the evening of the murder, while Roxie and Mary were burning the body in the parlor, the two boys amused themselves by playing checkers in an adjoining room.[52]

Noting that he had been besieged with arguments and petitions of every kind in favor of executive clemency, the governor divided such petitioners into four classes. First was the class of people who were always opposed to capital punishment and who petitioned the executive in favor of clemency in every capital case, not just those involving women. Second was the group of people who were not opposed to capital punishment for men but believed it should not be enforced against women. "The sentiment which actuates this class is entitled to respect when honestly held, although it is difficult to discover how it can be consistently entertained or defended so long as the law itself makes no distinction on account of sex," said Hill. He advised such people their petitioning efforts were better addressed to the legislature to change the law. In the third class were people seeking greater political rights for women and who insisted that as the women of New York State had no voice in making the laws, and so on, such laws should not be enforced against women. Again, he thought it was a problem to be dealt with by the legislature and, in any event, Hill reasoned, the same argument could be made about minors and native Indians, for example. The fourth and final class of people was one that had its sympathies aroused by this particular capital case only. With respect to capital punishment in general, Hill said, "The law which prohibits murder and declares that the life of the offender shall be forfeited is a Divine as well as a human law. The law of our State made by men is simply in harmony with the law of the Almighty. It would seem as though it should be obeyed by men, women, minors, Indians, and all classes and conditions of people so long as it exists, and that equal punishment should be meted out to all who disobey it, until at least the Legislature itself, in its wisdom, sees fit to direct, as it has the power to do, that distinction shall be made on account of sex."[53]

When the *New York Times* editor reviewed Hill's decision to grant no clemency, he noted the judge, the jury, and the prosecuting attorney in the Druse trial all declined to support any appeal for clemency for the woman. He declared Hill's decision "may not be the most courageous, but it cannot be severely censured." As far as what steps the legislature might take, the editor thought that would depend largely on public opinion and thus would be negligible in this case because "there has been no evidence of any effective public opinion in the murderess's favor" and "therefore, no evidence that public opinion is aroused in favor of an exception to the law." The editor concluded that the idea "Mrs. Druse ought not to suffer the penalty the law provides, or that the law should be changed for any reasons presented by her case are propositions which appear as untenable."[54]

Early in January 1887 a reporter called on the Reverend Dr. Powell of Herkimer, who was one of the advocates working for a commutation of the Druse sentence. Powell denied that the reason for his recent resignation from his church was due to the objection of members in his congregation to the interest he had taken in the Druse case, as rumor had it. However, he admitted he had incurred the displeasure of some people but said he had also made friends.[55]

Legislative action was taken finally, but Assemblyman Hadley's bill exempting women from the provisions of the capital punishment act was reported on unfavorably by the Judiciary Committee on February 16, by a vote of six to four. A motion to table that unfavorable report was lost by a vote of 60 to 44. While it was not a retroactive bill and therefore would not have applied to Druse directly, had it passed, observers felt it would have been all the incentive Hill needed to recognize public sentiment and grant an executive commutation to Roxie.[56]

During general debate on the Hadley bill, Assemblyman Baker (in favor of commutation) said he thought Christian civilization had advanced far enough to prevent the "awful and revolting spectacle of hanging a woman." A very few of the politicians favored abolishing capital punishment for all but most favored the death penalty and believed if it was to exist it should be applied equally to the sexes. When a vote on the bill came, the adverse report was accepted by a vote of 72 to 29; that is, Hadley's bill failed to pass.[57]

Reviewing the refusal of the legislature to pass a bill to save Druse, an editor with the *Brooklyn Eagle* applauded the decision, feeling it "will meet with general approval." According to him the principal advocate of the measure was Baker, "whose plea in favor of it was wholly of an emotional character and entirely illogical. Every one knows that the appeals to sentiment which are made in favor of women in courts and in the jury room are all powerful and frequently cause a miscarriage of justice, but to engraft such unjust distinctions on the law itself would be an intolerable outrage." He added, "Why should there be a distinction made between men and women in regard to the punishment for the crime of murder? While there is no object in the world more beautiful or more charming than a good woman, there is none more vile and detestable than a bad one. Shall every wanton or virago have free license to kill because she belongs to what is termed the gentler sex?" Arguing 999 women out of a thousand needed no such immunity as the bill proposed, he mused, "Shall it be granted for the benefit of the thousandth woman who is a bad woman, a criminal and a murderess who lies in wait to slay and turns the sacred hearth of the home into a shambles? Such sickly sentimentalism should have no place in legislation and the Assembly of this State has done right in putting it down."[58]

On February 24, a few days before the execution, Roxie's son George arrived at the Herkimer County Jail to remain with his mother until a day or two before the execution. The sheriff's office was said to be "besieged" by people asking for permission to visit the condemned woman, but he was firm in refusing admission to all. The dress Roxie was to wear on her final day was black and trimmed with colored ribbons.[59]

On February 25 Sheriff Cook received a communication from Governor David B. Hill reiterating that he would not interfere with the execution. A day later the gallows was erected in the jail yard at the rear of the Herkimer County Jail. Roxie's cell window had a view of the area wherein the gallows was situated. On February 26 Hill refused to allow the convict daughter Mary to visit her mother before the execution. Disclosed that day was that some two weeks earlier Hill appointed a committee of experts, three doctors from nearby asylums, to examine Druse with respect to sanity and submit a report to him. That course was quickly taken by the governor after it became evident the legislature would refuse to change the law. Without publicity, that committee of three visited the Herkimer Jail and conducted its investigation. In their report to Hill on February 15 they declared unanimously that she was sane then and was sane at the time of the murder. At the trial it took the jury five hours to agree on a verdict; nine favored guilty of murder in the first degree; three were for murder in the second degree. Those three were "adverse to hanging a woman," but, said a journalist, "they could not resist the pressure of public opinion, which demanded the woman's life. The most bitter against her were those of her own sex, who gathered in large numbers in the courtroom and plainly showed by their words and action that they demanded the woman's life."[60]

A day or two before the execution a photo of Druse, nameless, was placed in the window of a local shop in Herkimer (population 3,000) and drew much attention. It was, commented a reporter, "a face stamped with determination, but not a good face. The mouth was large and sensuous, the nose well formed and straight, but also too large, the cheek bones high, a broad, high forehead, straight heavy eyebrows, and apparently black sinister-looking eyes." Added the newsman, "Illiterate and of a low order of intelligence, the woman committed the crime in a manner that could not possibly avoid detection, yet before her arrest she possessed sufficient boldness to threaten with suits for slander all who pointed the finger of suspicion at her." Her army of sympathizers was said to be small indeed as three petitions for clemency had been circulated near her home but had then only five signatures in total affixed to them. "Though to many the idea of hanging a woman is repugnant, this woman's crime was so deliberate, so cold-blooded, that only those not thoroughly acquainted with its details or who are utterly opposed to capital punishment have interested themselves in her fate," concluded a reporter. One time an Episcopal clergyman of Herkimer, Mr. Edmunds, visited her and asked to pray with her. She threw his Bible across the cell and ordered him out. However, her current spiritual adviser, Reverend George W. Powell, was said to have much influence with her. Governor Hill sent Sheriff Cook a copy of the law detailing the maximum number of people who could be admitted to a private execution such as Druse's — the county judge, the district attorney, two physicians, the county clerk, two clergymen, 12 "respectable citizens" and seven deputy sheriffs. None of her relatives were to attend. Her brother — a tugboat captain who lived in New York City — had visited her once at the jail but said he would not return. Another worry for some was what happened after the execution. Said a reporter, "A scene of unpleasant and perhaps unseemly, excitement is expected if Mrs. Druse is given a public funeral. The woman is vain as well as bad. She requested the Rev. Dr. Powell to insure her a public funeral, and he promised to do so."[61]

One day before the execution, on Sunday, February 27, it was reported, "In every pulpit here [Herkimer] today allusion was made to the case of Mrs. Druse, who is to be hanged tomorrow, and the hope was generally expressed that the proceeding would be averted. Mrs. Druse has passed most of the day in tears. She contends that she is in reality innocent of the murder of her husband. Telegrams have been sent from here by scores today requesting the Governor to commute her sentence."[62]

Later on February 27 Roxie took part in an evening church service and choir hymn sing in the Herkimer Jail, led by the Rev. Powell, who brought in a six-voice choir. Druse also wrote a series of letters on her last day, to Powell, to the sheriff (expressing thanks), and one to Mary, bequeathing to her daughter her only possession, a cabinet organ, which was delivered to Mary in her prison. As to the attitude of Powell, a reporter remarked, "Though he spends hours with Mrs. Druse daily, he stands alone in the belief that she is an innocent woman." As well, this journalist commented on the character of Roxie and Mary, describing them as "utterly heartless, their morality is of the lowest character, and they impressed all who have come in close contact with them as lacking even in a desire to tell the truth where a lie will answer their purpose. Mother and daughter possess a spirit of vanity that, under less painful circumstances, would be ridiculous. Though their means were very limited, they delighted in aping their superiors in matters of dress." As a girl Roxie was said to have been noticeable for a "brilliant display of gaudily colored ribbons, though her dresses were of the commonest material and ill made at that." Roxalana Tefft was always known as Roxie Tefft, and after her marriage always as Roxie Druse. It was only at the time of her trial that she was referred to by her full Christian name of Roxalana. She first met her husband-to-be in 1863. William then lived alone on a big farm in the town of Warren. The farm was near the hop-growing district, and in the hop-picking season girls and men came from all parts to gather the crop and earn a few dollars. Among Farmer Northrup's pickers in 1863 was Roxie Tefft. She was described then as "of medium height, rather spare, but of good figure; had an abundance of long black hair and a pair of eyes that exercised over Bill Druse the fascination of a serpent." William first saw her in the hop field and his advances, "slow and uncouth as they were, were not repelled." She was afraid; she told a friend one day that Bill would not ask her to marry her, slow as he was, so she popped the question to him.[63]

Years and years later, when Mary was 16 years old, Druse noticed that

5. 1880s

his house was a favorite visiting place at night for some of his male neighbors. He went to bed early himself but was often awakened by sounds of laughter and the clinking of glasses. He put up with that situation for a year but then made a stand against that behavior only to find that his wife and daughter had formed an alliance against him and were determined to live as they pleased. As his temper soured, quarrels between the couple became a frequent occurrence. Neighbors, except for some of the men, gave his household a wide berth as it became common talk in the farming community that, said a reporter, "Bill Druse's house was the scene of nightly orgies in which he took no part, and in which Roxie Druse and her daughter were the ruling spirits." Druse began to threaten reprisals as the quarrels between the pair became increasingly heated. By this account, at the time of the murder Bill Druse was about 60 and Roxie about 45. As her end neared, Roxie continued to tell different stories about what had happened on the night of the murder, always contradictory tales. Two weeks or so before her execution she declared the murder was done by three masked men who threatened to return and kill her if she disclosed the manner of Bill's death.[64]

Editorializing on the day of the execution, the *New York Times* remarked that if the crime had been committed by a man it would have aroused no great interest. "It is the criminal's sex that has aroused general horror over the extraordinary offense of which she was guilty, while it has enlisted so large and varied a number of persons in the effort to save her life." Attempts to represent Roxie as the victim of an abusive husband failed, thought the editor, due in no small part to the revelations in other articles (such as the one cited directly above that portrayed Roxie and Mary as, more or less, sluts), which "shows that in the long quarrel of their married life the provocation came as often from her as from her victim, while her personal baseness and viciousness were the scandal of the neighborhood." Also, he argued that nobody appealed to for clemency, such as the governor, the appeals courts, and so on, had been swayed by the gender argument. "The unhealthy and essentially immoral movement to arrest the arm of the law or to divert it has found many supporters, chief among whom have been a limited number of clergymen and an indefinite number of women, many of them advocates of what is known as 'women's rights,'" fumed the editor. "The pleas they have presented have been urged with a zeal quite out of proportion to their soundness either as to facts or reasoning." Smugly he observed, "The tradition that public opinion would not permit the hanging of a woman, no matter how atrocious her claim was found, when brought to the sudden and sharp test of this actual case, to be without foundation. That, of itself, we regard as a wholesome and encouraging fact." One benefit arising from the Druse case, thought the editor, was the passage of a law making executions in New York State private instead of public, making executions come more within the conditions imposed by "decency and common sense." Making the executions private went a long way "toward depriving executions of that character of demoralizing shows they have so long possessed." But just as important to the editor as the removal of the executions from the public realm for "decency" was the idea that it would prevent the victim, and supporters, from gaining notoriety, fame, and so on. "It still remains possible for a criminal condemned to death to become the object of a morbid curiosity and sentimental demonstrations of sympathy such as have been much too frequent in Mrs. Druse's experience," said the editor. "Thanks largely to the foolish conduct of her 'spiritual adviser [Powell],' she has kept up to the last her apparent feeling that she is a distinguished and not undeserving person."[65]

Her last confession involved the naming of Charles Gates (father of Frank) as her accomplice. After a restless, sleepless night, one of Roxie's first visitors on February 28, execution day, was Superintendent Irving Terry of the Onondaga Penitentiary, who brought a farewell and a bouquet of flowers from Mary, serving life at Syracuse. At 9:00 A.M. Druse, joined by Powell, sang several hymns in her cell. "The morning was spent in praying, writing, and singing, with now and then hysterical periods on the part of the condemned," said an account. "At this point the prisoner again showed signs of collapse and began to scream and shriek at the top of her voice in a hysterical manner, but the drop of the 213 pound weight choked off her cries in her throat and the body of the murderess, whose awful crime has shocked the entire country, was sent flying upward about four feet, shooting forward to the right and settling back to within one foot and a half of the platform.... After the lapse of one minute a spasmodic clenching of the fingers occurred, followed by efforts to draw up the legs." The drop fell at 11:48 A.M.; death was pronounced at 12:00, and the body was cut down at 12:14. "When the black cap was drawn back it was found that death had resulted from asphyxia. The neck and lower

5. 1880s

portions of the face were much discolored, and the rope marks were plainly visible." It was said she was only the fifth woman executed in New York State. Margaret Houghtaling, alias Peggy Dinsmore, was hanged at Hudson County on October 17, 1817, six weeks after her indictment for the murder of her child. A few years later a woman on her deathbed confessed she was guilty of the murder and not Peggy. The other three were Van Valkenburg, Runkle, and Hoag. Roxie's final confession came on the morning of February 27. Around December 1, 1885, she said, Charles Gates asked her if she did not want to get rid of her husband. To which she replied that she was so fed up she did not care what happened. Charles came again on December 17, the night before the murder, and told her to hurry up, to take the first chance she got. On the morning of the 18th the married couple had their breakfast quarrel and Roxie got a gun and shot him once. Then Charles shot him three or four times from outside, through the window. Added Roxie, "I killed Druse because I couldn't stand it any longer. He was a brute and I hadn't slept with him in twelve years. That is all I can tell. Gates put up Frank to tell what he did to shove it all on me but he will get his reward some time."[66]

An editorial in the *Brooklyn Eagle* condemned the "sermon" delivered by Powell from the scaffold in which he professed to believe Druse was innocent despite that her last confession had been made to Powell. On the scaffold the clergyman proselytized against capital punishment in general even though only a couple of dozen people were on hand to hear it at the private execution. With respect to that sermon, said the editor, "It was of a nature well fitted to disgust rational people and in a fashion that has become common of late. It is time that such exhibitions were brought to a close. Religious services on the scaffold are not necessary. Whatever is to be done may as well be performed in the cell of the prisoner." He added, "And they are a public scandal when they become the means of exalting a great criminal into the position of a saint. In truth, Powell appears to have used his opportunity as a sensational advertisement ... of having his moral swash and his rhetorical atrocities act as a sort of 'boom' for himself."[67]

Execution day was a bitterly cold day with a temperature of zero degrees Fahrenheit, and an icy wind made it worse. With respect to the large crowd gathered outside the jail in that weather — they could see nothing — a reporter wrote, "The country yokels, fearless of the biting temperature, posted themselves close to the jail on all sides, only to be disturbed by the military. They simply changed their ground and stared at the stone wall of the jail for hours at a time, expressing their feelings in discordant and senseless howls."[68]

On the evening of March 3, 1887, at the regular monthly meeting of the New York City Woman Suffrage League, a resolution was passed condemning Governor Hill for his "brutal obstinacy" in refusing to commute the Druse sentence. Another resolution passed congratulated the Reverend George Powell for his unselfish care of and constant attention to Roxie.[69]

At Herkimer, New York, on March 6, Powell preached Druse's funeral sermon and it was described as follows: "It was a remarkable discourse, giving the preacher's views against capital punishment, and expressing his belief that the commission of the crime was due to an evil nature engendered by the husband's atheism. He denied the stories about Mrs. Druse's impure life." Also, Powell characterized the execution as a "murder." Reportedly, his sermon drew a large audience and made a sensation.[70]

Roxie's death certificate was filed on March 17. It said she was born in Marshall, Oneida County, and, reportedly, the place of death was stated to be "on the ghastly gallows at Herkimer, N.Y.," while the cause of death was listed as "asphyxia, caused by judicial hanging by the neck." If those things were true it was likely due to the two people who signed the certificate (and filled out the form). One was Dr. Cyrus Kay, jail physician; the other was the Reverend Dr. George W. Powell.[71]

Matilda Jones

On the night of January 27, 1885, Mrs. Henrietta Cole, a widow past 70 years of age, was strangled to death at her residence in Plaquemine, Louisiana. The house had been thoroughly ransacked and the woman's valuables stolen. Then it was learned that four black people had suddenly left the area — Matilda Jones, George Wilson, Charles Davis, and Sol Price. Evidence soon surfaced that linked them to the crime and all but Price were captured within a few days. At the trial held in June the three accused were all convicted and sentenced to death. Matilda Jones was described as "a coarse, stout negress of vicious habits." Her connection to the murder consisted in leading the men to the house, showing them how to enter, and revealing where Cole kept her money, jewelry, and other valuables hidden. Jones had once been employed by Cole.[72] She was executed on July 31, 1885, at Franklin, Louisiana.

Sarah Jane Robinson

Mrs. Sarah Robinson (about 48 years old) of Somerville, Massachusetts, was arrested on August 11, 1886, and charged with poisoning several members of her family. Thomas R. Smith, 45, was arrested as an accomplice. In March 1886 Elizabeth Robinson, the 22-year-old daughter of Sarah, died suddenly, despite being in apparent good health. Talk and rumors floated about the community but they all faded away fairly quickly. Then in July 1886 an adopted son in the family, Thomas Freeman, aged seven, was taken suddenly ill and he died in great agony after two days of suffering. He was buried without any suspicions being raised. On August 10, 1886, William J. Robinson, the 20-year-old son of Sarah, became suddenly ill, manifesting symptoms similar to those displayed by Thomas. His friends advised him to call in a certain well-respected physician. Sarah objected but the medical man was summoned without Sarah's knowledge. His investigations, and one by a Harvard professor, revealed and confirmed arsenic in both food and medicines. Results were made known to the police and then the body of Thomas was exhumed. Arsenic was found in his remains. William was then thought to be recovering but he took a turn for the worse and died a few days later. No doubts existed in the minds of the police that the deaths were planned by Sarah and her accomplice Smith — the body of Elizabeth was to be exhumed. All three of the above named were each insured for $2,000, all with the same company, United Order of Pilgrim Fathers. In all cases Sarah paid the premiums herself and collected on the two who were already dead. Sarah's husband had died some four years earlier; he was also insured. Such revelations resulted in her being named, in at least one news account, as "the new Lucrezia Borgia. She is a hard-looking woman, and is of a very grasping nature." Smith had been a constant visitor at the Robinson house for nearly a year. Stated a journalist: "He has a bad reputation in the town where he lives. It is said that he was to be married to Mrs. Robinson next month. Both are in good circumstances, but the greed for gold prompted them to commit two horrible murders and to attempt a third."[73]

Allegations against Sarah Robinson of having poisoned other people began to pour in as another media frenzy took hold. Most bizarre of those allegations held that the woman was responsible for the poisoning of 109 people at the strawberry festival in Somerville in June 1886 at which all of those 109 people ate ice cream and all became ill. Fifty of them were so badly taken that they vomited all night, but there were no deaths. Rumor had it that Sarah had been one of the ice cream servers at the affair. However, there was no evidence Sarah was even at the picnic and that charge was soon forgotten. Other allegations, though, stuck longer to the woman. Among the murders attributed to Sarah were those of her husband some four years earlier, followed by a 10-year-old daughter, Emma, who died soon after. Shortly thereafter the sister of Sarah married a man named Prince Arthur Freeman and that pair, and Freeman's two young children, went to board with Robinson. One of those children, an infant, promptly died. Prince Freeman died next, not long after making her the beneficiary of a $2,000 life insurance policy, taken out at Sarah's earnest solicitation. Then Elizabeth died. Deaths then ceased for a time at the Robinson household, perhaps, it was speculated, because a fair amount of suspicion was raised in the wake of Elizabeth's death, suspicions that had not been raised in any of the earlier deaths. After that brief hiatus came the deaths of Robinson's two children, first Thomas and then William. In his ante-mortem statement William declared his mother and Smith were the only people that gave him nourishment and medicines during his final illness. Among other facts unearthed about Sarah during the investigation was that she regularly failed to pay her bills and that she had a penchant for swindling furniture dealers. In some cases she leased large lots of furniture and then arranged chattel mortgages on the goods, up to three loans or more, on the same lot of furniture.[74]

Near the end of August, supposedly new evidence led to the indictment of a Dr. Beers, who had an earlier romantic involvement with Sarah and whose intimacy with the woman could be traced back to before the death of Prince Freeman. The authorities were convinced Robinson had an accomplice in all the murders, for no obvious reason, and the problem with naming Smith as that figure was that he had only known and associated with Robinson for a relatively short period of time, a time span that only covered the last two deaths. The hapless physician found himself indicted and behind bars.[75]

Sarah, Smith and Beers were all indicted, in October 1886, for trial on murder charges in the deaths of Elizabeth and William. But postponements kept pushing back trial dates. Early in March 1887, Sarah was indicted on four new counts of murder, involving Thomas, Prince Freeman, a new victim named Olive Sleeper, and her husband (also named William). But, in an unprecedented move, bail was allowed to Beers and to Smith with the understanding that their cases would be not prosecuted when the trial of Sarah got underway, although the charges would not necessarily be dropped. There was no evidence against Smith, who, while he did help nurse William, had known Sarah for such a short time. Even less "evidence" existed against the luckless Beers, who was 75 years old and in ill health after six months in jail. He had only known the woman for two years or so in his intimate phase with her, prior to Smith, but he never tended any of the many people listed as her victims. Also, he was entirely absent from the scene during the earliest murders. He was only arrested because he was a physician and the authorities stubbornly felt Sarah must have gotten instructions in the art of poisoning from someone. Not a shred of evidence existed against him.[76]

When Sarah stood trial in December 1887 for the murder of her son William she was acquitted. Following that she was placed on trial for the murder of Prince Arthur Freeman, who died on June 29, 1885. In July 1888 she was convicted of Freeman's murder and sentenced to be executed by hanging on November 11, 1888. Just days before her scheduled execution the sentence was commuted to life imprisonment in solitary confinement in the state prison.[77]

On January 4, 1906, Sarah Robinson died in the Middlesex County Jail in East Cambridge, Massachusetts. She was 68 years old and had been in solitary confinement for close to 18 years. Her obituary noted her conviction for killing Freeman, and added, "but it was established at the trial that she had also murdered her son William, 23 years old, her daughter Elizabeth, 22 years old, her husband and her nephew, Thomas A. Freeman."[78]

Sadie Hayes

Sadie Hayes (black) shot and killed Police Sergeant Jenks dead in the streets of St. Louis, Missouri, on the night of October 8, 1883. At her trial she was found guilty of murder in the first degree and sentenced to be executed by hanging on January 15, 1886. On the afternoon of January 1 Missouri Governor Marmaduke visited her incognito in her cell, being introduced to her by Deputy Jailer Waters as a personal friend of his who desired to talk with her about her case. After Marmaduke left, a reporter quizzed her about the conversation. Hayes said she discovered after the visitor left that he was the governor and she thought she should have been told in advance since her life was at stake. Marmaduke asked her about the particulars of her case and she told him, said Sadie, the whole story and insisted she had committed the murder while drunk and without knowing whom it was that she had shot. As well, the governor inquired as to her previous life, listened to all the details and then went away without making any remark or comment. An impression was said to then prevail that Hayes would not hang. Marmaduke had, of course, visited her to assess whether or not to commute her sentence. He was spared that decision when the state Supreme Court granted Hayes a new trial. At that new trial in January 1887 she was allowed to plead guilty to murder in the second degree and was sentenced to 99 years' imprisonment. Earlier, in March 1886, William Lacey, a black burglar from St. Louis, who had recently begun a two-year jail term, cut off a portion of one of his fingers and sent it, together with the ring he wore on that finger, as a keepsake to Sadie Hayes, of whom he was said to have become deeply enamored.[79]

Mary Garrett

Neighbors were drawn to the Garrett residence at Spencer, Medina County, Ohio, early on the morning of November 1, 1887, when they saw the farmhouse in flames. The first persons to arrive found Mrs. Mary Garrett hastily removing articles of furniture from the burning building. She said that someone had murdered her two stepdaughters and then set fire to the place. Those neighbors rushed in and extinguished the flames, which had been started in many places. In the room occupied by the two adult stepdaughters (aged 26 and 32, and described as "imbeciles") their bodies were found in bed with their heads beaten in and the bedclothes covered in blood. Their nightclothes and the bedding had been soaked in coal oil, and dry leaves had been soaked with the same fluid and heaped upon the bodies. Mrs. Garrett had not bothered to awaken her husband

and his son, who were sleeping in another part of the house. Suspicion pointed strongly to Mary and she was quickly arrested. Her trial was delayed because she was found to be in a "delicate" condition. On July 27, 1888, while awaiting trial in Medina, Ohio, she gave birth to a boy in jail whom she named Warden Coffin Garrett, in honor of Warden Coffin of the state prison. In the early part of September Garrett was tried for murder in a trial that lasted only a few days, there being almost no evidence presented in her defense. After five hours of deliberation on September 17 the jury returned a verdict of guilty on both counts and Garrett was sentenced to be executed by hanging on January 24, 1889. When she came to the area three years before the murders she met and soon after married Alonzo Garrett, a well-to-do widower with at least three children, including those two "imbecile" daughters. Mary had often complained she was tired of looking after her two stepdaughters and wished to be rid of the burden. About a week before the slated execution, Ohio Governor Foraker commuted the death sentence of Garrett to one of life imprisonment at the Ohio State Prison. Thus, the governor's intervention saved her life and answered the question so often raised over the course of the case, said a reporter, "Will Ohio hang a woman?"[80]

Axey Cherry

Axey Cherry was sentenced at the Barnwell, South Carolina, courthouse in mid–July 1887 to be executed by hanging on the third Friday in September for the murder of an infant white child that belonged to Amos Williams, of Allendale, South Carolina; she was just 12 years old. Axey was hired out by her mother, much against the child's will, as nurse to Mrs. Williams' baby. According to a news report, "She pouted around the house and attended to her duties in so neglectful a manner that she had to be constantly scolded. After a scolding one day she was overheard muttering to herself that she wasn't going to bother with that baby much more." A few days later concentrated lye was used in scouring the floor, and as Mrs. Williams left the room she told Axey that the lye was poison and that she mustn't touch it. On her return Mrs. Williams was horrified to find the baby's mouth full of concentrated lye. Cherry ran out of the house, saying as she left, "I don't reckon I will have to nurse that baby much longer now." All through her trial the girl seemed to have no idea of the nature of the deed or of the legal process then in progress. "When she was sentenced to be hanged she gazed stupidly at the Judge and grinned as she played with the buttons on her dress," said a reporter. "As she was being carried back to jail she saw her father and made an effort to go to him. She cried for the first time when she was told that she could not go home, but must go back to jail to await the day for her execution."[81]

South Carolina Governor Richardson received a large number of communications from all over America, pleading for mercy for the child. When the governor sought opinions from the judge who passed sentence and the prosecutor at the trial, he found the latter would not recommend a commutation of the death sentence, reminding Richardson that the girl had run away when hired out to nurse the child; that she had been brought back by her father, and that she undoubtedly knew the consequences of giving lye to the child. As far as the prosecutor was concerned it was "a cold-blooded, premeditated murder" and he could not recommend mercy. The judge who sentenced the girl said the case for murder had been made out but because of her youth he felt she should not be executed, but the "wretched little villain" should be jailed for a term of years. On August 26, 1887, Richardson commuted Axey's sentence to one of imprisonment in the penitentiary for five years. It was a commutation made solely because of Cherry's youthfulness.[82]

Chiara Cignarale

In broad daylight at the corner of First Avenue and 11th Street in Manhattan, on October 20, 1886, Chiara Cignarale shot and killed her husband Antonio Cignarale. She shot him from a distance of a few feet, firing directly into his back. Some 14 years earlier the couple had married in Italy, where they had one child and where Antonio worked as a stonemason. Four or five years before the murder he became dissatisfied with his life in Italy and often said he wanted to go to America — he had heard the tales of streets of gold from some of his migratory countrymen. In 1885 he made up his mind to emigrate. On March 28, 1885, the family landed at New York City and went to live in the Little Italy section, around 110th Street. He got work but soon quit and showed little interest in finding other work. Then he wanted Chiara to become a female bootblack, thinking the novelty value of a female shoe shiner would translate into financial success. She refused and he beat her, explained Chiara. "He always had done that." Married life, she said, was one long period of misery. Antonio was very cruel and whenever she refused to comply with his unreasonable demands he beat her, with his fists or any handy object. More than once he ordered her to leave the house but she stayed, because of the child. Finally, four months before the murder, Antonio said he would kill her if she did not leave him, and so she moved out. At first she roomed in a house wherein also dwelt Antonio D'Andrea, her cousin. Then she moved on, staying for short periods of time in other rooming houses.[83]

On the morning of the day she fired the fatal shot she said her husband came to her room on 125th Street and tried to get in. She would not admit him and he went away swearing that day would be her last. He had come to the other rooming houses she had lived in during her four months away from home, threatening her. With her husband's threat in her ears she armed herself with a revolver Antonio had bought some months before and which she had kept. Chiara went out shopping and was accosted by her husband, who slapped her twice in the face and accused her of having improper relations with D'Andrea. She denied the accusation. Then he said he wanted to kill her and drew a razor from his pocket. Chiara drew the gun from under the folds of her dress and fired a warning shot into the ground. But he kept coming with the open razor in his hand. She then shot him once and killed him. Chiara admitted she had never carried the revolver before that day. At least that was her story. Police Officer Hickey testified a razor was found in Antonio's pocket after his death but that it was wrapped in a piece of newspaper tied around with a string and the whole thing was then enclosed in a handkerchief. Since he died almost instantly he had no time to have wrapped up the razor after being shot. Another problem with Chiara's story was that the medical examiner testified her story of shooting her husband while face to face was false because the deceased had been shot from a distance of several feet, directly in the back. When she was on the stand she was described as follows: "She is a small, rather attenuated, sallow-faced woman, with little, restless black eyes. She talks excitedly and with extravagant gestures. She is dressed in deep mourning, presumably for the death of her husband."[84]

Her trial on a charge of murder in the first degree was held in May 1887, and on May 27 Recorder Smyth began to hear the summing up of the case by the attorneys. Chiara was represented by William F. Howe, who suddenly claimed the razor in the dead man's pocket was not the one he used to threaten his wife, but a second razor had been used and it had never been found. However, the claim of self-defense was still difficult to believe considering several independent and disinterested witnesses all testified that Antonio was walking quietly down the street, whistling to himself and unconscious of danger, when he was deliberately shot in the back by his wife. Howe attacked the assistant district attorney for saying in his opening remarks that he would prove that D'Andrea (shown at the trial to be Chiara's paramour) induced the woman to kill her husband by telling her that they did not hang women in America. When Recorder Smyth delivered his charge to the jury he specifically pointed out that women were to be tried and judged in the same way as men and that no distinction was to be made between the case of a woman and the case of a man. After deliberating for 70 minutes the jury returned a verdict of guilty against Chiara, arriving at that conclusion on the sixth ballot. On the first ballot the vote was eight to four in favor of conviction; nine to three on the second ballot; and 10 to two on the third, fourth, and fifth ballots.[85]

With a popular belief at the time of her conviction being that she had killed at the instigation of her paramour, D'Andrea then stood indicted as an accessory before the fact. Commenting on the case, an editor with the *Brooklyn Eagle* said, "Her conviction is an additional proof that juries are overcoming that 'sickly sentimentalism' which for so many years has given point to the sneer that no woman could be convicted of a capital crime in the State of New York." He pointed out that before the execution of Druse, New York State had not witnessed the execution of a woman for nearly 30 years. Continuing, he argued, there was no chivalry in espousing the cause of a deliberate murderess. "Cold blooded assassination effectually obliterates the respect which every properly conditioned man feels for members of the opposite sex." And, "If it is to be conceded that the majority of men shrink from the thought of hanging a woman with a repugnance which they do not feel in the case of a man, it must also be admitted in view of the cases of Mrs. Druse and Mrs. Cignarale that the disposition to permit that repugnance to override the law and defeat the ends of justice is rapidly yielding to a more rational view of the duties of jurymen."[86]

Shortly before Recorder Smyth passed sentence, Howe was making arguments to try to save his client. Smyth said to Howe, "This woman was guilty of deliberate, premeditated assassination. She went out armed with the determination to kill her husband if she met him. She did meet him; met him in a crowded thoroughfare in broad daylight and fired at him while he was walking away from her, entirely ignorant of her presence. A pedestrian called to him to look out or he would be shot and as he turned around she fired again, inflicting a wound from which he almost immediately died. Nothing now remains for me but to perform the duty imposed upon me by law; one of the most painful a judge can be called upon to do." Chiara Cignarale was sentenced to be executed by hanging on July 22, 1887.[87]

In the *Deseret News* an editorial remarked that for some time there had been agitation in New York State in opposition to capital punishment "and especially against hanging women." The editor thought the developments in the Cignarale trial would likely be a setback to those who opposed the infliction of the death penalty. As a reinforcement to that idea the editor presented a very different version of the case. Mrs. Cignarale deserted her husband to establish criminal relations with her second cousin, D'Andrea, went this variation. The wronged husband repeatedly called upon his wife after her desertion of him and implored her to return. His visits annoyed his wife and her paramour and the latter urged her to kill her husband, saying that he would do it himself, only that in America they hanged men but did not hang women. One day in October 1886 the husband called upon the unfaithful woman and renewed his importunities for her to return. She refused, and when he left her rooming house she followed him without his knowing it and shot him dead. Since, argued the editor, it seemed evident Chiara killed her husband in the belief they did not hang women in America and would not have done so if she knew that was not true, "It must be admitted that this case affords a strong argument in favor of capital punishment, and for women as well as men."[88]

Delegates from 56 Italian societies representing a constituency of over 20,000 people held a mass meeting on June 30 in New York City to help along the movement to commute the death sentence of Chiara. A delegation of five women was selected to go before New York State Governor Hill to ask for mercy for Cignarale. Petitions for a commutation were then being circulated and signed all over town. More mass meetings were also scheduled.[89]

That delegation met with Governor Hill on July 11 to make their plea for executive clemency, at a time Chiara's health was reported to be poor. Said Hill to the delegates, "This application should not be granted solely because the convict is an Italian; nor can it be granted upon the sole ground that she is a woman, nor upon the ground that she is temporarily ill.... Nor can it be granted because a large class of people desire it, nor because immense petitions are presented in favor of it, nor solely because influential people are urging it." Hill said the determination had to be made on the merits of the case, whether the person was properly convicted, whether new evidence had surfaced, and so on. Trying to please everyone, he concluded, "It is true that nearly all the jurymen have asked for a commutation of sentence. I cannot understand how jurymen can render a verdict saying that they are satisfied that a person is guilty of willful and premeditated murder and then turn around and immediately beseech the Executive to interfere to prevent the enforcement of the sentence." Hill promised to consider all aspects of the case carefully but he warned the delegation, "I cannot hold out much encouragement to you."[90]

When an appeal to the Court of Appeals went against the woman and affirmed her conviction, her execution date was rescheduled to August 17, 1888. Actor Pearl Eytinge appeared before Hill to plead for mercy on behalf of the murderess, also on July 11. Although Hill appeared "moved" by the actor's emotional pleas, he "commented rather severely on Chiara Cignarale's conduct in pushing her way through the crowd to see if her husband were dead after she had shot him." Many other people appeared before the governor on missions of mercy.[91]

A letter to Hill by District Attorney Fellows late in July expressed the district attorney's opinion that Chiara was guilty of the crime and that her sex should not be considered either in extenuation of her crime or in mitigation of the punishment. However, he felt Hill should take into consideration the fact that at an earlier trial Chiara offered a plea of guilty of murder in the second degree, which was accepted by the district attorney and the court; the punishment for this crime was life imprisonment. Fellows therefore recommended to Hill a commutation of the death sentence to one of life in jail. (Chiara had been allowed to change her original plea—from guilty of murder in the second degree to not guilty of murder in the first degree—because she spoke next to no English and there had been translation problems initially.)[92]

Under enormous and unrelenting pressure, Governor Hill finally relented and on July 27, 1888, he commuted her sentence to one of life imprisonment. On July 30 she was removed from the Tombs jail and taken to the county penitentiary on Blackwell's Island. A crowd of about 1,000 people gathered around the Tombs' gate to catch a glimpse of her being transferred. One of those spectators was Antonio D'Andrea.[93]

Sarah Jane Whiteling

Early in June 1888 in Philadelphia in the coroner's office Mrs. Sarah Jane Whiteling voluntarily confessed that she had poisoned her two children, a girl of nine and a boy of three, and that she had furnished her husband with the poison with which she declared he took his own life. The victims were husband John (38, who died on March 20), Bertha (April 24), and Willie (May 26). Said Sarah, "I gave Bertie the first dose of poison on April 21 and on April 24 she died. I put one spoonful of the stuff in a glass of water and called the child to me and said: 'Now Bertie, here is some medicine; you must take it like a good girl,' and I gave her one spoonful. It made her sick, and when the doctor prescribed some powders to be given in water I bought the medicine but gave her a spoonful of the poison every half hour instead. It made her so very sick and she suffered so much that I felt sorry, and the day before she died I stopped giving her poison and gave her the medicine, but it was too late. Little Willie died the same way. I had the insurance placed on each child only a short time before they died." Asked if she had poisoned her husband she strongly denied the accusation. Sarah said she did not tell the doctor her husband had taken poison because the insurance policy would not pay out for a suicide. As to why she murdered her children, she said, "I killed Bertie because I was afraid she would grow up to sin and crime, as she was a bad child and had stolen pennies from the neighbors, and once she stole her school teacher's pocket-book. The boy I killed because he was in the way. I am sorry now for what I have done and want people to pray for me." Sarah collected insurance money on all three deaths but the amount was said to have totaled just about $800.[94]

A few days later, on June 15, Whiteling confessed that she had also murdered her husband John by poisoning him. She explained how she went to the druggist to get something to use to kill cockroaches. The druggist sold her Rough on Rats, warning her to be careful as it would kill a human being if ingested. From that moment, said Sarah, the "devil put a fiendish impulse" into her head to destroy her husband — saying no such idea had crossed her mind up to and including the time when she purchased the poison. At home she took half a teaspoon of the powder and stirred it up in an eggnog. John drank it and after a prolonged and violent agony succumbed.[95]

Explaining her motivation further, Sarah said her husband had been ill recently and she had been feeding him eggnog and whiskey punches to strengthen him. Then she gave him the poison. "I did this on account of our poverty. I had a hard time getting along, and I thought as my husband was sick he would be better off out of the way, and I could pay off all our debts and have some money to live on." But after John's funeral she soon ran out of cash. "I paid the funeral expenses, bought a sewing machine and a watch, and paid off what we owed. When the money ran out I was tempted to get more by killing Bertha. After Bertha was dead the baby was a burden to me, and I knew that I would have enough money to bury it and have some left, so I gave him the poison too. Now, since I have confessed everything, I am ready to meet my husband and children in heaven." After the Coroner's inquest a crowd gathered waiting for her to come out, and threats of lynching were freely made. As she came out of the door two of the women in the crowd tried to strike her but a wall of police officers kept them back.[96]

On November 28 in Philadelphia, Sarah was convicted on three counts of murder in the first degree; her defense was insanity. According to this account the amount of insurance money she collected was about $125 on each of her three victims. Sarah was described as follows: "Mrs. Whiteling is a stout, middle-aged, rather pleasant-faced woman. During the trial she was dressed in deep mourning, and created a rather favorable impression on the spectators. Her husband was an invalid and they were very poor." She was sentenced to be executed by hanging on March 27, 1889.[97]

Legal maneuverings moved the date back but on June 25, 1889, Sarah was executed in Philadelphia at the Moyamensing Prison at 10:07 A.M. Reportedly, on the day before, "she was in the happiest mood, and repeatedly declared she was glad she would soon be in heaven to meet her beloved husband and children." And, "The woman's bearing throughout the terrible ordeal was a most remarkable exhibition of fortitude and resignation to her fate.... The several physicians who were present at the execution agreed that she had at no time shown any evidence of unsound mind." By this account John's life was insured for $145, Bertha's for $122, and Willie's for $47. As well, a benevolent organization John belonged to paid out an additional $85. "Every effort had been made by Mrs. Whiteling's counsel to save her life, first by proving her to be insane and also on the sentimental ground that, being a woman, the extreme penalty of the law should not be administered," explained a reporter, "and a number of philanthropic women also interested themselves in her behalf and endeavored to secure a commutation of the death sentence, but these efforts were unavailing, and the miserable woman had to hang, the only clemency extended her being a short respite by the Governor."[98]

Milly Poteat

Sometime in November 1887, James Henry Slade's residence in Caswell County, North Carolina, was burned to the ground. After an investigation a black couple, Milly and Pink Poteat, were arrested, indicted, and tried for the crime of arson. In court Milly swore that her husband Pink robbed the house and burned it, bringing home lots of loot from the Slade residence. But Pink proved he was in Danville, Virginia, attending a church service with many other people at the very time the house was being burned. Due to the strength of his alibi he was acquitted of the charge. The main evidence against Milly was given by Henry Tom Slade (no relation to the home owner), her paramour, who confessed he and Milly did the crime together. He swore that on the morning before the fire Milly sent for him, told him that James Slade had gone from home, left the house locked with nobody to tend it, and proposed that they together should plunder and burn the building. And so they did. On his testimony Milly was convicted while the equally guilty Henry Slade, because he had turned state's evidence, was set free. The crime for which Milly was convicted was the last in a series of incendiary fires that occurred within the three years before her trial and had the community residents up in arms to put an end to the firebugs. They even went so far as to employ professional detectives to find the culprit but to no avail. When James Slade's residence was burned the people rose in a general and determined effort to find the perpetrator. And, said a report, "A number of Negroes were arrested, all of whom on examination proved their innocence except Milly." Poteat's trial began and concluded in one day, August 17, 1888, with the all-white male jury finding her guilty "without hesitation." Milly was sentenced to be hanged on Friday, October 19, 1888. North Carolina Governor Seales granted her a 30-day reprieve a day or so before that date. It was said, "The event had drawn to the town fully 5,000 people, mostly colored, and morbid curiosity had been roused to such an extent that bitter disappointment was expressed when it was announced that the hanging would not occur — at least, for thirty days." Later, Seales commuted Milly's sentence to life imprisonment.[99]

Pauline McCoy

Pauline McCoy, a 22-year-old black woman, was executed by hanging at Union Springs, Bullock County, Alabama, on October 15, 1888. She was convicted of having murdered Annie Jordan, a 15-year-old "demented" white girl, on February 15, 1888. Pauline confessed to having killed Jordan, who had wandered away from her home, at a lonely place in the country by choking her to death. Some 5,000 people reportedly attended the execution.[100]

Executions of Women in the 1880s[101]

(All were executed by hanging and all for murder, except as noted.)

1881, April 22, Lucinda Fowlkes, black, Lunenberg, Virginia.
1881, February 3, Catherine Miller, 29, white housewife, Lycoming, Pennsylvania.
1881, January 6, Margaret Meierhofer, 40, white housewife, Essex, New Jersey.
1882, January 13, Matilda Carter, black farmhand, Rockingham, North Carolina.
1882, October 20, Ella Moore, black, Dodge, Georgia.

5. 1880s

1882, June 22, Lucinda Teasdale, black, Wiliamsburg, South Carolina.
1883, October 19, Margaret Harris, black, Gordon, Georgia.
1883, March 30, Emeline Meaker, 44, white housewife, Washington, Vermont.
1883, September 14, Barbara Miller, black (accessory), Henrico, Virginia.
1885, July 31, Matilda Jones, black servant, Franklin, Louisiana.
1887, February 28, Roxalana Druse, 40, white housewife, Herkimer, New York.
1888, October 15, Pauline McCoy, 22, black, Bullock, Alabama.
1889, June 25, Sarah Whiteling, white housewife, Philadelphia, Pennsylvania.

6

1890s

Elizabeth Potts

Elizabeth Potts, her husband Josiah Potts, and their three children moved to Carlin, Elko County, Nevada, around 1886. Josiah was employed as a machinist in the Central Pacific Railroad shops located in that community. Miles Fawcett was a carpenter who boarded with the family for several months and in 1887 he purchased a ranch seven miles from Carlin, known as the Hot Springs Ranch. After he moved there Elizabeth baked his bread and did his washing for him, which made it necessary for Fawcett to visit the Potts' home in Carlin frequently. On January 1, 1888, Fawcett told a friend the couple owed him some money and he was going there to collect it. Also, Miles stated that he knew enough about the past life of Elizabeth to compel her to pay up. When he went to the Potts' home that day he had over $100 on his person. Miles and his friend, an Elko businessman named Linebarger, both dropped in on the couple. Fawcett was invited to stay the night but Linebarger left a couple of hours after arriving, after seeing Fawcett's horses put in the stable at the Potts' residence. Miles was never seen alive again. His sudden disappearance raised concerns and questions, causing Josiah to show around town a bill of sale from Fawcett, which purported to show the latter had sold all of his effects to the Potts. According to the couple, Miles had been suddenly called east on business. In the summer of 1888 the couple moved to Rock Springs, Wyoming, and a family named Brewer rented the former home of the Potts.[1]

On the night of January 1, 1888, Josiah was observed driving Fawcett's horses and sleigh, and later those horses were seen attached to another of Fawcett's wagons, again driven by Josiah. The explanation presented by the couple about Miles suddenly rushing east on business and selling everything to the Potts was not believed by most people in the community. Suspecting foul play, the community organized a search party to search for the missing man but no trace was ever found. There the matter rested until the Brewers moved in. Rumors then spread that the house was haunted. Mrs. Brewer wrote an occasional column for the *Elko Free Press* and in her column dated January 5, 1889 (under her usual pen name of "Busy Bee"), described how for the past few weeks they kept hearing strange noises such as tapping, footsteps, and so on, with the greatest concentration of those strange noises coming from the cellar. Because of that, Mr. Brewer went to the cellar and began poking around, digging and investigating. On January 19, 1889, he found the remains of Miles Fawcett buried in that cellar. The body had been cut into pieces. The head was charred and fleshless and had been cut up and partially burnt; the legs, arms, and body were in small fragments. One or two small items were found on the remains that were specifically identified as the property of Miles. Fawcett was a well-to-do 70-year-old bachelor born, like the Potts, in Manchester, England. At the trial evidence showed that for the sake of money Elizabeth had struck her victim on the head with an axe and then crushed his skull to prevent identification. Not satisfied with those steps she and her husband then cut up the body. Elizabeth tried to boil the body down but had to give up the effort on account of the stench. She tried to feed the remains to the household farm animals but when that did not work the couple ended up burying the body under the house.[2]

Immediately upon the discovery of the remains, Sheriff Barnard of Elko telegraphed to Rock Springs to have the Potts placed under arrest. They were quickly returned to Elko, indicted for murder in the first degree, tried, convicted, and both sentenced to be executed by hanging on June 20, 1890. She was described as follows: "Elizabeth Potts was a native of England, 42 years of age. She was of large physique, with a ruddy complexion, light blue eyes, and weighed probably 200 pounds. Her maiden name was Atherton. From the time of her arrest at Rock Springs, Wyoming, and during the trial for murder she maintained a stolid indifference." At the trial Elizabeth testified she had discovered Fawcett in an attempt to assault her little daughter (her son was 17, and the two girls were six and 13) a "long time" before his disappearance and that Miles had threatened to kill Elizabeth if she exposed his behavior. Soon afterwards she wrote a

6. 1890s

letter to the constable at Carlin informing him of Fawcett's attempt and demanding the man's arrest. However, the letter, she said, was discovered by Josiah and kept by him. When Miles came to visit on January 1 a violent scene took place between the two men. And to settle the matter Fawcett offered her husband a bill of sale for all his possessions and his ranch. But her husband refused the offer and threatened to expose Miles and have him lynched. As Josiah was leaving the house to make good his threat to expose Fawcett, the latter, in a fit of depression, drew a pistol and shot himself dead. Fearful of being accused of murder, the Potts hid Fawcett's body in the cellar of their house. That story, told by Elizabeth, said a reporter, was "received with incredulity." As to her conduct at the trial and during sentencing, it was observed, "Mrs. Potts was a woman of wonderful nerve and self-control. When the verdict of conviction was rendered she seemed the coolest person in the room, and when the sentence of death was pronounced she displayed no emotion. Once or twice while in prison awaiting execution she shed tears, but with these exceptions she showed an unmoved outward appearance. Her husband exhibited considerable firmness, though not so much as did she."[3]

At Elko, Nevada, on Friday, June 20, 1890, Elizabeth and Josiah Potts were executed together, in a procedure that went horribly wrong, technically. In town that day, said an account, "an air of feverish excitement seemed to prevail." On Wednesday night, June 18, Elizabeth tried to commit suicide. The deathwatch sentry heard her rapping on her cell and her husband answering in some fashion. Later she called for water. Her voice was so weak it alarmed the sentry and he called for the jailer. When they entered her cell they discovered three incisions in her left wrist that she had made with a penknife. Blood was spurting out from the cuts and the prisoner was very weak. A physician was summoned and her life was saved "to meet a more awful fate." A sharp knife was also found in Josiah's possession. Josiah slept well throughout Thursday night but Elizabeth was restless until about 3:00 A.M. when she, too, fell asleep. At 10:30 A.M. on execution day the guards arrived at the cells with a flask of spirits. After a short prayer was read by Reverend Porter, a little spirits was administered to the pair. Then the death warrants were read to each of them during which Mrs. Potts raised her right hand and exclaimed, "Innocent, so help me God." Then more spirits were administered. At 10:38 A.M. the group walked to the scaffold. "Mrs. Potts was dressed in white and black silk bows at the throat and wrists; Potts in a business suit." Both had their legs and arms pinioned, both had their shoes removed. First, though, the couple embraced and kissed. As the ropes were being adjusted they were urged to look to Christ. As a last step the black caps were drawn over their faces. At 10:43 A.M. Sheriff Barnard cut the rope that held the trap door spring. His drop was six feet, hers was 5.5 feet. "Mrs. Potts never struggled or turned around. Her neck was broken and the blood streamed down the front of the white dress. The head was almost severed from the body. Her pulse never beat after she fell," said one account.[4]

A news account in a different newspaper described Elizabeth's last couple of days in a quite different fashion, remarking, "The conduct of Mrs. Potts for the last few days has been marked by alternate hysterical weeping and swearing at her husband, who spent his time in his own cell playing solitaire."[5]

Describing the execution in far more detail, and graphically gruesome detail, was yet another newspaper. "One of the most terrible scenes in the history of death by the noose was witnessed in the Elko (Nevada) jail yard.... Hardened men shuddered and turned pale as they saw the woman's head nearly cut off by the rope and the blood drench her clothing, while beside her swung in fearful contortions, the body of her husband." Continued the account, "The scene which followed the springing of the trap was awful and the spectators turned away, pale and sickened. Mrs. Potts was so heavy and her flesh so soft and flabby that when the rope became taut it cut through her neck severing the carotid artery. A stream of blood gushed out from under her chin and coursed down over the white dress she had made with so much care. It was a spectacle not soon to be forgotten. The woman's form hung motionless covered with blood and at its side swayed the body of her husband drawn up in frightful contortions which continued for fourteen minutes." When the bodies were cut down it was found the rope had cut so deep into her throat that had the drop been a little longer "her head would have been severed from her body. The muscles of the back of the neck alone kept head and trunk together. The blood was hurriedly wiped off the wife's face and the remains placed in a coffin." Half an hour after the bodies were cut down, in the absence of anyone to claim the bodies, the remains of Elizabeth and Josiah Potts were deposited in the Potter's Field section of the Elko cemetery. Elizabeth had died instantly from a broken neck while Josiah had died from strangulation, a process that took an agonizing 14 minutes in his case.[6]

Emily Boon

On September 13, 1890, in Gordon County, Georgia, Rufus B. Collins and Emily Boon were sentenced to be executed by hanging on November 7, 1890, in a public execution. Collins was a white man who hired Steve Custer to kill his wife, for which crime Custer was sentenced to life imprisonment. Apparently Boon was not executed.[7]

Margaret Lashley

Margaret Lashley and Jim Lyles (blacks) were hanged in Danville, Virginia, on January 22, 1892, for the murder of George Lashley, the woman's husband.[8]

Amanda Umble

Judge White in Kansas City, Missouri, sentenced Amanda Umble in June 1893 to be executed by hanging on August 19, 1893. That sentence was passed after Umble was convicted of murder in the first degree with the victim being Effie Jackson; both women were black. Back in 1892 Umble waylaid Jackson and stabbed her to death; she was jealous and believed the woman had alienated the affections of her lover. To that date no woman had ever been hanged, reportedly, in Missouri. And Umble did not become the first. Said a reporter, "The whole city united in a protest against the hanging of a woman. Clergymen denounced it from the pulpits and yard-long petitions were handed around everywhere until they united in one monster protest as big around as a hogshead." The governor stepped in and commuted the death sentence to one of life imprisonment.[9]

Anna Tribble

Anna Tribble, an unmarried black woman, was hanged at Newberry, South Carolina, on October 7, 1892, for the murder of her infant son on

February 23, 1892. She was convicted of having secreted the child in a field on the day of its birth and having deserted it, thereby causing its death. The hanging took place in the jail building with death said to have been almost instantaneous. Anna raved continuously during her last night and on the morning of October 7; she had to be forced onto the scaffold. To the end she protested her innocence.[10]

Milbry Brown

Milbry Brown was a black teenager, aged 14 or 15, who was executed by hanging at Spartanburg, South Carolina, on October 7, 1892. She was convicted of killing the one-year-old infant of W. Carpenter of Gaffney City, South Carolina, in June 1892. Milbry was hanged at 11:00 A.M. at the same time and on the same scaffold as was John Williams (black), who had committed a murder in 1891. Those two were complete strangers to each other and faced the gallows for unrelated crimes. The hangings took place within the jail yard enclosure in the presence of about 20 people, exclusive of the physicians, clergymen, attorneys, and the officers of the court. The drop was six feet and Brown died instantly from a broken neck. A short reprieve was granted to both prisoners when the original date of August 9 was changed to October 7. During that time the governor investigated both cases but declined to intervene with either a commutation or a pardon. Public sentiment was said to approve the hanging of Williams but "many people are of the opinion that the case of Milbry Brown was one that called for executive clemency," said an account. On the scaffold Brown said, "I am going home to die no more" and showed little feeling. Reportedly, she was one of the youngest women ever executed in the United States. Her crime was described as "peculiarly atrocious and ferocious." One day her employer, Mrs. Carpenter, reproved her for sweeping slowly. As soon as Mrs. Carpenter's back was turned Milbry deliberately went to the mantle, took down a bottle of carbolic acid, went to where Mrs. Carpenter's baby was sleeping, opened its lips, and poured the deadly poison down its throat. The infant died in the greatest agony. Brown expressed no contrition for her crime and after she had been sentenced and returned to jail she informed the keeper that if she ever got out of there she would poison the judge and the entire Carpenter family.[11]

Caroline Shipp

Condemned to be executed for infanticide, Caroline Shipp was taken from jail at Raleigh, North Carolina, on January 22, 1892, at 1:00 P.M. and led to the gallows. On the scaffold she talked for eight minutes, reaffirming her innocence and declaring that a man named Mack Farrar committed the crime. The drop fell at 1:55 P.M. and, said a news account, "death resulted in twenty minutes by strangulation."[12]

Lizzie Halliday

Early in September 1893 the bodies of two women were found in the barn on the farm property owned by Paul and Lizzie Halliday at Burlingham, Sullivan County, New York. The women had been murdered and were not identified for about one day. When found the bodies had their feet tied and their hands crossed and tied. Eight bullets had been fired into the older of the two; seven bullets were in the body of the younger woman. The older woman had been dead for a week when discovered, with the other female having been dead for some 48 hours. Paul Halliday was missing and unaccounted for. Suspicion fell on the only other resident of the property, Mrs. Paul Halliday, and she was taken into custody. So violent did she become that handcuffs had to be applied. She tore her dress in strips and attempted to undress herself. According to one account, "Her talk is incoherent, and she is either insane or feigns insanity." Crowds of neighbors gathered around the Halliday property as the news spread and threats of lynching were frequently heard.[13]

By September 6 the dead women had been identified as the wife and daughter of Thomas McQuillan of Newburg, New York; Mrs. Margaret McQuillan had been 50 years old, Sarah McQuillan 19. Investigators had pieced together the following story. On Monday, August 28, Lizzie drove up to the door of the McQuillan home and said her name was Mrs. Smith, that her home was at Walden and that she had come to Newburg in search of a good woman to do housecleaning. A friend had recommended Sarah as an excellent cleaner and thus Smith had come to offer the girl a job that might last a week, offering the very good pay of $2 per day with board and transportation both ways. Sarah declined the tempting offer but Mrs.

McQuillan, surprised at the refusal, exclaimed, "Well, if Sarah won't take the job, I will." A neighbor by the name of Mrs. Charles Wright heard the conversation but had taken a dislike to Lizzie and advised the mother to have nothing to do with "Smith." Despite that warning the older woman took the job anyway. The pair left shortly thereafter, supposedly going to Smith's home in Walden. Several days later, on a Saturday at about 5:00 P.M., Smith drove up to the door of the McQuillan home again, but in great haste this time, to tell Sarah her mother had fallen from a ladder and seriously injured herself. The mother wanted Sarah to come at once. Mr. McQuillan also wanted to go but Smith persuaded him there was no room in her vehicle for him and that the mother specifically requested the daughter's presence. Neighbor lady Mrs. Wright somehow again became involved in the conversation and asked Smith exactly where her house was in order that friends of Mrs. McQuillan could find her if required. Smith said, as she drove off with Sarah, it was seven miles beyond Walden, but gave no other specific information. When nothing had been heard from the McQuillan women by Monday, Mr. McQuillan hired a vehicle and drove 50 miles all over the place trying to locate them but no one near Walden or neighboring communities knew of such a person as Mrs. Smith. It was not until a description of the murdered women — at that stage not identified — and their clothing was circulated that McQuillan suspected they were his family members. Identification followed and the two pistols used in the murders were found secreted in an outhouse on the Halliday property.[14]

On September 7 the body of Paul Halliday was dug up from beneath the floor in the kitchen by investigators. His head had been bashed in by a blunt instrument and he had been shot three times in the heart. Although the ages of the couple were not given he was described as old and she was called young. Lizzie was Paul's second wife. The couple had no children and Paul's children from his first marriage were adults who had long been gone from the family home. Meanwhile in her prison cell it was said that Lizzie "spends her time in insane antics or feigns she is insane by action and word."[15]

A couple of days after the body of Paul was discovered his sons James and Robert came back home to settle their father's affairs. James admitted he had been on bad terms with his father and that he had never spoken to his stepmother. Both sons related the story about how the Halliday home had been destroyed by a fire on May 6, 1891, and how their crippled brother John had died in that fire. James speculated that Lizzie had killed John with an axe and then burned down the building to cover up the crime.[16]

Charged with three counts of murder, Lizzie was placed in the Sullivan County Jail on September 8. The trip to Monticello from Burlingham, a distance of 25 miles, was made across the county in a wagon. "Her arrival in Monticello was hailed by the people much as a hand organ is received by small boys. Hundreds lined the streets to get a glimpse of the face of the murderess," said a news account. "She was placed in her cell without resistance except a deafening shriek now and then to apprise the public on the outside that she was in confinement. Her face shows no evidence of insanity and her eyes have no cold, wild look in them.... Sheriff Beecher allowed the reporter for the *New York Times* to see her, but her language was incoherent and the interview was closed." Two coroner's juries declared Lizzie had murdered all three; Margaret McQuillan on or about August 30, Sarah McQuillan on or about September 2, and Paul Halliday on or about August 28.[17]

William Greve was a neighbor with a farm directly opposite the Halliday farm. He said, "Mrs. Halliday was not favorably regarded by her neighbors. She is a short, thick-set woman, with a repulsive face, and the most peculiar nose I ever saw. She has great muscular strength.... I warned my children not to go into her house, because I distrusted her. They never did, though she often invited them. I am glad now that they did not."[18]

By September 12, 1893, according to an editorial in the *New York Times*, the chief interest in the case centered around the issue of Lizzie's sanity. "There is nothing whatever about the conduct of Mrs. Halliday to establish the plea of insanity. When not under the observing eye of the county officials or newspaper men, her demeanor is that of a person in sound health, but more or less exhausted by unusual strain or excitement," said the editor. As further proof of her sanity he cited the fact she ate all the usual food served to prisoners and she slept well and she had none of the nervousness displayed by so many women who were "candidates for the guardianship of the State Commissioners of Lunacy. In fact, Mrs. Halliday, since her arrival at the Monticello jail, has exhibited almost all of the feints and resources usually gone through with by ignorant people who are endeavoring to feign insanity." Her conversation was said to be entirely unconnected with the subject of the murders and her answer to any question pertaining to the matter "is utterly foreign. She tears her bed ticking to pieces and makes shreds of her apparel whenever the Sheriff allows a visitor to approach the door of her cell, but when watched unknown to herself, she sits moodily and lost in thought on the cot prepared for her to rest upon." Local physicians who had examined Lizzie were said to have pronounced her to be "a clear case of feigned insanity." As well, the editor said she only ate one meal a day — despite a seeming contradiction earlier that she ate well — and, worried over the effects that might have on the prisoner's health, the jailers "administered nourishment to her forcibly." Hundreds of people were said to daily visit Monticello in the hope of seeing the prisoner.[19]

She was born Eliza Margaret McNally in County Antrim, Ireland, around 1864 and came to America with her parents in 1867. Around 1879 she married Charles Hopkins, by whom she had her only child, a boy who was in a Pennsylvania institution at the time of Lizzie's arrest. Upon the death of Hopkins, around 1881, she married Artemas Brewer, a veteran and a pensioner who died within a year. Next was marriage to Hiram Parkinson but he deserted her within a year. She then married George Smith (although Parkinson was likely alive), a veteran and comrade of her second husband Brewer. A few months after the wedding ceremony she reportedly tried to kill Smith by giving him poisoned tea. Failing in that effort, she fled from Smith to Bellows Falls, Vermont, taking with her every item from the house that was portable. While in Vermont she married Charles Playstel, who was described as "the only one of her husbands who could be called young." However, they only lived together for about two weeks. Lizzie next surfaced in Philadelphia in the winter of 1888. She called on the McQuillans (relatives of the Newburg McQuillans), who kept a saloon at 1218 North Front Street, and asked if she could stay with them for a bit, pointing to an old family friendship, since the McNallys and the McQuillans had been neighbors in Ireland. Lizzie opened a small retail shop in Philadelphia that, after having it insured on the 10-cents-a-week installment plan, she burned down, together with the houses of her two neighbors on either side of the shop. For that crime she served two years in the Eastern Penitentiary. Her next appearance was in Newburg, where she met and married Paul Halliday, a farmer living at Burlingham, about 20 miles from Newburg. Married life with Halliday did not go well and she soon eloped with a neighbor, stealing a team of horses to hasten their flight. In Newburg her companion deserted her and Lizzie was arrested. Her lawyer entered a plea of insanity and she was sent to an asylum. From there she persuaded Paul to secure her release. Shortly after her return to the Halliday farm from the asylum came the fire in which Paul's "idiotic" son perished. In August 1893 Paul disappeared. Lizzie claimed he had gone away but the neighbors were suspicious and one day when Lizzie was absent they searched the farm. They did not find Paul but they did find the bodies of the McQuillan women. After the discovery of the bodies Mrs. Halliday, it was said, "suddenly developed evidence of insanity."[20]

A few months later further investigation into her past revealed she was known in Philadelphia as Maggie Hopkins and that while imprisoned in that city at the Eastern Penitentiary she became insane. Warden Michael J. Cassidy of that institution said Lizzie was sent there (as Hopkins) in 1888 after receiving a two-year term for arson and she was received at the prison on May 4. She was five feet and one-half inch tall, weighed 117 pounds, was "fairly good-looking" and claimed to be 25 years old. Cassidy described her as a model prisoner with no infractions of the rules against her and said that she used to worry about her little boy and often inquired about him, then in a home of some kind. About two months before her sentence expired, explained Cassidy, she became insane, was diagnosed as such by prison physicians and transferred to the Department for the Insane at Blockley. After that, Cassidy heard no more about her.[21]

Meanwhile, as Lizzie waited in her cell for her trial her behavior became more and more bizarre and more and more violent. On November 14 she attacked Mrs. Beecher, wife of Sheriff Beecher, and tried to strangle her. Mrs. Beecher was saved by the sheriff. During a search of her cell it was found the steel shanks had been removed from her shoes, sharpened by rubbing them on the stone floor of her cell, and then hidden in her cell. Then she refused to take any solid food and Dr. F.A. McWilliams, jail physician, pumped food into her stomach for four days "under a strong protest on her part." One night she tried to kill herself by setting fire to the jail. A coal stove had been placed in her cell — the only means of heating it — and she ignited the bedclothes from the burning coals. Sheriff Beecher and his deputies extinguished the fire. During December 1893 she tried once to hang herself with the binding torn from the bottom of her dress. On December 15 she tried to kill herself by gashing her throat and arms with glass broken from her cell window. Some time later it was reported, "For the last three months it has been necessary to keep her chained to the floor."[22]

At Monticello, New York, on June 21, 1894, Lizzie Halliday was convicted by the jury of murder in the first degree. The jury deliberated for 190 minutes before reaching its decision. A key witness as to the woman's sanity was Dr. E.C. Mann of the sanitarium in New York, who testified she showed insanity symptoms off and on and he thought "there was no insanity about her, and that her actions during the last year could easily be performed by a sane person who was a pretty good actor."[23]

A day later Justice Edwards sentenced Halliday to be executed by electrocution on a day in the week beginning August 6, 1894. It was, reportedly, the first time in America that a woman had been sentenced to death by that method. Her conduct in court during sentencing was marked by the shaking of her head and hands, as in previous court appearances. She made no response to the judge's questions and seemed to be entirely out of it.[24]

Commenting on the outcome of her case an editorial in the *Washington Post* declared her conviction was a matter of course and "there was found to be nothing whatever in her plea of insanity. She is evidently a woman of low order, mentally as well as morally, but she was intelligent enough to commit a terrible crime for the most mercenary of motives, and then to seek immunity at the hands of the courts. There will be few persons, however, to object to a term of life imprisonment as the penalty. There is a well-defined prejudice against the hanging of women."[25]

While the *New York Times* had maintained an editorial consistency that Lizzie was faking madness it suddenly declared it had some doubts, wondering whether or not a jury should be left to make the decision on a prisoner's sanity, thinking perhaps it should be left to experts. "It is impossible to doubt that the jury, in reaching its conclusion was consciously or unconsciously affected by the prejudice against the accused that prevailed very bitterly in the community," explained the editor. "It was openly threatened that if the jury cleared the woman a mob would take the law into its hands and lynch her. This feeling was reflected in the testimony of the local physicians and other witnesses, and it is a psychological truism that the jury must in some degree have shared in it."[26]

Her behavior continued to deteriorate. Around the time of her conviction she got out of bed one night at 11:00 P.M. in her cell, took a position near the foot of her bed, raised her skirts as far as she could get them, and stood for two hours that way without moving. She started to insist on putting her left shoe on her right foot, she kicked over chairs and water pails in her cell, and "She continued the very filthiest habits of which she is capable."[27]

Finally, Lizzie's sentence was commuted and she was transferred to a psychiatric facility. While Sheriff Beecher was transferring her from one institution to another in 1894 she bit him on the hand. Over time the wound began to itch and burn and within weeks it was swollen as far up as the elbow. For a time it was feared Beecher would lose his arm.[28]

Even in an asylum Lizzie continued to produce havoc. On September 2, 1895, at the Mattawan State Asylum for the Insane in New York, Halliday attacked Catherine Ward, a facility attendant. Lizzie grabbed Ward by the throat and tried to strangle her.[29]

Maria Barberi (Barbella)

In broad daylight on the streets of Manhattan on April 26, 1895, in front of 428 East 13th Street, a woman killed a man, with jealousy reported as being the motivation. The throat of Dominico Cataldo, around 30 years of age, was cut from ear to ear with a razor. Wielding the blade was Maria Barberi, about 22 years of age. (Her birth name was Barbella but for unreported reasons Maria mostly went by the name of Barberi.) Five minutes after he was slashed he was dead. Her explanation was that she had killed the man she had lived with for the previous three months because he said he was going to leave her to marry another woman. Dominico first came to America around 1892 with his two brothers and first met Barberi some 18 months before his death. She was a seamstress then and lived with her family at 163 Mott Street. After a brief courtship she was induced to leave her home and move in with Cataldo, who promised to marry her. It was a promise he never kept and it led to frequent quarrels between the pair at their residence at 424 East 13th. Finally, a week before the slaying, Dominico told Maria that he was tired of her, had never intended to marry her, and was going to leave her for another woman. Shortly after 9:00 A.M.

on April 26 people in the neighborhood heard the pair quarrelling. Half an hour later he left the house and went to a nearby saloon. Dominico was playing cards there when Maria appeared at the door and beckoned him to come out. He did. She demanded, "Are you going to marry me?" and when he said no she pulled out the razor and slashed him. Within minutes she was arrested.[30]

Two days later an irritated editor of the *New York Times* declared, "A great deal of maudlin sentiment has already expressed itself in favor of Maria Barberi." He found in some respects the situation was similar to the Chiara Cignarale case in which "Herculean efforts"—ultimately successful—had been made to save her from the gallows. "There is some indication that a similar course may be pursued in regard to Maria Barberi" because she had been visited in her cell in the Essex Market Police Court Prison the day before "by a very large number of persons, the majority of whom are women," the editor worried.[31]

In her confession Maria said she first met Dominico in the streets near her family home where he worked as a bootblack. Being apprised about her new boyfriend, Maria's father warned her to stay away from him. Nevertheless the pair continued to meet. He told her he had $400 in the bank and with a view to hastening the marriage she matched his funds, giving him $800 in total in the bank. It was shortly after that transaction that she went to live with him at 424 East 13th Street. And it was soon after that the pair started to quarrel as he kept stalling on the promise of a wedding.[32]

On July 15, 1895, the jury returned a verdict of guilty of murder in the first degree against Barberi; the jury had taken 90 minutes to reach its decision. In New York City on July 18, Recorder Goff sentenced her to be executed by electrocution on a day in the week beginning August 19, 1895. She was just the second woman in America to be condemned to death by that method, after Lizzie Halliday. A huge crowd of spectators and would-be spectators was in and around the courthouse on sentencing day with a lineup having formed an hour in advance of the time the doors opened. In passing sentence Goff said, "The sentence of this court is that you, Maria Barberi, for murder in the first degree of Dominico Cataldo be and you are hereby sentenced to death. Within ten days from this date the sheriff of the county of New York shall deliver you to the warden or agent of the state prison at Sing Sing, who shall keep you in solitary confinement until the week beginning Monday, August 19, and on a day within that week, the said warden or agent shall do execution upon you in the manner prescribed by the laws of the state of New York."[33]

Maria was immediately transferred to Sing Sing and spent the night of July 19 there. Before that transfer, though, Warden Sage telegraphed the New York State governor, Levi P. Morton, to say he had no female attendant at the prison to tend to Barberi, asking the governor to address the situation. He did so by notifying the superintendent of prisons to make a requisition to hire two attendants through the civil service commission. That rush hiring was done and two women were appointed. Barberi was placed at the prison in a room that had been especially prepared for her in the hospital building. She was not to be put in the death house where six condemned murderers, all male, were awaiting execution. While one of those new matrons attended to the prisoner, a male guard was on duty night and day at the door leading to Maria's room. Warden Sage expressed much sympathy for his new charge and hinted he hoped something would happen to keep him from being compelled to kill the girl in the electric chair.[34]

On the afternoon of July 18, before her transfer to Sing Sing, Maria met with her parents, her sister, her aunt, and a titled supporter, the Countess di Brazzi, and the latter's secretary. A stiletto with a five-inch-long blade was taken from the aunt and two pocketknives were confiscated from the sister, during the pre-visit search. Within a few days of her conviction, letters were pouring in to Morton's office asking for clemency. Di Brazzi was circulating petitions for clemency and urging as many people as possible to get out and sign one. "Not only the quality of the names of the supplicants, but the quantity of them, will impress his Excellency and no one in this case is too humble or too poor to help save a human life," she explained. One who signed the Countess's petition was actor Lillian Russell, who was spending the summer with her mother near Yonkers, New York. Unlike most of the petitions circulated for other condemned women profiled in this book, the one sponsored by di Brazzi asked for a pardon (freedom) and not for a commutation to a term of some years' imprisonment.[35]

And it was the pardon aspect of the petition that caused a *New York Times* editor to declare he was appalled by the illogic of such a petition. "Meanwhile, the facts in this case are self-evident to all but the mentally blind. A savage murder was committed to avenge a wrong for which the law offers redress. There is absolutely nothing more to the case than that. Doubts as to the adequacy of the law's redress, doubts as to the utility or the righteousness of capital punishment, doubts as to the propriety of executing women — even if men convicted of the same crime should be executed — these have no bearing on the matter," he fumed. Continuing on, he scored those who signed such petitions: "About illogical actions, of course, it is impossible to reason. The mere pleasure of seeing their names on an official-looking document is so great, for a not inappreciable portion of humanity, that to acquire it they are willing to subscribe to any statements, no matter how absurd, and to demand, or command, as the case may be, any action, no matter how indefensible."[36]

Taking a different position was an editorial in the *Chicago Tribune* that came out with reasons why the state should not execute Barberi. Included was, "The thought that men are to gather about this wretched and distraught girl, strap her, a woman, to a chair, and then stand by to watch her killing by an electric current is horrible in the extreme. No decent man would be willing to take part in such a proceeding. No Governor ought to subject manhood to it. Killing a woman in cold blood is not a business for men. It outrages humanity." Summarizing the case, the editor said, "Maria Barberi is an ignorant, low-born, passionate Italian girl ... whom fate had left stranded in the squalid tenement district of New York. She was betrayed by an Italian lover, a vulgar, brutal fellow. Her ruin accomplished," she killed him. Always in the past the *Chicago Tribune* had been in favor of the equal application of capital punishment to the sexes — and no exemptions for women. And so, to avoid a seeming contradiction with its own policy if it advocated commutation for Barberi, the editor used a painfully distorted attempt at logic. He argued the execution of a woman for avenging her honor was discriminatory since men were never executed when they killed a man who had ruined the honor of, say, their sister. (No examples, or details, were cited.) Going even further into strange realms, he went so far as to compare Barberi to Thomas Hardy's famed fictional character Tess of the D'Urbervilles. "But where is the difference between Tess of D'Urberville [*sic*] in Hardy's fiction and Maria Barberi in the slums of New York visiting her vengeance upon Domenico Cabaldo, the sneering libertine?" (At the end of Hardy's novel Tess was executed for murdering the man who ruined her honor years earlier, sending her on a long and winding downward path.) He was convinced Maria's sentence would be commuted.[37]

One day later an article in the *Chicago Tribune* published a sentence or two drawn from editorials in nine major newspapers, all of them against, usually emphatically, the execution of Barberi. Those papers were: *Memphis Commercial Appeal, Detroit Tribune, Cincinnati Commercial-Gazette, Washington Times, New York Advertiser, New York World, New York Sun, New York Recorder,* and *Philadelphia Record.*[38]

There were a few dissenters, though. A mass meeting of black men under the auspices of the Colored Republican Association of the State of New York was held in Manhattan on July 29, 1895. C.E. Davis got a large, positive reaction from the crowd when, in his speech, he said the people who sympathized with Barberi, "a red-handed murderess, never raised their voice when colored women were lynched in the South."[39]

Meetings to protest the pending execution, and the signing of petitions, continued into August. One petition, circulated by Mrs. Frank du Sauchet, had over 4,000 signatures and asked for Maria's pardon. Said Mrs. du Sauchet, declaring the prisoner should be pardoned outright, "She was not a bad girl. She wanted to get Cataldo to do what was right. Was it not better than, under a sense of shame, she should take the life of her betrayer than take her own, like the poor girl did who was found dead at Washington Heights? ... There are now 60,000 signatures to petitions for her pardon, and I will sign no other kind."[40]

Almost alone in being staunchly against Maria was the *Brooklyn Eagle*. It published an article in August purporting to show the woman was not the innocent she was portrayed to be. According to this account their quarrels near the end were not about marriage at all, but about $400 that Cataldo had promised to give her but did not. When the live-in relationship began he had $825 in the bank and promised Barberi half. After a month she demanded her half but he would not give it to her. (The story of the $800 in the bank, how it got there, who contributed to it, how it was to be split, and so on, was mentioned often in news reports but in hopelessly confusing and contradictory versions.) Portraying the woman in that light was a rationale for the editor to declare, "But it is just as well to have it understood that if any woman is to be executed under sentence of death Maria deserved the punishment as much as any of her sisters can ever do. Then the appeal to the governor can be made upon grounds which apply in the case of all women and not upon the theory that a wronged innocent has been sentenced in defiance of justice."[41]

Barberi's case caused the *New York Times* to bring up the issue of voting for women in an editorial. The "question is whether the fact that the leading advocates of immunity for Maria Barberi, who killed her unfaithful lover, are women does or does not constitute an argument against the extension to women of the suffrage." Having posed the question, the editor, however, declined to answer it. He did go on to raise an incidental question: "Would a woman in Maria Barberi's position be better off with a jury of women than with a jury of men?" While women led the movement to free the prisoner, the editor wondered if they were really representative of their sex. First, though, he speculated what would have happened if the positions were reversed and it was the man who did the killing. "The movement for the pardon of Maria Barberi is distinctly incompatible with the demand for equal rights and equal privileges for each sex, for it is a movement for the pardon of a woman as a woman under conditions which would not give rise to a movement for the pardon of a man as a man. It is a distinct infringement of the principle that what is sauce for the goose is sauce for the gander." As to the outcome if the jury had comprised only women, the editor declared it as settled that upright women held animosity toward women who had fallen and the effect upon a jury of average women to the revelation of the relations between Barberi and Cataldo would have been "a firm conviction that the culprit was 'a brazen hussy,' and that upon a brazen hussy some punishment that she would feel acutely ought to be inflicted, not necessarily instantaneous death by electricity, but something painful and lingering."[42]

With an appeal filed in the case, an automatic stay of execution existed with Barberi confined, as of March 1896, in the same makeshift cell at Sing Sing that she had been transferred to the previous summer. Because she was the only female prisoner at Sing Sing and because she remained under a death sentence it remained necessary to have two special prison matrons appointed whose duties continued to be limited to guarding her alone. And that made her a very costly prisoner to maintain, at a cost to the State of $3,500 to $4,000 a year. Said one reporter, "She gets better treatment and food than the other convicts."[43]

A month later, in April 1896, the New York Court of Appeals, in a unanimous decision, ordered a new trial for Barberi, declaring errors had been made by the trial judge in his charge to the jury. Unhappy with the idea of a new trial was the editor of the *Brooklyn Eagle*, who went on to comment more generally, "It is not pleasant to think that a woman may be put to death by process of law, but the fact of her womanhood aggravates rather than excuses her brutality, and the sentiment that would save her from the consequences of her crime is sentimentality."[44]

Nor was it easy to secure a jury for that second trial because, as a journalist explained, "Talesman after talesman was excused because he did not believe in capital punishment, or did not believe in applying it to a woman."[45]

Nonetheless a jury was assembled and Maria's trial got underway in November 1896. Barberi's family tree was introduced by her lawyer in defense of his client — presumably to show what defective stock she had sprung from. "All her family shown in the history are tainted with alcoholism or insanity or epilepsy, or else are common, inconspicuous peasants. Several are now in asylums in Italy. Others have died in them."[46]

On December 10, 1896, after being a prisoner for one year, seven months, and 16 days, Maria was acquitted by the jury in her second trial, with the jury taking just 45 minutes to reach its verdict. Evidence and testimony at the second trial were mostly the same as it had been the first time. "The lowness of her type pleaded for her. Had there been luster in her eye instead of heavy-lidded dullness, had there been intelligence in her face instead of vacancy, she might not have fared so well," concluded an article in the *Chicago Tribune*. "Her acquittal is hardly a triumph for anybody, though the ingenious showing of the girl's descent from a race of epileptics and degenerates furnished an excuse on which to hang an acquittal." In the opinion of a *Brooklyn Eagle* editorial, "The shrieking sisterhood will see in all this a triumph for their sex against the tyrant man. Tyrant man will see nothing of the kind, for he is not apt to regard questions of age or sex in criminal cases. He simply knows that a grievous offense against the laws has been committed, and that it has not been punished." This editor would have been content if Barberi had been convicted of manslaughter and punished accordingly.[47]

Maggie Tiller

Maggie Tiller, said to be the first woman upon whom the death penalty was passed in the state of Illinois, was a 19-year-old mulatto. She was born July 27, 1875, in Wilmington, North Carolina. After passing through the elementary schools she attended the North Carolina Normal Institute at Goldsboro for two years, leaving without graduating. Then she went on the stage and in 1893 she became associated with Freida Huntington in a sketch performance. The two girls played in some of the variety halls in Chicago. They were said to be "strongly attached" to each other and Tiller was jealous if any attentions were paid to her associate. Sometime in November 1894 Freida left Tiller and went to live with Charles Miller. Maggie was angry over the situation and on the morning of December 14 she surprised the couple in their room at 115 State Street, Chicago. Maggie drew a revolver while Miller rushed to a window trying to escape. As he leapt to the sill Tiller fired two shots into him. The mortally wounded man's foot caught and he hung upside down from the second-floor window into the street with blood from his wounds dripping down to the ground. A huge crowd quickly gathered and traffic on State Street was blocked for half an hour until the police arrived and removed the body. Miller died soon after help arrived.[48]

On March 26, 1895, Tiller was convicted of the murder of Miller and condemned to be executed by hanging. Blacks in Chicago banded together to oppose the hanging of Tiller and to lobby for a new trial for the woman. Mass meetings were held and collections taken to raise funds for a new trial. White women were not so enthusiastically behind Tiller. As to the question of why should Tiller not be hanged if she was guilty of the crime just the same as a man would be under the circumstances, the socially prominent Mrs. J.M. Flower said the "new woman" had to resign herself to take her chances with the man, "for the day of sentiment is rapidly waning, at least that sort which used to consider petticoats a protection from deserved punishment." A new trial was granted. At her first trial her defense had been insanity; at her second it was claimed she had been hypnotized. As a result of her second trial Maggie Tiller was sentenced, on May 4, 1895, to a term of 25 years' imprisonment.[49]

6. 1890s

Elizabeth Nobles

In 1895 Mrs. Elizabeth Nobles lived on a small place some 12 miles from Jeffersonville, Georgia. She and her husband had two children, Deborah, 18, and John, 10. According to a news account, they lived in squalor and the story of the crime revealed a picture of "life among the lowly" in Georgia. "They were Georgia crackers of the most ignorant and depraved type, living without knowing or caring anything about the great world outside. Their life was hard and monotonous with the drudgery of work in the fields from morning till night. Nor were the relations of the family pleasant. Mrs. Nobles complained that her husband cruelly mistreated her, but neighbors said the woman was anything but kind to her husband." There were three blacks living on the farm who worked for the Nobles — Gus Fambles, his wife Mary Fambles, and Dalton Joiner. Mrs. Nobles labored in the field as a common hand and while so engaged she talked over her troubles with Gus, complaining bitterly about her husband. One day Gus suggested that the old man be put out of the way; thus the murderous conspiracy was hatched. Over the following three weeks the plans were perfected. It was surmised that the other three adults on the farm, including Deborah, assisted the two principals in the conspiracy. On a Sunday morning in early 1895 Elizabeth aroused her husband from sleep to tell him somebody was stealing corn from the barn. Robberies of that kind had been frequent and the old man was eager to catch the culprits. At once he started for the barn but he did so unarmed as his wife had first hidden his gun before she awoke her husband. Outside, Gus crept up behind him and struck him in the head from behind with an axe. While Mr. Nobles lay on the ground, Elizabeth arrived and delivered a second blow with the axe. The pair then carried the body to a secluded spot, dug a shallow grave, and buried the remains. With the husband absent, neighbors began to ask as to his whereabouts. Elizabeth explained he had gone to the neighboring town of Danville and would return in the evening. But when he was still not back on Monday morning the alarmed neighbors launched a search for the missing man and soon found his body. All five of the adults on the farm were arrested. Elizabeth and Gus were convicted of the murder and were each sentenced to be executed by hanging on August 16, 1895. Joiner had an alibi, was acquitted, and immediately left the state. Deborah Nobles was also acquitted. Mary

Fambles was sentenced to life imprisonment and set to work in the coal mines operated by the convicts.[50]

Legal maneuverings put the execution on hold. Many women petitioned on her behalf for a commutation of the sentence with a strong split between the sexes: men favored imposing the penalty; women wanted a commutation. On December 1, 1897, a bill was introduced in the Georgia House of Representatives in Atlanta to prevent the execution of Nobles. It was introduced by Representative Berry of Whitefield at the insistence of Governor Atkinson, who wished to evade the responsibility of making a decision in the case of Elizabeth. By that time her last legal resort had been exhausted — the United States Supreme Court had just refused to intervene in her case. A reporter observed that Atkinson had been deluged with petitions from women for a commutation, and some pleas from men as well, but that he did not feel competent to set a precedent. Gus Fambles, whose execution was also stayed, would not gain anything from the bill even if it passed; he would still hang. "Only one woman [Eberhart] has been legally executed in this State in the last forty years, and popular sentiment seems to oppose strongly the death penalty in this case, although the circumstances of the crime are especially horrible."[51]

On February 12, 1898, Elizabeth Nobles was taken quietly to Jeffersonville and sentenced by Judge Smith to hang in April. It marked the fifth time a date for execution had been passed on the woman. Few people knew the court had convened for that purpose, according to a reporter, "the precautions being taken in consequence of threats of violence frequently heard on account of the long delay in executing the oft-repeated sentence." Elizabeth Nobles had no options left to her except executive clemency.[52]

Her sentence was commuted to a term of life imprisonment. Elizabeth died of natural causes in prison on February 7, 1916, aged about 71 years. At her request her remains were buried on the prison farm. At her death Nobles was supervisor of the prison sewing room. Gus Fambles also had his sentence commuted to a term of life imprisonment. He was still in jail when Elizabeth died.[53]

6. 1890s

Mary Snodgrass

On July 10, 1896, Mrs. Mary Snodgrass, 28, was hanged at Coburn, Virginia, for the murder of her child. She was described in one account as a "disreputable character" that had been compelled to leave Pikeville, Kentucky, on that account. When she moved on to Coburn, her child was left in the care of others until it was returned to her when it was about one month old. But Mary did not want it and tried unsuccessfully to get rid of the child in various ways. The county judge was called in and he told Snodgrass who would have to keep the child and provide for it. Subsequently, she was caught holding the child in a fire, cremating the infant. She was married at the age of 16 to what was described as a "worthless man" but the pair soon separated. She was promptly tried, convicted and executed. Mary Snodgrass was the last woman put to death by hanging in the United States in the 19th century.[54]

Martha Place

A series of crimes was committed in Brooklyn, New York, by Mrs. Martha Place on the night of February 7, 1898. Fueling those crimes was the woman's jealousy of her 17-year-old stepdaughter Ida Place. Brooding over her perception that her husband William cared more for Ida than for her, she worked herself up into a rage. She then got some vitriol that she tossed into Ida's face, some of which she forced down the girl's throat. Then she split her head open with an axe and, to make sure of the job, smothered Ida with some bedclothes. A later medical examination found Ida had been rendered blind by the acid and that death was due to suffocation. After murdering Ida, Martha waited for William, an insurance agent, to return home. When he arrived she rushed at him with an axe, chopped both sides of his head and crushed his skull. Somehow, though, he managed to escape into the street; he survived his injuries. With William having escaped from the house, Martha went upstairs and turned on the gas in a suicide attempt but the police arrived to save her, and to arrest her.[55]

William and Martha had married some five years earlier; it was a second marriage for both. Just a few months after the wedding Martha began to evince a hatred for the girl; Ida tried to pay no attention to her rages.

Things continued that way until about one year before the murder when Martha's conduct became unbearable, with her going so far as to threaten to kill William. He caused her to be arrested and arraigned in police court over that threat. Meanwhile, William sent Ida away to stay with relatives. The case dragged on in court until it was finally dismissed due to the non-appearance of William in court. But Martha's conduct improved dramatically afterward and a few months before the murder William had his daughter return to the family home. For a time Martha showed a kindly disposition to her stepdaughter. Then one night she went into a tirade at home, accusing William of loving Ida altogether too much and even lashing out at Ida's boyfriend (present at the time). Several times after that Martha verbally abused the three. Just a few days before the murder Martha had discharged the household servant, saying the family had no further use for her services. Then came February 7th. (Martha's first husband was Frank Lavcole and she was a widow for six years before she married Place. There were no children from that first marriage but she had adopted a boy, then 14. She took charge of him some 10 or 11 years earlier and claimed William would not let him live in the Place family home. The boy was then living in Orange, New Jersey, where he worked as an apprentice harness maker.[56])

On July 8, 1898, Martha Place was convicted of murder in the first degree with the jury returning a verdict after deliberating for two hours and 45 minutes. At that time she was described by a reporter as follows: "She is rather tall and spare, with a pale, sharp face. Her nose is long and pointed, her chin sharp and prominent, her lips thin and her forehead retreating. There is something about her face that reminds one of a rat's, and the bright, but changeless eyes somehow strengthen the impression." And, "She looks like a woman of great strength of mind and relentless determination. The only time her expression changed during the trial was when her husband William W. Place, testified to the attack made upon him. Then her thin lips parted in a sardonic grin, and she fixed her eyes upon him. The smile hardly ever left her face while she was on the stand. He did not look at her." Place lived in one of the better neighborhoods in Brooklyn. As a widower with a young daughter he felt the need of a woman to care for her. Some time before he and Martha married he had hired her to be a live-in housekeeper. "She soon began to show an ungovernable temper, which was frequently excited by the fact that her husband's friends and relatives refused to recognize her as an equal." William tried for years to reconcile Martha and Ida but in vain. For three years Ida and her stepmother rarely spoke to each other, and in her father's absence the girl was generally away from home.[57]

On July 12 Martha was sentenced to be executed in the electric chair on a day in the week beginning August 29, 1898. The 41-year-old woman had been born in New Jersey and had never before been convicted of a crime. She was immediately dispatched to Sing Sing Prison, which would be the execution site. When she arrived there she was taken to the old hospital building and placed in a room on the top floor formerly occupied by Maria Barberi while she had been under a death sentence. As in the case of Barberi, Martha was watched day and night by a police matron who was constantly in the room with her while a male guard was always stationed outside of the door.[58]

In the opinion of one reporter the woman's "stolid, indifferent demeanor" during the trial went a long way to securing the conviction as jurors looked upon that as evidence of "an abandoned and malignant heart." Place stood to be the first woman in America put to death by electrocution, after the two sentenced to that fate before her were saved from the death chamber. With respect to the question as to whether it was right to execute women, New York Assistant District Attorney Daniel O'Reilly said, "I believe that life imprisonment is sufficient punishment for a woman convicted of a capital offense. I am opposed to the infliction of the death penalty upon a woman. It is barbarous and opposed to the teachings of our Christian civilization." Taking an opposite view was New York Assistant District Attorney James Lindsay Gordon, who remarked, "If women begin to think they can commit crime with impunity there will be a fearful increase of unnatural murders like that committed by Mrs. Place. The only way to avoid such a contingency is to enforce the law regardless of sex." One journalist thought that electrocution was the most dreaded form of taking a life devised in modern times: "It is doubtless this repulsiveness more than anything else which is causing the public and press to take so active a part in the case spoken of. No woman has yet been so dispatched, and the procedure is certainly indelicate as well as savoring of barbarism."[59]

Various legal appeals would stay the execution and push the date back a number of times. As a prisoner Martha was said to have caused prison attendants no trouble. She spent much of her time reading scriptural books and professed to be devoutly religious. None of her relatives ever came to see her and Martha's only visitor was the Reverend Dr. Coles of Yonkers, who was formerly her Sunday school teacher.[60]

Her case garnered much media attention with public sympathy not entirely on her side. It may have been close to evenly divided. An example of the unsympathetic side could be seen in an editorial in the *Salt Lake Tribune* that stated, "A great many people believe that she should be pardoned because she is a woman; we believe it would be a mercy to her to shock her to a painless death."[61]

Many of those petitions to commute Place's sentence were directed, of course, to New York State Governor Theodore Roosevelt (later U.S. president). He put himself on record as being against the commutation of sentence for women under sentence of death for murder. Roosevelt declared, in February 1899, that he would be influenced by no "mawkish sentiment" in any case, nor would he be influenced by the sex of the criminal. The governor insisted he would decide each case on its merits.[62]

New York State legislators got involved again. In Albany on February 6, 1899, Assemblyman Harburger of New York City introduced a bill into the legislature that sought to save Place from the chair. The bill was a proposed amendment to the Penal Code of New York State that made murder in the first degree, when committed by a woman, punishable by life imprisonment. The measure, all agreed, had no chance of being enacted into law.[63]

A month later another bill in the legislature—from Assemblyman Maher—that also would have abolished capital punishment for women got as far as being voted on in the Assembly. In the debate on the measure, Maher said his bill, if passed, would not affect Martha Place since it would not be a retroactive measure, but it would in the future prevent the execution of women, "which was an insult to womanhood." The bill was voted down by a count of 78 to 47.[64]

Famed feminist Elizabeth Cady Stanton wrote a letter to the editor of the *New York Sun* in February 1899 in which she said Martha should not be executed because she belonged to a disenfranchised sex, that she had no voice in making the laws under which she was convicted and that, anyway, capital punishment was barbarism. That caused an editor on the *Brooklyn Eagle* to go off on a tirade, declaring that if Stanton was right then women should be favored in every crime by way of a discriminatory sentence. Calling her position an "absurdity" he went on to say, the "law has made woman a privileged character." Granting women did not have the right to vote he noted the law allowed them to control their own property and a woman could make a will without her husband's interference. "It may be that the State of New York will eventually see fit to abolish capital punishment, especially so far as women are concerned, but the case of Mrs. Place is the very last to put forth on which to base an appeal for a change in the law. The woman is a monster who deserved to die and the community will be the better off when she is executed," he concluded. "The last people to urge clemency in her behalf should be women, and the last women should be those who are advocating the extension of the franchise to the sex. It is a matter of rare good fortune that we have at this time in the Governor's chair a hard headed man to whom the sentimentalists will look for assistance in vain and who will take the ground that there is no sex in crime, just as there ought to be no discrimination in law."[65]

When the Medico-Legal Society of New York held its monthly meeting in February 1899, it decided Place should be executed, adopting a resolution that it was the sense of society that the question of the sex of the criminal convicted of homicide should be eliminated from the consideration of the executive in the exercise of the clemency power. Secretary of the Society Clark Bell remarked that it was a matter of fact that every time a woman had been sentenced to death in New York State, "a great public agitation had been started to induce the Governor to exercise the pardoning power on the ground the prisoner was a woman." This time, he felt, the voice of the people seemed to be all one way — against her execution. The only woman who spoke on that subject at the meeting was Mrs. Ida Trafford Bell, who exclaimed that Martha Place had "just as much right to be electrocuted as a man." According to a reporter, "The other women present applauded her sentiments."[66]

Expert medical men brought in to examine her all declared she was sane then and had been sane at the time of the murder. Meanwhile, strong pressure continued to be brought to bear on Governor Roosevelt from all over America and even from Europe to save the woman. On March 15, 1899, Roosevelt declined to interfere on her behalf. He explained that no more painful case could come before a governor than an appeal to save a woman from capital punishment when her guilt had been clearly established and there were no circumstances whatever to mitigate the crime.

"All that remains is the question as to whether I should be justified in interfering to save a murderess on the ground of her sex when no justification would exist to interfere on behalf of a murderer," said Roosevelt. "This murder was one of peculiar deliberation and atrocity. To interfere with the course of the law in this case could be justified only on the ground that never hereafter, under any circumstances, should capital punishment be inflicted upon any murderess, even though the victim was herself a woman, and even though that victim's torture preceded her death. There is but one course open to me. I decline to interfere with the course of the law."67

Martha Place was executed by electrocution at Sing Sing Prison on March 20, 1899. The first shock was one of 1,760 volts delivered for four seconds. It was then reduced to 200 volts for 56 seconds, and then a second shock was given. "Mrs. Place was calm beyond expectation. No one has walked into the death chamber as serenely as she. Death came with less struggle than was ever witnessed here before. Death was instantaneous," said a news report. She was dressed in black, having made the plain gown herself. "The electrode was fastened in a moment. Another was placed under her thick, light hair, turning gray, a small circle of which had been clipped away. The straps were adjusted over her face and a pad over her forehead. Only her mouth was visible. In her hand Mrs. Place carried a prayer book, and when the shock came she gripped it tightly. The other held fast to the chair handle. The woman's mouth merely closed, the face a trifle livid. Her heart ceased to beat within a minute."68

In an editorial on the Place execution, the *New York Times* noted first that on the Sunday prior to the execution at a Central Federated Union (a trade union group) meeting, a motion was made to petition Governor Roosevelt to commute Place's sentence on the ground that the Union in its constitution opposed capital punishment completely. However, the motion was almost unanimously rejected with its opponents taking the position that while they did not believe in capital punishment they did believe in the full and impartial enforcement of the law. They wanted the death penalty law abolished, not selectively evaded. Especially they objected to an exception in the case of Place on the ground she was a woman. With respect to the Central Federated Union activity, the newspaper editor concluded, "This strikes us as a peculiarly interesting and significant expression of public sentiment." He added, "But the general sentiment against the death penalty is certainly no stronger than it was a score of years ago. We very much doubt it is as strong." A total of 18 witnesses (over and above the attending officers of the court) were present at that execution.[69]

After Martha was executed her brain was removed and placed in a jar. It was regarded by Dr. Irvine, the prison physician, as a "valuable specimen" because of the questions raised as to Place's responsibility for her crime. Dr. Irvine intended to present the brain to Columbia University but sometime before February 1, 1900, it was consumed in a fire in the new hospital building at the prison, where it was being stored.[70]

Cordelia Poirier

At St. Scholastique, Quebec, on March 10, 1899, Mrs. Cordelia Poirier and Samuel Parslow (paramours) were hanged at 8:05 A.M. Both suffered broken necks and were dead almost instantly. She was described as "firm and collected throughout." The condemned were taken to the scaffold separately and were prevented from seeing each other by a screen placed between them. The pair was hanged for the murder of Cordelia's husband, Isador Poirier, which had occurred in the Poirier home in St. Canute, Quebec, in 1897. Cordelia, 33, was the organist at the Roman Catholic church at St. Jerome, Quebec, where Parslow sang. Both confessed their guilt but each sought to blame the other. According to one account she, "though not especially attractive in appearance, possessed more than the ordinary accomplishments of women in her situation in life. She had a fair education, and was the organist of the Roman Catholic Church at St. Jerome, where Parslow sang in the choir. Poirier, who was an industrious workman, built his wife a neat little cottage and maintained her in comfort." Behavior of the crowd at the execution was of an almost unimaginable ugliness. One problem stemmed from the fact the sheriff had given out something like 600 admission tickets to the execution while the tiny jail yard could accommodate nowhere near that number. "The crowd outside the jail jeered at her, but even then her composure did not desert her, and at the suggestion of the executioner she turned and faced the jeerers, and stood erect and prayed to the last," observed a reporter. Besides those who squeezed into the jail yard, "Outside the jail, there were two thousand more, who, with a beam, tried to batter down the gate of the jail yard, and could only be made to desist by the provincial police firing their revolvers in the air. The behavior of the crowd inside was such that one of the priests, Reverend Father Melroche, had to reprove them from the scaffold." Hundreds of people stayed up all night in anticipation of the spectacle. Cordelia was the third woman out of 11 condemned since Canadian confederation (1867) to receive capital punishment — the others were Phoebe Campbell and Elizabeth Workman, in 1872 and 1873, respectively. The sentences of the other eight were all commuted to life imprisonment. Six of the 11 were convicted of murdering their husbands.[71]

Emily Hilda Blake

The case of Emily Hilda Blake added one more to the Canadian totals right at the end of 1899. On December 27 in Brandon, Manitoba, Blake, a domestic servant, was executed by hanging in a private procedure that was witnessed by only a few people. Emily, although only 22 years old, was said to have walked calmly and firmly to the scaffold. She was convicted of having murdered her employer, Mrs. Robert Lane of Brandon, on July 5, 1899. Lane was found dying with a gunshot to the chest. Blake was the one who gave the alarm, saying a tramp had killed her mistress. Later she was charged with the crime, and then she confessed, saying she did it because she loved Mrs. Lane's children and was jealous of the mother's love. Emily's trial was brief as she refused all offers of counsel and pled guilty.[72]

Executions of Women in the 1890s[73]

(All were executed by hanging and all for murder, except as noted.)
1890, July, Mary O'Cammon, white, San Francisco, California.
1890, July, Kate McShane, white, San Francisco, California.
1890, June 20, Elizabeth Potts, white housewife, Elko, Nevada.
1892, October 7, Milbry Brown, 14, black servant, Spartanburg, South Carolina.

6. 1890s

1892, October 7, Anna Tribble, black, Newberry, South Carolina.
1892, January 22, Caroline Shipp, 18, Gaston, North Carolina.
1892, January 22, Margaret Lashley, black (accessory), Danville City, Virginia.
1893, July 28, Ada Heirs, black, Colleton, South Carolina.
1895, November 22, Amanda Cody, black, Warren, Georgia.

> Amanda and Florence English (black male) were executed together at Warrenton, Georgia, for the murder of Amanda's husband Cicero.

1896, July 10, Mary Snodgrass, 28, white, Wise, Virginia.
1899, March 20, Martha Place, 44, white housewife (electrocuted), Kings, New York.

Chapter Notes

Chapter 1

1. "American female executions 1900–2005." geocities.com/trctl11/amfem/html? 200726; Stephen J. Leonard, *Lynching in Colorado, 1859–1919* (Boulder, Colorado: University Press of Colorado, 2002), p. 74.
2. "Capital punishment." *Leadville Evening Chronicle* [Colorado], January 18, 1892, p. 2.
3. "Illumination at Flatlands." *Brooklyn Eagle*, November 27, 1844, p. 2.
4. "Accident on the Long Island Railroad." *Brooklyn Eagle*, June 27, 1855, p. 2.
5. "Hanging a woman." *New York Times*, July 21, 1855, p. 4.
6. "European chit-chat." *Brooklyn Eagle*, June 23, 1856, p. 2.
7. "Should women be hung for murder?" *Fort Wayne Sentinel* [Indiana], November 13, 1858.
8. "Executive clemency denied in the case of Mrs. Hartung." *New York Times*, April 9, 1859, p. 11.
9. "Proposition to abolish capital punishment of females in England." *Brooklyn Eagle*, July 12, 1866, p. 4.
10. "Minor topics." *New York Times*, May 6, 1871, p. 4.
11. "The Hyde case." *Brooklyn Eagle*, April 22, 1872, p. 2.
12. "Female murderers." *Rocky Mountain News Weekly* [Denver], May 8, 1872, p. 1.
13. "A plea for clemency." *St. Louis Globe Democrat*, December 4, 1875, p. 4.
14. "Character in murder." *St. Louis Globe Democrat*, December 17, 1875, p. 5.
15. No title. *Hartford Courant*, July 31, 1879, p. 2.
16. "The president on capital punishment." *New York Times*, March 26, 1880, p. 2.
17. "Gleanings from the mails." *New York Times*, January 10, 1881, p. 3.
18. Henry Ward Beecher. "Mr. Beecher on hanging." *Brooklyn Eagle*, January 23, 1887, p. 11.
19. "Hanging of men and women." *New York Times*, February 20, 1887, p. 8.
20. No title. *New York Times*, March 1, 1887, p. 4.
21. "Another woman on the way to the gallows." *Brooklyn Eagle*, May 28, 1887, p. 4.
22. "The hanging of women." *Hartford Courant*, May 30, 1887, p. 2.
23. "Political notes." *Brooklyn Eagle*, June 24, 1887, p. 4.
24. No title. *Reno Weekly Gazette and Stockman*, November 28, 1889, p. 4.
25. "The hanging of women." *Brooklyn Eagle*, June 11, 1896, p. 6.
26. "No sex in crime." *Brooklyn Eagle*, June 28, 1896, p. 6.
27. "Women and the death penalty." *Brooklyn Eagle*, December 2, 1897, p. 6.
28. "A woman may hang." *Montezuma Journal* [Cortez, Colorado], February 8, 1898, p. 4.
29. "Sentiment versus reason." *Washington Post*, July 19, 1898, p. 6.
30. "Sex in crime." *Washington Post*, March 16, 1899, p. 6.
31. "The death penalty for women." *New York Times*, August 20, 1899, p. 17.

Chapter 2

1. "The way of the transgressor is hard." *The Ohio Repository* [Canton], February 28, 1846.
2. Ibid.
3. "Murder." *Brooklyn Eagle*, August 27, 1847, p. 2.
4. Ibid.
5. "Mary Runkle, the murderess." *The Sandusky Clarion* [Ohio], December 7, 1847.
6. "New mode of hanging." *The Adams Sentinel* [Gettysburg, Pa.], November 29, 1847.
7. "Mary Runkle, the murderess," op. cit.
8. "A double tragedy." *New York Times*, July 31, 1852, p. 3.
9. "A woman sentenced to death at Poughkeepsie." *Brooklyn Eagle*, March 27, 1852, p. 2.
10. "Ann Hoag, the murderess." *New York Times*, April 21, 1852, p. 2; "To be executed." *Brooklyn Eagle*, July 22, 1852, p. 2.
11. "Execution of a murderess—letter from Governor Hunt." *New York Times*, July 24, 1852, p. 4.
12. Ibid.
13. "A double tragedy." *New York Times*, July 31, 1852, p. 3.
14. Ibid.
15. "Death of a murderess." *Tioga County Agitator* [Wellsboro, Pa.], November 29, 1855.
16. "A woman sentenced to death." *Liberty Weekly Tribune* [Missouri], January 6, 1854, p. 2.
17. "Female convicted of murder." *Brooklyn Eagle*, December 9, 1853, p. 4.
18. "Death of a murderess." *New York Times*, November 13, 1855, p. 8.
19. "Death of a murderess." *Tioga County Agitator* [Wellsboro, Pa.], November 29, 1855.
20. "Murder trials." *New York Times*, May 26, 1854, p. 3.
21. Ibid.
22. "Vessel crushed to pieces by the ice." *Brooklyn Eagle*, May 29, 1854, p. 2.
23. "Henrietta Robinson—the prisoner at Troy." *New York Times*, June 9, 1854, p. 1.
24. "Sentence of Henrietta Robinson." *Brooklyn Eagle*, June 20, 1855, p. 2.
25. "Hanging a woman." *New York Times*, July 21, 1855, p. 4.
26. "Mrs. Henrietta Robinson not Mrs. Wood—who is she?" *New York Times*, November 14, 1856, p. 5.
27. "Sing Sing state prison." *Brooklyn Eagle*, July 20, 1858, p. 1.
28. "Life in Sing Sing prison." *Brooklyn Eagle*, August 23, 1860, p. 1.
29. Ibid.
30. "The veiled murderess." *New York Times*, April 22, 1875, p. 2.
31. "The veiled murderess disclosed." *Ogden Standard Examiner* [Utah], July 30, 1898.
32. "History's mysteries." *Davis County Clipper* [Utah], August 8, 1922.
33. "Veiled murderess dead." *Eureka Reporter* [Utah], May 19, 1905.
34. "Miscellaneous items." *Brooklyn Eagle*, May 8, 1857, p. 1.
35. "The double murder at Keesport, Pa." *Hartford Courant*, May 6, 1857, p. 3.
36. "The double murder near Pittsburg." *Brooklyn Eagle*, May 11, 1857, p. 2.
37. "Poetry and murder." *Brooklyn Eagle*, July 13, 1857, p. 2.
38. "Verdict." *Hartford Courant*, July 13, 1857, p. 3.
39. "Confession of two of the McKeesport murderers." *Brooklyn Eagle*, December 1, 1857, p. 2.
40. "Execution." *Hartford Courant*, February 13, 1858, p. 3; "Various items." *Brooklyn Eagle*, February 25, 1858, p. 2.
41. "Execution of a woman." *Defiance Democrat* [Defiance, Ohio], November 6, 1858.
42. "Execution of a woman at Danville, Pa." *Chicago Tribune*, October 27, 1858, p. 2.
43. "Execution of a woman." *Defiance Democrat* [Defiance, Ohio], November 6, 1858.
44. "Some notable trials." *New York Times*, November 10, 1895, p. 32.
45. "Arrest of the Albany murderers." *New York Times*, July 14, 1858, p. 1.
46. "Evidence of a party." *New York Times*, February 9, 1859, p. 4; "The case of Mrs. Hartung." *New York Times*, February 8, 1859, p. 5.
47. "Albany matters." *New York Times*, March 4, 1859, p. 1.

48. "Sentence of death upon Mary Hartung." *New York Times*, March 5, 1859, p. 2.
49. "Executive clemency denied in the case of Mrs. Hartung." *New York Times*, April 9, 1859, p. 11.
50. "Mrs. Hartung's case." *New York Times*, April 9, 1859, p. 4.
51. "Mrs. Hartung." *Brooklyn Eagle*, April 9, 1859, p. 2.
52. "Mrs. Hartung's case." *New York Times*, April 11, 1859, p. 4.
53. "The hanging of women." *New York Times*, April 15, 1859, p. 4.
54. "Affairs at Albany." *New York Times*, April 19, 1859, p. 4.
55. "The case of Mrs. Hartung—a new trial denied." *New York Times*, December 20, 1859, p. 2.
56. "Mary Hartung cast down." *New York Times*, December 21, 1859, p. 3.
57. "From Albany." *New York Times*, January 27, 1860, p. 5.
58. "Webb on hanging women." *New York Times*, February 16, 1860, p. 4.
59. "The diamond murder." *Brooklyn Eagle*, August 4, 1863, p. 2.
60. "The case of Mrs. Hartung." *New York Times*, December 21, 1861, p. 4; "Discharge of Mary Hartung." *New York Times*, March 26, 1863, p. 5.
61. "Mary Hartung discharged." *Brooklyn Eagle*, March 26, 1863, p. 2.
62. "Some notable trials." *New York Times*, November 10, 1895, p. 32.
63. John D Bessler, *Legacy of Violence: Lynch Mobs and Executions in Minnesota* (Minneapolis: University of Minnesota Press, 2002), p. 67.
64. Ibid., pp. 68–69.
65. Ibid., pp. 70, 74, 80–81.
66. Ibid., pp. 82–85.
67. Ibid., pp. 86–88.
68. Ibid., pp. 88–89.
69. Ibid., pp. 89–91.
70. "Execution of a murderess." *The Daily Gazette* [Davenport, Iowa], March 29, 1860.
71. "Female executions, the Espy file, 1632 to 1962." users.bestweb.net/~rg/executions/females/htm.
72. "Female hangings 1632 to 1900." geocities.com/trct11/femhang.html?200726.

Chapter 3

1. "The wholesale Pittsburgh poisoner." *Brooklyn Eagle*, August 30, 1865, p. 2.
2. "Insanity in criminal cases." *Chicago Tribune*, August 31, 1865, p. 2.
3. "Sketch of the life of Mrs. Grinder." *New York Times*, September 3, 1865, p. 3.
4. "Mrs. Grinder—further developments." *Brooklyn Eagle*, September 18, 1865, p. 4.
5. "More about Mrs. Grinder." *Chicago Tribune*, September 21, 1865, p. 3.
6. "The Grinder poisoning case." *Chicago Tribune*, October 26, 1865, p. 3.
7. "The Pittsburgh Borgia." *Brooklyn Eagle*, October 27, 1865, p. 4.
8. "The Pittsburgh Borgia." *New York Times*, October 31, 1865, p. 5; "From Pittsburgh." *Chicago Tribune*, November 27, 1865, p. 3.
9. "The Pittsburgh poisoner." *Brooklyn Eagle*, December 2, 1865, p. 2.
10. "The American Borgia." *New York Times*, January 20, 1866, p. 8.
11. "The execution of Mrs. Grinder." *New York Times*, January 21, 1866, p. 1.
12. Ibid.
13. "The execution of women." *New York Times*, January 22, 1866, p. 4.
14. "The female Borgia." *Chicago Tribune*, September 22, 1866, p. 2.
15. "The assassination conspiracy." *Chicago Tribune*, May 4, 1865, p. 1.
16. "The night before the murder." *Brooklyn Eagle*, May 3, 1865, p. 2.
17. "The criminals and their counsel." *Brooklyn Eagle*, May 13, 1865, p. 3.
18. "From Washington." *Chicago Tribune*, May 15, 1865, p. 1.
19. "The trial of the conspirators." *Brooklyn Eagle*, May 31, 1865, p. 2.
20. "The trial of the alleged conspirators." *Brooklyn Eagle*, June 20, 1865, p. 2.
21. "Dr. Mudd, Arnold and O'Loughlin imprisoned for life." *Brooklyn Eagle*, July 6, 1865, p. 3.
22. "How they received the tidings." *Brooklyn Eagle*, July 7, 1865, p. 2.
23. "The sentence of the conspirators." *Brooklyn Eagle*, July 7, 1865, p. 2.
24. "Did she deserve to be hanged?" *Brooklyn Eagle*, July 8, 1865, p. 3.

25. No title. *Liberty Weekly Tribune* [Missouri], July 14, 1865, p. 2.
26. "The case of Mrs. Surratt." *Brooklyn Eagle*, July 18, 1865, p. 2.
27. "Mrs. Surratt." *Chicago Tribune*, July 18, 1865, p. 1.
28. "The president and Mrs. Surratt." *Chicago Tribune*, August 6, 1867, p. 2.
29. No title. *Liberty Weekly Tribune* [Missouri], September 4, 1868, p. 4.
30. "Who hung Mrs. Surratt?" *Chicago Tribune*, October 6, 1873, p. 1.
31. "The Surratt tragedy." *Liberty Weekly Tribune* [Missouri], November 21, 1873, p. 1.
32. "K.C. mail." *Liberty Weekly Tribune* [Missouri], December 2, 1881, p. 2.
33. "After thirty years' work." *Brooklyn Eagle*, March 23, 1895, p. 12.
34. "A horrible murder." *Chicago Tribune*, March 2 1867, p. 3.
35. "The Coriell murder." *New York Times*, May 21, 1867, p. 1.
36. "The Coriell murder." *New York Times*, June 1, 1867, p. 2.
37. "The Coriell murder." *New York Times*, June 3, 1867, p. 4.
38. "The Coriell murder." *New York Times*, June 3, 1867, p. 5.
39. "The Coriell murder." *New York Times*, June 18, 1867, p. 8.
40. "Mrs. Elizabeth Oakes Smith's account of a visit to Bridget Durgan." *New York Times*, August 25, 1867, p. 6.
41. "Topics of the day." *Brooklyn Eagle*, August 28, 1867, p. 2.
42. "Bridget Durgan." *New York Times*, August 28, 1867, p. 5.
43. "Execution of Bridget Durgan." *New York Times*, August 31, 1867, p. 8.
44. "The hanging of a woman." *Hartford Courant*, September 2, 1867, p. 4.
45. "The end of Durgan, the murderess." *New York Times*, August 31, 1867, p. 4.
46. "Execution of Bridget Durgan." *New York Times*, August 31, 1867, p. 8.
47. "The confession of Bridget Durgan, the New Jersey murderess." *Chicago Tribune*, September 2, 1867, p. 1.
48. "The scaffold." *Chicago Tribune*, March 8, 1868, p. 3.
49. "Trial at Cleveland, Ohio, of Mrs. Victor for the murder of her brother." *New York Times*, June 11, 1868, p. 5.
50. "The Cleveland tragedy." *New York Times*, June 27, 1868, p. 1.
51. "The sentence of Mrs. Victor — her appearance in the court-room." *Brooklyn Eagle*, July 8, 1868, p. 2.
52. "Mrs. Victor." *Brooklyn Eagle*, July 10, 1868, p. 2.
53. "The case of Mrs. Victor, the poisoner." *New York Times*, July 16, 1868, p. 2.
54. "Mrs. Victor, convicted of murder, reprieved by the Governor of Ohio." *New York Times*, July 17, 1868, p. 1.
55. "A singular case." *Liberty Weekly Tribune* [Missouri], July 6, 1877, p. 1.
56. "After eighteen years." *New York Times*, December 26, 1886, p. 1.
57. "The working women of New York." *New York Times*, November 25, 1868, p. 5.
58. "Meeting of women in behalf of Hester Vaughn." *Hartford Courant*, December 2, 1868, p. 3.
59. "Hester Vaughn." *New York Times*, December 2, 1868, p. 5.
60. "Personal and political." *Hartford Courant*, May 20, 1869, p. 2.
61. "Digest of news." *Galveston Daily News*, December 4, 1869.
62. "A murderess reprieved." *New York Times*, July 27, 1869, p. 5.
63. "Female executions, the Espy file, 1632 to 1962." users.bestweb.net/~rg/execution/females.htm; "Female hangings 1632 to 1900." geocities.com/trctl11/femhang.html?200726.

Chapter 4

1. "The gallows in Maryland." *New York Herald*, February 11, 1871, p. 6.
2. Ibid.
3. "The price of a vote." *Daily Register Call* [Central City, Colorado], April 28, 1871, p.1.
4. "Daily news." *Rocky Mountain News* [Denver], May 3, 1871, p. 2.
5. "Laura D. Fair." *Colorado Weekly Chieftain* [Pueblo], May 4, 1871, p. 1.
6. "The sentence of Mrs. Fair." *Daily Register Call* [Central City, Colorado], June 11, 1871, p. 1.
7. "A woman of the period." *Daily*

Notes—Chapter 4

Register Call [Central City, Colorado], June 15, 1871, p. 2.
8. "Mrs. Laura Fair." *New York Times*, July 18, 1871, p. 3.
9. "Putting prisoners to the torture." *New York Times*, September 17, 1871, p. 4.
10. "Laura Fair." *Colorado Daily Chieftain* [Pueblo], May 15, 1872, p. 2.
11. "The Pacific slope." *Colorado Daily Chieftain* [Pueblo], October 1, 1872, p. 1.
12. "The acquittal of Mrs. Fair." *New York Times*, October 1, 1872, p. 4.
13. "Western notes." *Deseret News* [Utah], October 30, 1872.
14. "Notice." *The Rolla Express* [Missouri], November 9, 1872, p. 3.
15. "California." *Rocky Mountain News* [Denver], November 22, 1872, p. 1.
16. "Telegrams in brief." *Rocky Mountain News* [Denver], February 8, 1873, p. 1.
17. "A murderer hanged." *Chicago Tribune*, June 21, 1872, p. 1.
18. "Hanging a woman." *Chicago Tribune*, June 24, 1872, p. 5.
19. "The execution of Phoebe Campbell." *The Globe* [Toronto], June 21, 1872, p. 4.
20. "A woman hanged in Georgia." *New York Times*, May 3, 1873, p. 3.
21. "Hanging a woman." *Chicago Tribune*, May 5, 1873, p. 8.
22. "News summary." *Brooklyn Eagle*, January 5, 1872, p. 2.
23. "The Paterson, N.J., tragedy." *Chicago Tribune*, January 8, 1872, p. 3.
24. "News summary." *Brooklyn Eagle*, January 9, 1872, p. 2.
25. "The Burroughs mystery." *New York Times*, January 9, 1872, p. 5; "The Burroughs murder." *New York Times*, April 26, 1872, p. 5.
26. "The Burroughs murder trial." *New York Times*, May 3 1872, p. 8.
27. "The Burroughs murder." *New York Times*, May 19, 1872, p. 5.
28. "News summary." *Brooklyn Eagle*, June 19, 1872, p. 2.
29. "Keeper Laverty's trial." *New York Times*, March 19, 1886, p. 5.
30. "Keeper Laverty's trial." *New York Times*, March 24, 1886, p. 5.
31. "A woman in prison twenty-nine years." *Ogden Standard Examiner* [Utah], November 21, 1901.

32. "Execution of a woman for the murder of her husband." *New York Times*, June 20, 1873, p. 1.
33. "The execution of Mrs. Workman." *The Globe* [Toronto], June 20, 1873, p. 1.
34. "A mother and son sentenced to death." *Fort Wayne Weekly Sentinel* [Indiana], December 1, 1875.
35. "Freed at last." *Brooklyn Eagle*, July 18, 1884, p. 4.
36. "The bill of fare." *Brooklyn Eagle*, August 17, 1880, p. 2.
37. "Freed at last." *Brooklyn Eagle*, July 18, 1884, p. 4.
38. "Beastly." *St. Louis Globe Democrat*, December 18, 1875, p. 1.
39. "A plea for clemency." *St. Louis Globe Democrat*, December 4, 1875, p. 4.
40. No title. *St. Louis Globe Democrat*, December 15, 1875, p. 4.
41. "High in air." *St. Louis Globe Democrat*, December 17, 1875, p. 1.
42. "Beastly." *St. Louis Globe Democrat*, December 18, 1875, p. 1.
43. "A woman sentenced to be hanged." *New York Times*, November 1, 1876, p. 2.
44. "A chivalrous judge." *New York Times*, November 2, 1876, p. 4.
45. "The mysterious assassination of Officer Smith." *Brooklyn Eagle*, August 3, 1878, p. 4.
46. Ibid.
47. "The murdered officer." *Brooklyn Eagle*, August 4, 1878, p. 4.
48. "The Jersey City mystery." *New York Times*, August 5, 1878, p. 8.
49. "Jennie Smith arraigned." *New York Times*, August 6, 1878, p. 8.
50. "Current events." *Brooklyn Eagle*, February 3, 1879, p. 2.
51. "One of the jury insane." *New York Times*, February 18, 1879, p. 3.
52. "Beginning the defense." *New York Times*, May 17, 1879, p. 8.
53. "Awaiting sentence for murder." *New York Times*, May 27, 1879, p. 2.
54. "To be hanged." *Brooklyn Eagle*, June 9, 1879, p. 4.
55. "Emma Abbott's appeal." *New York Times*, June 13, 1879, p. 8.
56. "A shocking defensive alliance." *Brooklyn Eagle*, June 14, 1879, p. 2.

57. "Acquitted." *Brooklyn Eagle*, February 1, 1880, p. 4.
58. "Feathers." *Brooklyn Eagle*, February 15, 1880, p. 2.
59. "Kate Sothern's crime." *Fort Wayne Daily Sentinel* [Indiana], May 9, 1878.
60. "A murder — and the sex." *Chicago Tribune*, May 19, 1878, p. 3.
61. "A shame to be avoided." *The Daily Constitution* [Atlanta], May 5, 1878.
62. "Ten years." *The Daily Constitution* [Atlanta], May 24, 1878.
63. "Kate Sothern." *The Daily Constitution* [Atlanta], May 30, 1878.
64. "Mrs. Sothern's triumph." *The Daily Constitution* [Atlanta], June 4, 1878.
65. "Kate Sothern." *New York Times*, June 21, 1878, p. 5.
66. "Quips." *Chicago Tribune*, July 14, 1878, p. 11.
67. "Kate Sothern pardoned." *Chicago Tribune*, April 1, 1882, p. 9.
68. "Killed while dancing." *New York Times*, September 9, 1883, p. 7.
69. "Female executions, the Espy file, 1632 to 1962."] users.bestweb.net/~rg/execution/females.htm; "Female hangings 1632 to 1900." geocities.com/trctl11/femhang.html?200726.

Chapter 5

1. "Strangled." *Brooklyn Eagle*, January 6, 1881, p. 4.
2. Ibid.
3. "Current events." *Brooklyn Eagle*, December 27, 1880. p. 2.
4. "The penalty paid." *Chicago Tribune*, January 7, 1881, p. 9.
5. "Trial by rope." *Reno Evening Gazette*, January 15, 1881.
6. "Strangled." *Brooklyn Eagle*, January 6, 1881, p. 4.
7. "A colored murderess hanged." *New York Times*, April 23, 1881, p. 2.
8. "Criminal news." *Chicago Tribune*, April 23, 1881, p. 2.
9. "A colored murderess hanged." *New York Times*, April 23, 1881, p. 2.
10. "Six murderers hanged." *New York Times*, February 4, 1881, p. 5.

11. "Sentences commuted." *Chicago Tribune*, November 22, 1882, p. 3.
12. "A confession of guilty." *Washington Post*, April 12, 1882, p. 4.
13. "A colored girl sentenced to death." *New York Times*, July 2, 1882, p. 1.
14. "Sentence commuted." *Chicago Tribune*, November 22, 1882, p. 3.
15. "United States." *Manitoba Daily Free Press* [Winnipeg], November 18, 1882.
16. "Sentence commuted." *Chicago Tribune*, November 22, 1882, p. 3.
17. "State news." *The Landmark* [Statesville, N.C.], January 20, 1882, p. 1.
18. "Finis for five." *The Atlanta Constitution*, October 21, 1882, p. 1.
19. "Wholesale hanging." *Fort Wayne Daily Gazette* [Indiana], June 24, 1882.
20. "Emiline Meaker hanged." *New York Times*, March 31, 1883, p. 2.
21. "The gallows." *Chicago Tribune*, March 31, 1883, p. 10.
22. "Emiline Meaker hanged." *New York Times*, March 31, 1883, p. 2.
23. "Latest telegrams." *Ogden Standard Examiner* [Utah], March 26, 1883.
24. "Unrepentant." *Chicago Tribune*, March 30, 1883, p. 12.
25. "Emiline Meaker hanged." *New York Times*, March 31, 1883, p. 2.
26. "The gallows." *Chicago Tribune*, March 31, 1883, p. 10.
27. "Frank Leslie's Sunday Magazine." *Denton Journal* [Maryland], April 14, 1883.
28. "Crimes and criminals." *New York Times*, March 3, 1883, p. 2.
29. "The gallows." *Chicago Tribune*, August 4, 1883, p. 7.
30. "Barbara Miller hanged." *New York Times*, September 15, 1883, p. 2.
31. "The gallows." *Brooklyn Eagle*, September 14, 1883, p. 4.
32. "A woman executed." *Chicago Tribune*, September 15, 1883, p. 7.
33. "An orgy at the gallows." *Chicago Tribune*, September 20, 1883, p. 4.
34. No title. *The Trenton Times*, September 17, 1883.
35. "The gallows." *Chicago Tribune*, October 20, 1883, p. 3.
36. "A woman hanged." *New York Times*, October 20, 1883, p. 2.

Notes—Chapter 5

37. "The gallows." *Chicago Tribune*, October 20, 1883, p. 3.
38. "A woman hanged." *New York Times*, October 20, 1883, p. 2.
39. "Hanging a woman in effigy." *Chester Times* [Pennsylvania], March 28, 1883.
40. "An aged wife's crime." *Chicago Tribune*, February 25, 1884, p. 1.
41. "A murderess doomed." *Chicago Tribune*, February 26, 1884, p. 1.
42. No title. *Decatur Weekly Republican* [Illinois], March 6, 1884.
43. "A death sentence commuted." *New York Times*, April 12, 1884, p. 5.
44. "Saved from the gallows." *New York Times*, April 13, 1884, p. 9.
45. "A horrible story." *Chicago Tribune*, January 17, 1885, p. 1.
46. "The murder of William Druse." *New York Times*, January 20, 1885, p. 5; "Mrs. Druse the murderer." *New York Times*, January 29, 1885, p. 3.
47. "Mrs. Druse sentenced to hang." *Brooklyn Eagle*, October 6, 1885, p. 4.
48. "A juror made insane." *New York Times*, January 5, 1886, p. 1.
49. "Governor Hill and the Druse murder case." *Brooklyn Eagle*, December 23, 1886, p. 2.
50. Ibid.
51. "Horrible crime of Mrs. Druse." *Chicago Tribune*, December 23, 1886, p. 1.
52. "Two months more of life." *New York Times*, December 23, 1886, p. 5.
53. Ibid.
54. "May a murderess be hanged?" *New York Times*, December 23, 1886, p. 4.
55. "The case of Mrs. Druse." *New York Times*, January 8, 1887, p. 2.
56. "Mrs. Druse likely to hang." *Brooklyn Eagle*, February 16, 1887, p. 6.
57. "She must hang." *Brooklyn Eagle*, February 18, 1887, p. 6.
58. "Women who murder to be hanged." *Brooklyn Eagle*, February 19, 1887, p. 2.
59. "The hanging of Mrs. Druse." *Chicago Tribune*, February 26, 1887, p. 14.
60. "No hope for Mrs. Druse." *Brooklyn Eagle*, February 27, 1887, p. 9.
61. "Mrs. Druse facing death." *New York Times*, February 27, 1887, p. 7.
62. "A murderess to hang." *Chicago Tribune*, February 28, 1887, p. 1.
63. "Roxie Druse's last Sunday." *New York Times*, February 28, 1887, p. 2.
64. Ibid.
65. "The Herkimer County murderess." *New York Times*, February 28, 1887, p. 4.
66. "The execution of Mrs. Druse at Herkimer." *Brooklyn Eagle*, February 28, 1887, p. 4.
67. "The Druse case." *Brooklyn Eagle*, March 1, 1887, p. 2.
68. "Roxalana Druse hanged." *New York Times*, March 1, 1887, p. 2.
69. "Petticoated politicians." *New York Times*, March 4, 1887, p. 5.
70. "A funeral sermon for Mrs. Druse." *New York Times*, March 7, 1887, p. 5.
71. "Death certificate of Mrs. Druse." *New York Times*, March 20, 1887, p. 6.
72. "Triple execution." *The Galveston Daily News*, August 1, 1885.
73. "Murderously poisoned." *Chicago Tribune*, August 12, 1886, p. 1.
74. "The Somerville Borgia." *New York Times*, August 14, 1886, p. 1.
75. "Charges against a doctor." *New York Times*, August 26, 1886, p. 1.
76. "Against all precedent." *New York Times*, March 6, 1887, p. 3.
77. "The Somerville poisoner." *New York Times*, February 7, 1888, p. 1; "To apply for commutation." *New York Times*, July 10, 1888, p. 5; "Her neck saved." *New York Times*, November 13, 1888, p. 1.
78. "Died in jail." *Ogden Standard Examiner* [Utah], January 5, 1906.
79. "Sadie Hayes' chances for life." *Chicago Tribune*, January 3, 1886, p. 11; "Missouri state news." *The Rolla New Era* [Missouri], March 20, 1886, p. 2; "Sentenced to ninety-nine years." *New York Times*, January 25, 1887, p. 3.
80. "Will not be hung." *Daily Advocate* [Newark, N. J.], January 22, 1889.
81. "Twelve-year-old girl to be hanged." *New York Times*, July 21, 1887, p. 2.
82. "Her sentence commuted." *Chicago Tribune*, August 27, 1887, p. 1.
83. "The murder rehearsed." *New York Times*, May 27, 1887, p. 10.
84. Ibid.
85. "Very near the gallows." *New York Times*, May 28, 1887, p. 8.
86. "Another woman on the way to the

gallows." *Brooklyn Eagle*, May 28, 1887, p. 4.

87. "Facing a noose." *Brooklyn Eagle*, June 3, 1887, p. 6.

88. "Capital punishment." *Deseret News* [Utah], June 15, 1887.

89. "Mrs. Cignarale's appeal." *New York Times*, July 1, 1887, p. 5.

90. "Pleading for a life." *New York Times*, July 12, 1887, p. 3.

91. "Pleading for Cignarale." *New York Times*, July 11, 1888, p. 8.

92. "Mercy for Mrs. Cignarale." *New York Times*, July 27, 1888, p. 8.

93. "Mrs. Cignarale on the island." *New York Times*, July 31, 1888, p. 8.

94. "A mother's confession." *Hartford Courant*, June 13, 1888, p. 1.

95. "She murdered her husband." *Hartford Courant*, June 16, 1888, p. 1.

96. "Killed her husband too." *New York Times*, June 16, 1888, p. 3.

97. "Convicted of murder." *New York Times*, November 29, 1888, p. 5.

98. "Without fear." *Brooklyn Eagle*, June 25, 1889, p. 6.

99. "Milly Poteat's crime." *Washington Post*, October 15, 1888, p. 1.

100. "First since the war." *Mitchell Daily Republican* [South Dakota], October 15, 1888.

101. "Female executions, the Espy file, 1632 to 1962." users.bestweb.net/~rg/execution/females.htm; "Female hangings 1632 to 1900." geocities.com/trctl11/femhang.html? 200726.

Chapter 6

1. "Miles Fawcett." *Deseret News* [Utah], June 28, 1890.

2. "The Potts tragedy." *Deseret News* [Utah], July 5, 1890.

3. Ibid.; "Miles Fawcett." *Deseret News* [Utah], June 28, 1890.

4. "A Nevada hanging." *Aspen Weekly Times* [Colorado], June 21, 1890, p. 1.

5. "Husband and wife on the gallows." *Chicago Tribune*, June 21, 1890, p. 5.

6. "Man and wife hanged." *Cranbury Press* [New Jersey], June 27, 1890, p. 4.

7. "Two will be hanged." *Manitoba Daily Free Press* [Winnipeg], September 15, 1890, p. 2.

8. "Dead on the gallows." *Los Angeles Times*, January 23, 1892, p. 5.

9. "A man was to hang today." *San Antonio Daily Light*, June 22, 1893, p. 1; "Mrs. Agnes Myers' life in the hands of Governor Folk." *Washington Post*, July 15, 1906, p. 8.

10. "Three of a kind." *Sandusky Daily Register* [Ohio], October 8, 1892, p. 1.

11. "Young girl hanged in South Carolina." *Brooklyn Eagle*, October 7, 1892, p. 12; "Three of a kind." *Sandusky Daily Register* [Ohio], October 8, 1892, p. 1; "One state's five hangings." *Washington Post*, October 8, 1892, p. 1.

12. "Dead on the gallows." *Los Angeles Times*, January 23, 1892, p. 5.

13. "The Burlingham murders." *New York Times*, September 6, 1893, p. 1.

14. "The Halliday murder case." *New York Times*, September 7, 1893, p. 8.

15. "Paul Halliday's body found." *New York Times*, September 8, 1893, p. 8.

16. "Mrs. Halliday is in Monticello jail." *Chicago Tribune*, September 9, 1893, p. 6.

17. "Mrs. Halliday in jail." *New York Times*, September 9, 1893, p. 5.

18. "Distrusted Mrs. Halliday." *New York Times*, September 12, 1893, p. 9.

19. "Mrs. Halliday not insane." *New York Times*, September 12, 1893, p. 9.

20. "Mrs. Halliday's case called." *New York Times*, June 19, 1894, p. 9.

21. "Mrs. Halliday was insane." *New York Times*, November 7, 1893, p. 5.

22. "Mrs. Halliday tries to burn jail." *New York Times*, November 24, 1893, p. 1; "Mrs. Halliday's case called." *New York Times*, June 19, 1894, p. 9.

23. "Mrs. Halliday found guilty." *New York Times*, June 22, 1894, p. 5.

24. "Mrs. Halliday must die." *New York Times*, June 23, 1894, p. 9.

25. No title. *Washington Post*, June 23, 1894, p. 4.

26. "Criminal law and the insane." *New York Times*, June 24, 1894, p. 4.

27. "Lizzie Halliday eats nothing." *Brooklyn Eagle*, June 24, 1894, p. 24.

28. "Bitten by Lizzie Halliday." *Brooklyn Eagle*, August 24, 1894, p. 10.

Notes—Chapter 6

29. "Assault by lunatics." *Chicago Tribune*, September 2, 1895, p. 2.
30. "Cuts his throat with a razor." *Brooklyn Eagle*, April 26, 1895, p. 16.
31. "Maudlin sentiment in parallel." *New York Times*, April 28, 1895, p. 16.
32. "Maria Barberi at the bar." *Brooklyn Eagle*, July 11, 1895, p. 2.
33. "Maria Barberi sentenced." *Brooklyn Eagle*, July 18, 1895, p. 4.
34. "The Barberi case appealed." *Brooklyn Eagle*, July 19, 1895, p. 12.
35. "Maria Barbella to die." *New York Times*, July 19, 1895, p. 2; "Trying to save Maria Barbella." *New York Times*, July 23, 1895, p. 8.
36. No title. *New York Times*, July 24, 1895, p. 4.
37. "The case of Maria Barberi." *Chicago Tribune*, July 25, 1895, p. 6.
38. "To save Maria Barberi." *Chicago Tribune*, July 26, 1895, p. 10.
39. "Conference of colored men." *New York Times*, July 30, 1895, p. 6.
40. "In behalf of Maria Barbella." *New York Times*, August 1, 1895, p. 3.
41. "Maria Barberi not an innocent." *Brooklyn Eagle*, August 3, 1895, p. 6.
42. "Woman suffrage and the Barberi case." *New York Times*, August 8, 1895, p. 4.
43. "Maria Barberi a costly prisoner." *New York Times*, March 13, 1896, p. 11.
44. "Maria Barberi." *Brooklyn Eagle*, November 17, 1896, p. 6.
45. "Barbella jury completed." *New York Times*, November 18, 1896, p. 7.
46. "Maria Barberi's family tree." *Chicago Tribune*, November 21, 1896, p. 4.
47. "Maria Barberi is free." *Chicago Tribune*, December 11, 1896, p. 5; "Maria Barberi's acquittal." *Brooklyn Eagle*, December 11, 1896, p. 6.
48. "The hanging of a woman." *Lincoln Evening News* [Nebraska], April 15, 1895; "Morning telegraph briefs." *Ogden Standard Examiner* [Utah], December 15, 1894.
49. "The hanging of a woman." *Lincoln Evening News* [Nebraska], April 15, 1895; "Will serve twenty-five years." *Brooklyn Eagle*, May 5, 1895, p. 8.
50. "Woman to be executed." *The Daily Light* [San Antonio], February 5, 1898.
51. "Will execute a woman." *New York Times*, December 2, 1897, p. 3.
52. "Mrs. Nobles sentenced again." *New York Times*, February 13, 1898, p. 2.
53. "Husband-slayer dies." *The Constitution* [Atlanta], February 7, 1916.
54. "An inhuman mother hanged." *The News* [Frederick, Maryland], July 17, 1896.
55. "Crime of a female fiend." *Daily Journal* [Telluride, Colorado], February 8, 1898, p. 1.
56. "A woman's triple crime." *New York Times*, February 8, 1898, p. 5.
57. "Mrs. Place convicted." *New York Times*, July 9, 1898, p. 4.
58. "Martha Place sentenced." *New York Times*, July 13, 1898, p. 12.
59. "The Place murder case." *Deseret News* [Utah], July 23, 1898.
60. "Mrs. Place's appeal in vain." *New York Times*, January 11, 1899, p. 3.
61. No title. *Salt Lake Tribune*, January 18, 1899.
62. "Woman faces death in the chair." *Chicago Tribune*, February 4, 1899, p. 2.
63. "Bill to save Mrs. Place from death." *New York Times*, February 7, 1899, p. 5.
64. "Capital punishment bill." *New York Times*, March 14, 1899, p. 3.
65. "Women and discrimination in law." *Brooklyn Eagle*, February 15, 1899, p. 4.
66. "No mercy for Mrs. Place." *New York Times*, February 16, 1899, p. 5.
67. "Mrs. Martha Place must die." *Chicago Tribune*, March 16, 1899, p. 1.
68. "Woman electrocuted." *Ogden Standard Examiner* [Utah], March 20, 1899.
69. "Capital punishment." *New York Times*, March 21, 1899, p. 6.
70. "Mrs. Place's brain cremated." *New York Times*, February 2, 1900, p. 3.
71. "Hanging of a woman." *Ogden Standard Examiner* [Utah], March 10, 1899; "Disorder at woman's hanging." *Chicago Tribune*, March 11, 1899, p. 13.
72. "Young girl hanged." *Ogden Standard Examiner* [Utah], December 27, 1899.
73. "Female executions, the Espy file, 1632 to 1962." users.bestweb.net/~rg/execution/females.htm; "Female hangings 1632 to 1900." geocities.com/trctl11/femhang.html?200726.

Bibliography

"Accident on the Long Island Railroad." *Brooklyn Eagle*, June 27, 1855, p. 2.
"The acquittal of Mrs. Fair." *New York Times*, October 1, 1872, p. 4.
"Acquitted." *Brooklyn Eagle*, February 1, 1880, p. 4.
"Affairs at Albany." *New York Times*, April 19, 1859, p. 4.
"After eighteen years." *New York Times*, December 26, 1886, p. 1.
"After thirty years' work." *Brooklyn Eagle*, March 23, 1895, p. 12.
"Against all precedent." *New York Times*, March 6, 1887, p. 3.
"An aged wife's crime." *Chicago Tribune*, February 25, 1884, p. 1.
"Albany matters." *New York Times*, March 4, 1859, p. 1.
"The American Borgia." *New York Times*, January 20, 1866, p. 8.
"American female executions 1900–2005." geocities.com/trctl11/amfem.html?200726.
"Ann Hoag, the murderess." *New York Times*, April 21, 1852, p. 2.
"Another woman on the way to the gallows." *Brooklyn Eagle*, May 28, 1887, p. 4.
"Arrest of the Albany murderess." *New York Times*, July 14, 1858, p. 1.
"The assassination conspiracy." *Chicago Tribune*, May 4, 1865, p. 1.
"Assault by lunatics." *Chicago Tribune*, September 2, 1895, p. 2.
"Awaiting sentence for murder." *New York Times*, May 27, 1879, p. 2.
"Barbara Miller hanged." *New York Times*, September 15, 1883, p. 2.
"Barbella jury completed." *New York Times*, November 18, 1896, p. 7.
"The Barberi case appealed." *Brooklyn Eagle*, July 19, 1895, p. 12.
"Beastly." *St. Louis Globe Democrat*, December 18, 1875, p. 1.
Beecher, Henry Ward. "Mr. Beecher on hanging." *Brooklyn Eagle*, January 23, 1887, p. 11.
"Beginning the defense." *New York Times*, May 17, 1879, p. 8.
Bessler, John D. *Legacy of Violence: Lynch Mobs and Executions in Minnesota*. Minneapolis: University of Minnesota Press, 2002.
"The bill of fare." *Brooklyn Eagle*, August 17, 1880, p. 2.
"Bill to save Mrs. Place from death." *New York Times*, February 7, 1899, p. 5.
"Bitten by Lizzie Halliday." *Brooklyn Eagle*, August 24, 1894, p. 10.
"Bridget Durgan." *New York Times*, August 28, 1867, p. 5.
"The Burlingham murders." *New York Times*, September 6, 1893, p. 1.
"The Burroughs murder." *New York Times*, April 26, 1872, p. 5.
"The Burroughs murder." *New York Times*, May 19, 1872, p. 5.
"The Burroughs murder trial." *New York Times*, May 3, 1872, p. 8.
"The Burroughs mystery." *New York Times*, January 9, 1872, p. 5.

Bibliography

"California." *Rocky Mountain News* [Denver], November 22, 1872, p. 1.

"Capital punishment." *Deseret News* [Utah], June 15, 1887.

"Capital punishment." *Leadville Evening Chronicle* [Colorado], January 18, 1892, p. 2.

"Capital punishment." *New York Times*, March 21, 1899, p. 6.

"Capital punishment bill." *New York Times*, March 14, 1899, p. 3.

"The case of Maria Barberi." *Chicago Tribune*, July 25, 1895, p. 6.

"The case of Mrs. Druse." *New York Times*, January 8, 1887, p. 2.

"The case of Mrs. Hartung." *New York Times*, February 8, 1859, p. 5.

"The case of Mrs. Hartung." *New York Times*, December 21, 1861, p. 4.

"The case of Mrs. Hartung — a new trial denied." *New York Times*, December 20, 1859, p. 2.

"The case of Mrs. Surratt." *Brooklyn Eagle*, July 18, 1865, p. 2.

"The case of Mrs. Victor, the poisoner." *New York Times*, July 16, 1868, p. 2.

"Character in murder." *St. Louis Globe Democrat*, December 17, 1875, p. 5.

"Charges against a doctor." *New York Times*, August 26, 1886, p. 1.

"A chivalrous judge." *New York Times*, November 2, 1876, p. 4.

"The Cleveland tragedy." *New York Times*, June 27, 1868, p. 1.

"A colored girl sentenced to death." *New York Times*, July 2, 1882, p. 1.

"A colored murderess hanged." *New York Times*, April 23, 1881, p. 2.

"Conference of colored men." *New York Times*, July 30, 1895, p. 6.

"The confession of Bridget Durgan, the New Jersey murderess." *Chicago Tribune*, September 2, 1867, p. 1.

"A confession of guilty." *Washington Post*, April 12, 1882, p. 4.

"Confession of two of the McKeesport murderers." *Brooklyn Eagle*, December 1, 1857, p. 2.

"Convicted of murder." *New York Times*, November 29, 1888, p. 5.

"The Coriell murder." *New York Times*, June 1, 1867, p. 2.

"The Coriell murder." *New York Times*, June 3, 1867, p. 4–5.

"The Coriell murder." *New York Times*, June 18, 1867, p. 8.

"The Coriell murder." *New York Times*, May 21, 1867, p. 1.

"Crime of a female fiend." *Daily Journal* [Telluride, Colorado], February 8, 1898, p. 1.

"Crimes and criminals." *New York Times*, *New York Times*, March 3, 1883, p. 2.

"Criminal law and the insane." *New York Times*, June 24, 1894, p. 4.

"Criminal news." *Chicago Tribune*, April 23, 1881, p. 2.

"The criminals and their counsel." *Brooklyn Eagle*, May 13, 1865, p. 3.

"Current events." *Brooklyn Eagle*, February 3, 1879, p. 2.

"Current events." *Brooklyn Eagle*, December 27, 1880, p. 2.

"Cuts his throat with a razor." *Brooklyn Eagle*, April 26, 1895, p. 16.

"Daily news." *Rocky Mountain News* [Denver], May 3, 1871, p. 2.

"Dead on the gallows." *Los Angeles Times*, January 23, 1892, p. 5.

"Death certificate of Mrs. Druse." *New York Times*, March 20, 1887, p. 6.

"Death of a murderess." *New York Times*, November 13, 1855, p. 8.

"Death of a murderess." *Tioga County Agitator* [Wellsboro, Pa.], November 29, 1855.

"The death penalty for women." *New York Times*, August 20, 1899, p. 17.

"A death sentence commuted." *New York Times*, April 12, 1884, p. 5.

"The diamond murder." *Brooklyn Eagle*, August 4, 1863, p. 2.

"Did she deserve to be hanged?" *Brooklyn Eagle*, July 8, 1865, p. 3.

"Died in jail." *Ogden Standard Examiner* [Utah], January 5, 1906.

"Digest of news." *Galveston Daily News*, December 4, 1869.
"Discharge of Mary Hartung." *New York Times*, March 26, 1863, p. 5.
"Disorder at woman's hanging." *Chicago Tribune*, March 11, 1899, p. 13.
"Distrusted Mrs. Halliday." *New York Times*, September 12, 1893, p. 9.
"The double murder at Keesport, Pa." *Hartford Courant*, May 6, 1857, p. 3.
"The double murder near Pittsburg." *Brooklyn Eagle*, May 11, 1857, p. 2.
"A double tragedy." *New York Times*, July 31, 1852, p. 3.
"Dr. Mudd, Arnold and O'Loughlin imprisoned for life." *Brooklyn Eagle*, July 6, 1865, p. 3.
"The Druse case." *Brooklyn Eagle*, March 1, 1887, p. 2.
"Emiline Meaker hanged." *New York Times*, March 31, 1883, p. 2.
"Emma Abbott's appeal." *New York Times*, June 13, 1879, p. 8.
"The end of Durgan, the murderess." *New York Times*, August 31, 1867, p. 4.
"European chit-chat." *Brooklyn Eagle*, June 23, 1856, p. 2.
"Evidence of a party." *New York Times*, February 9, 1859, p. 4.
"Execution." *Hartford Courant*, February 13, 1858, p. 3.
"Execution of a murderess." *The Daily Gazette* [Davenport, Iowa], March 29, 1860.
"Execution of a murderess — letter from Governor Hunt." *New York Times*, July 24, 1852, p. 4.
"Execution of a woman." *Defiance Democrat* [Defiance, Ohio], November 6, 1858.
"Execution of a woman at Danville, Pa." *Chicago Tribune*, October 27, 1858, p. 2.
"Execution of a woman for the murder of her husband." *New York Times*, June 20, 1873, p. 1.
"Execution of Bridget Durgan." *New York Times*, August 31, 1867, p. 8.

"The execution of Mrs. Druse at Herkimer." *Brooklyn Eagle*, February 28, 1887, p. 4.
"The execution of Mrs. Grinder." *New York Times*, January 21, 1866, p. 1.
"The execution of Mrs. Workman." *The Globe* [Toronto], June 20, 1873, p. 1.
"The execution of Phoebe Campbell." *The Globe* [Toronto] June 21, 1872, p. 4.
"The execution of women." *New York Times*, January 22, 1866, p. 4.
"Executive clemency denied in the case of Mrs. Hartung." *New York Times*, April 9, 1859, p. 11.
"Facing a noose." *Brooklyn Eagle*, June 3, 1887, p. 6.
"Feathers." *Brooklyn Eagle*, February 15, 1880, p. 2.
"The female Borgia." *Chicago Tribune*, September 22, 1866, p. 2.
"Female convicted of murder." *Brooklyn Eagle*, December 9, 1853, p. 4.
"Female executions, the Espy file, 1632 to 1962." users.bestweb.net/~rg/execution/females.htm.
"Female hangings 1632 to 1900." geocities.com/trctl11/femhang.html?200726.
"Female murderers." *Rocky Mountain News Weekly* [Denver], May 8, 1872, p. 1.
"Finis for five." *The Atlanta Constitution*, October 21, 1882, p. 1.
"First since the war." *Mitchell Daily Republican* [South Dakota], October 15, 1888.
"Frank Leslie's Sunday Magazine." *Denton Journal* [Maryland], April 14, 1883.
"Freed at last." *Brooklyn Eagle*, July 18, 1884, p. 4.
"From Albany." *New York Times*, January 27, 1860, p. 5.
"From Pittsburgh." *Chicago Tribune*, November 27, 1865, p. 3.
"From Washington." *Chicago Tribune*, May 15, 1865, p. 1.
"A funeral sermon for Mrs. Druse." *New York Times*, March 7, 1887, p. 5.
"The gallows." *Chicago Tribune*, March 31, 1883, p. 10.
"The gallows." *Chicago Tribune*, August 4, 1883, p. 7.

"The gallows." *Brooklyn Eagle*, September 14, 1883, p. 4.

"The gallows." *Chicago Tribune*, October 20, 1883, p. 3.

"The gallows in Maryland." *New York Herald*, February 11, 1871, p. 6.

"Gleanings from the mails." *New York Times*, January 10, 1881, p. 3.

"Governor Hill and the Druse murder case." *Brooklyn Eagle*, December 23, 1886, p. 2.

"The Grinder poisoning case." *Chicago Tribune*, October 26, 1865, p. 3.

"The Halliday murder case." *New York Times*, September 7, 1893, p. 8.

"Hanging a woman." *Chicago Tribune*, June 24, 1872, p. 5.

"Hanging a woman." *Chicago Tribune*, May 5, 1873, p. 8.

"Hanging a woman." *New York Times*, July 21, 1855, p. 4.

"Hanging a woman in effigy." *Chester Times* [Pennsylvania], March 28, 1883.

"The hanging of a woman." *Hartford Courant*, September 2, 1867, p. 4.

"The hanging of a woman." *Lincoln Evening News* [Nebraska], April 15, 1895.

"Hanging of a woman." *Ogden Standard Examiner* [Utah], March 10, 1899.

"Hanging of men and women." *New York Times*, February 20, 1887, p. 8.

"The hanging of Mrs. Druse." *Chicago Tribune*, February 26, 1887, p. 14.

"The hanging of women." *Brooklyn Eagle*, June 11, 1896, p. 6.

"The hanging of women." *Hartford Courant*, May 30, 1887, p. 2.

"The hanging of women." *New York Times*, April 15, 1859, p. 4.

"Henrietta Robinson — the prisoner at Troy." *New York Times*, June 9, 1854, p. 1.

"Her neck saved." *New York Times*, November 13, 1888, p. 1.

"Her sentence commuted." *Chicago Tribune*, August 27, 1887, p. 1.

"The Herkimer County murderess." *New York Times*, February 28, 1887, p. 4.

"Hester Vaughn." *New York Times*, December 2, 1868, p. 5.

"High in the air." *St. Louis Globe Democrat*, December 17, 1875, p. 1.

"History's mysteries." *Davis County Clipper* [Utah], August 8, 1922.

"Horrible crime of Mrs. Druse." *Chicago Tribune*, December 23, 1886, p. 1.

"A horrible murder." *Chicago Tribune*, March 2, 1867, p. 3.

"A horrible story." *Chicago Tribune*, January 17, 1885, p. 1.

"How they received the tidings." *Brooklyn Eagle*, July 7, 1865, p. 2.

"Husband and wife on the gallows." *Chicago Tribune*, June 21, 1890, p. 5.

"Husband-slayer dies." *The Constitution* [Atlanta], February 7, 1916.

"The Hyde case." *Brooklyn Eagle*, April 22, 1872, p. 2.

"Illumination at Flatlands." *Brooklyn Eagle*, November 27, 1844, p. 2.

"In behalf of Maria Barbella." *New York Times*, August 1, 1895, p. 3.

"An inhuman mother hanged." *The News* [Frederick, Maryland], July 17, 1896.

"Insanity in criminal cases." *Chicago Tribune*, August 31, 1865, p. 2.

"Jennie Smith arraigned." *New York Times*, August 6, 1878, p. 8.

"The Jersey City mystery." *New York Times*, August 5, 1878, p. 8.

"A juror made insane." *New York Times*, January 5, 1886, p. 1.

"Kate Sothern." *The Daily Constitution* [Atlanta], May 30, 1878.

"Kate Sothern." *New York Times*, June 21, 1878, p. 5.

"Kate Sothern pardoned." *Chicago Tribune*, April 1, 1882, p. 9.

"Kate Sothern's crime." *Fort Wayne Daily Sentinel* [Indiana], May 9, 1878.

"K.C. mail." *Liberty Weekly Tribune* [Missouri], December 2, 1881, p. 2.

"Keeper Laverty's trial." *New York Times*, March 19, 1886, p. 5.

"Keeper Laverty's trial." *New York Times*, March 24, 1886, p. 3.

Bibliography

"Killed her husband too." *New York Times*, June 16, 1888, p. 3.
"Killed while dancing." *New York Times*, September 9, 1883, p. 7.
"Latest telegrams." *Ogden Standard Examiner* [Utah], March 26, 1883.
"Laura D. Fair." *Colorado Weekly Chieftain* [Pueblo], May 4, 1871, p. 1.
"Laura Fair." *Colorado Daily Chieftain* [Pueblo], May 15, 1872, p. 2.
"Life in Sing Sing prison." *Brooklyn Eagle*, August 23, 1860, p. 1.
"Lizzie Halliday eats nothing." *Brooklyn Eagle*, June 24, 1894, p. 24.
Leonard, Stephen J. *Lynching in Colorado, 1859–1919*. Boulder, Colorado: University Press of Colorado, 2002.
"Man and wife hanged." *Cranberry Press* [New Jersey], June 27, 1890, p. 4.
"A man was to hang today." *San Antonio Daily Light*, June 22, 1893, p. 1.
"Maria Barbella to die." *New York Times*, July 19, 1895, p. 2.
"Maria Barberi." *Brooklyn Eagle*, November 17, 1896, p. 6.
"Maria Barberi a costly prisoner." *New York Times*, March 13, 1896, p. 11.
"Maria Barberi at the bar." *Brooklyn Eagle*, July 11, 1895, p. 2.
"Maria Barberi is free." *Chicago Tribune*, December 11, 1896, p. 5.
"Maria Barberi not an innocent." *Brooklyn Eagle*, August 3, 1985, p. 6.
"Maria Barberi sentenced." *Brooklyn Eagle*, July 18, 1895, p. 4.
"Maria Barberi's acquittal." *Brooklyn Eagle*, December 11, 1896, p. 6.
"Maria Barberi's family tree." *Chicago Tribune*, November 21, 1896, p. 4.
"Martha Place sentenced." *New York Times*, July 13, 1898, p. 12.
"Mary Hartung cast down." *New York Times*, December 21, 1859, p. 3.
"Mary Hartung discharged." *Brooklyn Eagle*, March 26, 1863, p. 2.
"Mary Runkle, the murderess." *The Sandusky Clarion* [Ohio], December 7, 1847.

"Maudlin sentiment in parallel." *New York Times*, April 28, 1895, p. 16.
"May a murderess be hanged?" *New York Times*, December 23, 1886, p. 4.
"Meeting of women in behalf of Hester Vaughn." *Hartford Courant*, December 2, 1868, p. 3.
"Mercy for Mrs. Cignarale." *New York Times*, July 27, 1888, p. 8.
"Miles Fawcett." *Deseret News* [Utah], June 28, 1890.
"Milly Poteat's crime." *Washington Post*, October 15, 1888, p. 1.
"Minor topics." *New York Times*, May 6, 1871, p. 4.
"Miscellaneous items." *Brooklyn Eagle*, May 8, 1857, p. 1.
"Missouri state news." *The Rolla New Era* [Missouri], March 20, 1886, p. 2.
"More about Mrs. Grinder." *Chicago Tribune*, September 21, 1865, p. 3.
"Morning telegraph briefs." *Ogden Standard Examiner* [Utah], December 15, 1894.
"A mother and son sentenced to death." *Fort Wayne Weekly Sentinel* [Indiana], December 1, 1875.
"A mother's confession." *Hartford Courant*, June 13, 1888, p. 1.
"Mrs. Agnes Myers' life in the hands of Governor Folk." *Washington Post*, July 15, 1906, p. 8.
"Mrs. Cignarale on the island." *New York Times*, July 31, 1888, p. 8.
"Mrs. Cignarale's appeal." *New York Times*, July 1, 1887, p. 5.
"Mrs. Druse facing death." *New York Times*, February 27, 1887, p. 7.
"Mrs. Druse likely to hang." *Brooklyn Eagle*, February 16, 1887, p. 6.
"Mrs. Druse sentenced to hang." *Brooklyn Eagle*, October 6, 1885, p. 4.
"Mrs. Druse the murderer." *New York Times*, January 29, 1885, p. 3.
"Mrs. Elizabeth Oakes Smith's account of a visit to Bridget Durgan." *New York Times*, August 25, 1867, p. 6.
"Mrs. Grinder — further developments."

Bibliography

Brooklyn Eagle, September 18, 1865, p. 4.

"Mrs. Halliday found guilty." *New York Times*, June 22, 1894, p. 5.

"Mrs. Halliday in jail." *New York Times*, September 9, 1893, p. 5.

"Mrs. Halliday is in Monticello jail." *Chicago Tribune*, September 9, 1893, p. 6.

"Mrs. Halliday must die." *New York Times*, June 23, 1894, p. 9.

"Mrs. Halliday not insane." *New York Times*, September 12, 1893, p. 9.

"Mrs. Halliday tries to burn jail." *New York Times*, November 24, 1893, p. 1.

"Mrs. Halliday was insane." *New York Times*, November 7, 1893, p. 5.

"Mrs. Halliday's case called." *New York Times*, June 19, 1894, p. 9.

"Mrs. Hartung." *Brooklyn Eagle*, April 9, 1859, p. 2.

"Mrs. Hartung's case." *New York Times*, April 9, 1959, p. 4.

"Mrs. Hartung's case." *New York Times*, April 11, 1859, p. 4.

"Mrs. Henrietta Robinson not Mrs. Wood — who is she?" *New York Times*, November 14, 1856, p. 5.

"Mrs. Laura Fair." *New York Times*, July 18, 1871, p. 3.

"Mrs. Nobles sentenced again." *New York Times*, February 13, 1898, p. 2.

"Mrs. Place convicted." *New York Times*, July 9, 1898, p. 4.

"Mrs. Place must die." *Chicago Tribune*, March 16, 1899, p. 1.

"Mrs. Place's appeal in vain." *New York Times*, January 11, 1899, p. 3.

"Mrs. Place's brain cremated." *New York Times*, February 2, 1900, p. 3.

"Mrs. Sothern's triumph." *The Daily Constitution* [Atlanta], June 4, 1878.

"Mrs. Surratt." *Chicago Tribune*, July 18, 1865, p. 1.

"Mrs. Victor." *Brooklyn Eagle*, July 10, 1868, p. 2.

"Mrs. Victor, convicted of murder, reprieved by the Governor of Ohio." *New York Times*, July 17, 1868, p. 1.

"Murder." *Brooklyn Eagle*, August 27, 1847, p. 2.

"Murder." *St. Louis Globe Democrat*, December 9, 1875, p. 3.

"A murder — and the sex." *Chicago Tribune*, May 19, 1878, p. 3.

"The murder of William Druse." *New York Times*, January 20, 1885, p. 5.

"The murder rehearsed." *New York Times*, May 27, 1887, p. 10.

"Murder trials." *New York Times*, May 26, 1854, p. 3.

"The murdered officer." *Brooklyn Eagle*, August 4, 1878, p. 4.

"A murderer hanged." *Chicago Tribune*, June 21, 1872, p. 1.

"A murderess doomed." *Chicago Tribune*, February 26, 1884, p. 1.

"A murderess reprieved." *New York Times*, July 27, 1869, p. 5.

"A murderess to hang." *Chicago Tribune*, February 28, 1887, p. 1.

"Murderously poisoned." *Chicago Tribune*, August 12, 1886, p. 1.

"The mysterious assassination of Officer Smith." *Brooklyn Eagle*, August 3, 1878, p. 4.

"A Nevada hanging." *Aspen Weekly Times* [Colorado], June 21, 1890, p. 1.

"New mode of hanging." *The Adams Sentinel* [Gettysburg, Pa.], November 29, 1847.

"News summary." *Brooklyn Eagle*, January 5, 1872, p. 2.

"News summary." *Brooklyn Eagle*, January 9, 1872, p. 2.

"News summary." *Brooklyn Eagle*, June 19, 1872, p. 2.

"The night before the murder." *Brooklyn Eagle*, May 3, 1865, p. 2.

"No hope for Mrs. Druse." *Brooklyn Eagle*, February 27, 1887, p. 9.

"No mercy for Mrs. Place." *New York Times*, February 16, 1899, p. 5.

"No sex in crime." *Brooklyn Eagle*, June 28, 1896, p. 6.

No title. *Decatur Weekly Republican* [Illinois], March 6, 1884.

Bibliography

No title. *Hartford Courant*, July 31, 1879, p. 2.

No title. *Liberty Weekly Tribune* [Missouri], July 14, 1865, p. 2.

No title. *Liberty Weekly Tribune* [Missouri], September 4, 1868, p. 4.

No title. *New York Times*, July 24, 1895, p. 4.

No title. *New York Times*, March 1, 1887, p. 4.

No title. *Reno Weekly Gazette and Stockman*, November 28, 1889, p. 4.

No title. *Salt Lake Tribune*, January 18, 1899.

No title. *St. Louis Globe Democrat*, December 15, 1875, p. 4.

No title. *The Trenton Times*, September 17, 1883.

No title. *Washington Post*, June 23, 1894, p. 4.

"Notice." *The Rolla Express* [Missouri], November 9, 1872, p. 3.

"One of the jury insane." *New York Times*, February 18, 1879, p. 3.

"One state's five hangings." *Washington Post*, October 8, 1892, p. 1.

"An orgy at the gallows." *Chicago Tribune*, September 20, 1883, p. 4.

"The Pacific slope." *Colorado Daily Chieftain* [Pueblo], October 1, 1872, p. 1.

"The Paterson, N. J., tragedy." *Chicago Tribune*, January 8, 1872, p. 3.

"Paul Halliday's body found." *New York Times*, September 8, 1893, p. 8.

"The penalty paid." *Chicago Tribune*, January 7, 1881, p. 9.

"Personal and political." *Hartford Courant*, May 20, 1869, p. 2.

"Petticoated politicians." *New York Times*, March 4, 1887, p. 5.

"The Pittsburgh Borgia." *Brooklyn Eagle*, October 27, 1865, p. 4.

"The Pittsburgh Borgia." *New York Times*, October 31, 1865, p. 5.

"The Pittsburgh poisoner." *Brooklyn Eagle*, December 2, 1865, p. 2.

"The Place murder case." *Deseret News* [Utah], July 23, 1898.

"A plea for clemency." *St. Louis Globe Democrat*, December 4, 1875, p. 4.

"Pleading for a life." *New York Times*, July 12, 1887, p. 3.

"Pleading for Cignarale." *New York Times*, July 11, 1888, p. 8.

"Poetry and murder." *Brooklyn Eagle*, July 13, 1857, p. 3.

"Political notes." *Brooklyn Eagle*, June 24, 1887, p. 4.

"The Potts tragedy." *Deseret News* [Utah], July 5, 1890.

"The president and Mrs. Surratt." *Chicago Tribune*, August 6, 1867, p. 2.

"The president on capital punishment." *New York Times*, March 26, 1880, p. 2.

"The price of a vote." *Daily Register Call* [Central City, Colorado], April 28, 1871, p. 1.

"Proposition to abolish capital punishment of females in England." *Brooklyn Eagle*, July 12, 1866, p. 4.

"Putting prisoners to the torture." *New York Times*, September 17, 1871, p. 4.

"Quips." *Chicago Tribune*, July 14, 1878, p. 11.

"Roxalana Druse hanged." *New York Times*, March 1, 1887, p. 2.

"Roxie Druse's last Sunday." *New York Times*, February 28, 1887, p. 2.

"Sadie Hayes' chances for life." *Chicago Tribune*, January 3, 1886, p. 11.

"Saved from the gallows." *New York Times*, April 13, 1884, p. 9.

"The scaffold." *Chicago Tribune*, March 8, 1868, p. 3.

"Sentence commuted." *Chicago Tribune*, November 22, 1882, p. 3.

"Sentence of death upon Mary Hartung." *New York Times*, March 5, 1859, p. 2.

"Sentence of Henrietta Robinson." *Brooklyn Eagle*, June 20, 1895, p. 2.

"The sentence of Mrs. Fair." *Daily Register Call* [Central City, Colorado], June 11, 1871, p. 1.

"The sentence of Mrs. Victor — her appearance in the court-room." *Brooklyn Eagle*, July 8, 1868, p. 2.

Bibliography

"The sentence of the conspirators." *Brooklyn Eagle*, July 7, 1865, p. 2.

"Sentenced to ninety-nine years." *New York Times*, January 25, 1887, p. 3.

"Sentiment versus reason." *Washington Post*, July 19, 1898, p. 6.

"Sex in crime." *Washington Post*, March 16, 1899, p. 6.

"A shame to be avoided." *The Daily Constitution* [Atlanta], May 5, 1878.

"She murdered her husband." *Hartford Courant*, June 16, 1888, p. 1.

"She must hang." *Brooklyn Eagle*, February 18, 1887, p. 6.

"A shocking defensive alliance." *Brooklyn Eagle*, June 14, 1879, p. 2.

"Should women be hung for murder?" *Fort Wayne Sentinel* [Indiana], November 13, 1858.

"Sing Sing state prison." *Brooklyn Eagle*, July 20, 1858, p. 1.

"A singular case." *Liberty Weekly Tribune* [Missouri], July 6, 1877, p. 1.

"Six murderers hanged." *New York Times*, February 4, 1881, p. 5.

"Sketch of the life of Mrs. Grinder." *New York Times*, September 3, 1865, p. 3.

"Some notable trials." *New York Times*, November 10, 1895, p. 32.

"The Somerville Borgia." *New York Times*, August 14, 1886, p. 1.

"The Somerville Poisoner." *New York Times*, February 7, 1888, p. 1.

"State news." *The Landmark* [Statesville, N.C.], January 20, 1882, p. 1.

"Strangled." *Brooklyn Eagle*, January 6, 1881, p. 4.

"The Surratt tragedy." *Liberty Weekly Tribune* [Missouri], November 21, 1873, p. 1.

"Telegrams in brief." *Rocky Mountain News* [Denver], February 8, 1873, p. 1.

"Ten years." *The Daily Constitution* [Atlanta], May 24, 1878.

"Three of a kind." *Sandusky Daily Register* [Ohio], October 8, 1892, p. 1.

"To apply for commutation." *New York Times*, July 10, 1888, p. 5.

"To be executed." *Brooklyn Eagle*, July 22, 1852, p. 2.

"To be hanged." *Brooklyn Eagle*, June 9, 1879, p. 4.

"To save Maria Barberi." *Chicago Tribune*, July 26, 1895, p. 10.

"Topics of the day." *Brooklyn Eagle*, August 28, 1867, p. 2.

"Trial at Cleveland, Ohio, of Mrs. Victor for the murder of her brother." *New York Times*, June 11, 1868, p. 5.

"Trial by rope." *Reno Evening Gazette*, January 15, 1881.

"The trial of the alleged conspirators." *Brooklyn Eagle*, June 20, 1865, p. 2.

"The trial of the conspirators." *Brooklyn Eagle*, May 31, 1865, p. 2.

"Triple execution." *The Galveston Daily News*, August 1, 1885.

"Trying to save Maria Barbella." *New York Times*, July 23, 1895, p. 8.

"Twelve-year-old girl to be hanged." *New York Times*, July 21, 1887, p. 2.

"Two months more of life." *New York Times*, December 23, 1886, p. 5.

"Two will be hanged." *Manitoba Daily Free Press* [Winnipeg], September 15, 1890, p. 2.

"United States." *Manitoba Daily Free Press* [Winnipeg], November 18, 1882.

"Unrepentant." *Chicago Tribune*, March 30, 1883, p. 12.

"Various items." *Brooklyn Eagle*, February 25, 1858, p. 2.

"The veiled murderess." *New York Times*, April 22, 1875, p. 2.

"Veiled murderess dead." *Eureka Reporter* [Utah], May 19, 1905.

"The veiled murderess disclosed." *Ogden Standard Examiner* [Utah], July 30, 1898.

"Verdict." *Hartford Courant*, July 13, 1857, p. 3.

"Very near the gallows." *New York Times*, May 28, 1887, p. 8.

"Vessel crushed to pieces by the ice." *Brooklyn Eagle*, May 29, 1854, p. 2.

"The way of the transgressor is hard." *The*

Ohio Repository [Canton], February 28, 1846.
"Webb on hanging women." *New York Times*, February 16, 1860, p. 4.
"Western notes." *Deseret News* [Utah], October 30, 1872.
"Who hung Mrs. Surratt?" *Chicago Tribune*, October 6, 1873.
"Wholesale hanging." *Fort Wayne Daily Gazette* [Indiana], June 24, 1882.
"The wholesale Pittsburgh poisoner." *Brooklyn Eagle*, August 30, 1865, p. 2.
"Will execute a woman." *New York Times*, December 2, 1897, p. 2.
"Will not be hung." *Daily Advocate* [Newark, N.J.], January 22, 1889.
"Will serve twenty-five years." *Brooklyn Eagle*, May 5, 1895, p. 8.
"Without fear." *Brooklyn Eagle*, June 25, 1889, p. 6.
"Woman electrocuted." *Ogden Standard Examiner* [Utah], March 20, 1899.
"A woman executed." *Chicago Tribune*, September 15, 1883, p. 7.
"Woman faces death in the chair." *Chicago Tribune*, February 4, 1899, p. 2.
"A woman hanged." *New York Times*, October 20, 1883, p. 2.
"A woman hanged in Georgia." *New York Times*, May 3, 1873, p. 3.
"A woman in prison twenty-nine years." *Ogden Standard Examiner* [Utah], November 21, 1901.
"A woman may hang." *Montezuma Journal* [Cortez, Colorado], February 8, 1898, p. 4.
"A woman of the period." *Daily Register Call* [Central City, Colorado], June 15, 1871, p. 2.
"A woman sentenced to be hanged." *New York Times*, November 1, 1876, p. 2.
"A woman sentenced to death." *Liberty Weekly Tribune* [Missouri], January 6, 1854, p. 2.
"A woman sentenced to death at Poughkeepsie." *Brooklyn Eagle*, March 27, 1852, p. 2.
"Woman suffrage and the Barberi case." *New York Times*, August 8, 1895, p. 4.
"Woman to be executed." *The Daily Light* [San Antonio], February 5, 1898.
"A woman's triple crime." *New York Times*, February 8, 1898, p. 5.
"Women and discrimination in law." *Brooklyn Eagle*, February 15, 1899, p. 4.
"Women and the death penalty." *Brooklyn Eagle*, December 2, 1897, p. 6.
"Women who murder to be hanged." *Brooklyn Eagle*, February 19, 1887, p. 2.
"The working women of New York." *New York Times*, November 25, 1868, p. 5.
"Young girl hanged." *Ogden Standard Examiner* [Utah], December 27, 1899.
"Young girl hanged in South Carolina." *Brooklyn Eagle*, October 7, 1892, p. 12.

Index

Abbott, Emma 104–105
acquittals 83–84, 105, 175
admission, to executions 66, 185
adultery 20–21, 34–35, 43–44, 85–86, 100–102, 111–112, 114, 115, 121–122, 185
Alband, Christian 95–96
Alband, Wilhelmina 95–96
Albany Transcript 21
alcohol 93
Anthony, Susan B. 74
arsenic 70, 73
Atlanta Constitution 106
Atzerodt, George 57
axe murders 76, 94, 128–134

Barberi, Maria 169–175
beatings 18, 63–64, 70, 93
beauty 42, 81–84, 104
Beecher, Henry Ward 11
Bell, Clark 183
Bennett, Covert 100–102
Benyon, Elizabeth 7
Bilansky, Ann 43–47
Bilansky, Stanislaus 43–44
Blake, Emily Hilda 186
bludgeoning 114
Bodine, Polly 4
Boon, Emily 161
Booth, John Wilkes 56–57
Booth, Mary 115–117
Booth, Virginia 115–116
Brooklyn Eagle 4, 8, 11–12, 13, 51, 58, 104–105, 148–149
Brophy, John P. 60
Brown, Milbry 162
Buchanan, Jane P. 49–51
Burroughs, Ransom F. 89–91

Campbell, George 85–86
Campbell, Phoebe 85–87
Canada 85–87, 93, 185–186

Carpenter, W. 162
Carruthers, James 55
Carruthers, Mary C. 49, 51–52
Carson Tribune 12
Carter, Matilda 117
Cassidy, Michael J. 167
Cataldo, Dominico 169–171
celebrity status 84–85
Central Federated Union 184–185
Cherry, Axey 145–146
Chicago Tribune 50, 61, 172
Cignarale, Antonio 146–148
Cignarale, Chiara 11–12, 146–151
civil courts, replaced 56–62
Clampitt, John W. 62
Clark, Catharine Ann 33
Cleveland, Grover 127–128
Cleveland Plain Dealer 5–6
Cole, Henrietta 140
Collins, Rufus B. 161
Colorado Daily Chieftain 83–84
Colored Republican Association 173
Colquitt, Alfred 106–107
common-law relationships 29–31, 81–84, 169–171
commutations 22, 28, 37–28, 45–46, 59–61, 72, 92, 94, 97, 98, 106–107, 116–117, 127–128, 130–135, 143, 145, 146, 151, 154, 161, 178
concert, benefit 104
Confederacy, U.S. 56–62
confessions 17, 23, 32, 53, 54–55, 68, 76, 119
conspiracies 56–62
Coriell, Lester 62–64
Coriell, Mary Ellen 63–64
Cowan, Thomas 45
Cowart, Narcissa 105
Coyle, Thomas 85–87
Crittenden, A.R. 80–84
Crittenden, Harriet *see* Grier, Harriet
crowds at gallows *see* spectators at

Index

D'Andrea, Antonia 147–149
Davis, Charles 140
Davis, Orly 94
Deans, Isaac 114
death warrants 24
decapitation 98, 160
Deseret News 149
divorces 82–83
Druse, Mary 129–134
Druse, Roxalana 11, 128–140
Druse, William 128–133
Dukes, David 124–125
Durgan, Bridget 62–69
du Sauchet, Mrs. Frank 173

Eberhart, Susan 88–89
editorial comment 4
editorials 4–15, 55–56, 59, 64, 83–84, 91, 98–99, 104–105, 137–138, 148–149, 168, 171–173, 181; against 27, 37–38, 106; for 39–40, 40–41, 68–69, 81, 96
electrocution 168, 171, 184
Ewart, William 6
executions: Canada 186; descriptions 17, 19, 22–23, 33, 46–47, 54–55, 60, 67–69, 70, 80, 86, 87, 88–89, 93, 113, 115, 120, 122–123, 124–125, 138–139, 152–153, 159–160, 162, 184; numbers of 3–4; percentage female 3–4, 46; private versus public 45–46, 123, 138
Eytinge, Pearl 150

Fair, Laura 80–85
Fambles, Gus 177–178
Fambles, Mary 177–178
Fawcett, Miles 157–159
feedings, forced 71–72, 167
feminism 7–9
feminist writings 65–66, 143
Fife, Henry 31–32
Fletcher, Matilda 106
Flower, J.M. 176
foster children 118–119
Fowlkes, Lucinda 113–115
Fowlkes, Wilson 113–114
Fredenburg, Albert 94–95
Fredenburg, Lodecea 94–95
Freeman, Prince 142–143
Freeman, Thomas 141–142

gallows: trap door 23; upward jerk 23, 113
Garrabrant, Libby 89–93
Garrabrant, Peter J. 90
Garrett, Alonzo 145
Garrett, Mary 144–145
Gates, Charles 129–134

Gates, Frank 129–133
gender differences 4–15, 37–38, 41–42, 55–56, 96, 98, 127, 130–133, 148–149, 168, 175, 181, 182–184, 184–185
Georgia 75, 106–108
Gordon, James Lindsay 181
Gould, Jay 104
governors, state 17, 21–22, 37–39, 44–45, 72–73, 75, 106–107, 114, 127–128, 130–135, 149–150
Gray, R.C. 115–117
Greeley, Horace 74
Greve, William 165
Grier, Harriet 75–76
Grinder, Martha 49–56

Haight, Angenette 125–128
Haight, George W. 125–127
Halliday, Lizzie 163–168
Halliday, Paul 163–165
Harker, Elizabeth 23–25
Harrell, Pete 117–118
Harris, Margaret 123–125
Hartford Courant 10
Hartung, Emil 34–35
Hartung, Mary 34–42
Harvard, James 117–118
Hayes, Joe 117
Hayes, Rutherford 10, 72–73
Hayes, Sadie 143–144
Herbert, Charles 63
Herold, David 56–57
Hill, David B. 130–135, 149–150
Hoag, Ann 20–23
Hoag, Nelson 20
Hollenschied, Anna 9, 95–98
Hollenschied, Henry 95–98
House of Commons (U.K.) 5
Humbrick, Amarilla 107
Huntington, Freida 176

illegitimacy 74–75, 161–162
Indianapolis Journal 10–11
infanticide 74–75, 79–80, 145–146, 161–162, 163, 179
insanity 27–28, 52, 54, 71–73, 80, 84, 87, 119, 134, 165–168; and race 99
insurance proceeds 71–73, 126, 141–142, 151–152

Jackson, Effie 161
Johnson, Andrew 58
Johnson, Charles P. 9–10
Joiner, Dalton 177–178
Jones, Charlotte 31–32
Jones, Martha 115–116

Index

Jones, Matilda 140–141
Jones, Travis 116
Jordan, Annie 154
judicial remarks 36–37, 52–53, 91, 98, 127, 149
jury deliberations 44, 52, 64, 80–81, 86–87, 91, 105, 134–135, 148, 170, 180

Kilpatrick, Lucinda 43–44
Kirk, Eleanor 74

Lacey, William 144
Lammens, Frank 111–113
Lane, Robert 186
Lannagan, Timothy 25–26
Lashley, George 161
Lashley, Margaret 161
laws 41–42, 44–45, 133–134
lawyers 75
lecture circuit 85, 105
Lee, Charles 121–123
Lincoln assassination 56–62
lobbying efforts 30, 33, 59, 96–97, 103–105, 146, 161; by blacks 176; ethnic 149; by feminists 74–75, 106
Lubee, Catherine 25–26
Luckey, Reverend 29–30
Lyles, Jim 161
lynching 3–4

marriage, trust within 37
McCoy, Pauline 154
McMasters, Elizabeth 31–32
McQuillan, Margaret 163–165
McQuillan, Sarah 163–165
Meaker, Almon 118–119
Meaker, Emeline 118–120
media coverage, sensationalized 50–51, 141–143
Medico-Legal Society of New York 183
Meierhofer, John 111–112
Meierhofer, Margaret 111–113
mercy recommendations 61–62, 80, 98, 116
Meyers, Gertie 92
Miller, Andrew 115
Miller, Barbara 121–123
Miller, Catherine 115
Miller, Charles 176
Miller, Daniel 121–123
Minnesota 44–45
Minnesota Legislature 44–46
Missouri 161
Moon, Andrew 32
Moore, Ella 117–118
Morgan, Edwin 37–39
Morey, Alonzo H. 21–23

Morgan, Edwin D. 6
murder, rates by women 3–4
murders, political 56–62

New York Standard 8–9
New York State 21–22, 28, 37, 126–127, 130–135
New York State Legislature 38–39, 41–42, 130–134, 181
New York Times 8, 11, 27, 37–38, 64, 68–69, 84, 91, 98–99, 137–138, 168
newspapers, opinions on 4–25
Nicola, Felix 72–73
Nobles, Elizabeth 13, 177–178

O'Reilly, Daniel 181

Paine, Lewis 57–58
pardons 30, 73, 108, 171
Parnell, Lucy 69–70
Parquet, William 70–72
Parslow, Samuel 185
Payne, Mary Jane 82–83
Pearson, John C. 112
Pennsylvania 24
petitions 33, 46, 80, 91–92, 93, 108, 124, 132, 135, 161, 171–173, 178
Phillips, Mary 103
Place, Ida 179–181
Place, Martha 14, 179–185
Place, William 179–181
Poirier, Cordelia 185–186
Poirier, Isador 185
poisonings 17, 20, 24, 25–26, 34–35, 43–44, 49–51, 71–73, 79–80, 89–90, 116, 118–119, 123–124, 141–142, 151–152
Poteat, Milly 153–154
Poteat, Pink 153
Potts, Elizabeth 157–160
Potts, Josiah 157–160
Powell, George W. 135–136, 139–140
pregnancy and executions 21, 66–67, 145
Price, Sol 140
prison life, descriptions 28–29, 30–31, 40, 65, 94, 108–109, 120, 128
prison matrons 171
prisoners, leased out 108
public opinion 178

racism 99, 117–118
Ramsey, Alexander 44–45
Read, Albert M. 79–80
religion 6, 36, 53, 115, 135–136, 139–140
reputations 100
Rhineman, William 34–41
Riley, Gilbert 89–90

211

Index

riots 117–118
Robbins, Hanson 69–70
Robinson, Elizabeth 141–142
Robinson, Henrietta 4–5, 25–31
Robinson, Sarah Jane 141–143
Robinson, William J. 141–142
Roosevelt, Theodore 182
rumors 19
Runkle, Elizabeth 18
Runkle, John 18–19
Runkle, Mary 18–20
Russell, Lillian 171

St. Louis Globe Democrat 9, 96
Scales, Eldridge 117
sentencings, descriptions 36, 52–53, 65, 71, 82, 91, 103, 126–127, 129
servants 79–80, 115–117, 123–124, 145–146, 162
Seward, William 57
sexual abuse, of prisoners 92
sexual double standard 100–101
Shipp, Caroline 163
shootings 81–82, 111–112, 126, 143–144, 146–148, 163–165, 176, 186
Sibley, Henry 44–45
Singleton, Anderson 118
Slade, Henry 153
Smith, Elizabeth Oakes 65–66
Smith, George 113
Smith, Jennie 99–105
Smith, Richard Harrison 99–101
Smith, Thomas 141–142
Snodgrass, Mary 179
Sothern, Kate 105–109
Sothern, Robert 105–108
South Carolina 146
Southern belle, media myth 105–108
Spann, Enoch F. 88
The Spectator (U.K.) 15
spectators at 19, 32, 33, 46, 54, 67–69, 80, 87, 89, 96–98, 114–115, 122, 124, 139–140, 154, 185–186
spousal abuse 137, 147–149
spy, planted in prison 103
stabbings 63–64, 100, 105–106, 169–171
Stanton, Elizabeth Cady 74, 182–183
Steele, Eva 92
Stewart, Monroe 31–32

Stone, William 82–83
strangulation, on gallows 54, 89, 113, 122–123, 160, 163
subjugation, wife to husband 96
Sumners, William 20–21
Surratt, Anna 59–60
Surratt, John 56–57
Surratt, Mary 56–62
Sweet, G.W. 44–45

Teasdale, Lucinda 118
Tiller, Maggie 176
Tribble, Anna 161–162
tribunals, military 56–62
Turbin, Johanna 98–99
Twigg, Mary 33–34

Umble, Amanda 161
Union Woman Suffrage Association 7–8

Van Valkenburgh, Elizabeth 17
Van Winkle, Bogert 89–91
Vaughn, Hester 7, 74–75
Victor, Sarah 70–74
Virginia 114, 116–117

Walker, John 43–44
Wallis, Mary 79–80
wardens, prison 92
Washington Post 14, 168
Webster, Mary 10
Weichman, Louis 60–62
Whiteling, Bertha 151–152
Whiteling, John 151–152
Whiteling, Sarah Jane 151–153
Whiteling, Willie 151–152
Williams, John 162
Williams, Jonas 22–23
Wilson, George 31–32, 140
witnesses, official 22, 32, 113, 114
Woman's Christian Temperance Union 92–93
Woman's Suffrage Society 106
women, as different 4–15, 21–22, 37–39, 41–42, 52–53, 99, 120, 133–135
women's suffrage 174
Wood, William F. 26–27
Workman, Elizabeth 93
Wright, Nancy 75–76

www.ingramcontent.com/pod-product-compliance
Lightning Source LLC
Chambersburg PA
CBHW032056300426
44116CB00007B/764